GOD'S SMUGGLER
TO CHINA

Brother David

with Dan Wooding and Sara Bruce

A cry to the Chinese to let us love them

HODDER & STOUGHTON
LONDON SYDNEY AUCKLAND TORONTO

British Library Cataloguing in Publication Data

David, *Brother*
 God's smuggler to China.
 1. Missions – China
 I. Title   II. Wooding, Dan   III. Bruce, Sara
 266'.00951   BV3415.2

 ISBN 0–340–33902–0

CONTENTS

DEDICATION
To Julie and the 3 D's
With all my love.

ACKNOWLEDGEMENTS

This book tells more than my story. It is the story of God at work. It tells of a team of His people and their identification with me, with Brother Andrew, with the Lord Himself and His people in China. Together with the church in China, we have been His witnesses, and this is the story He has shown us.

I am grateful to God for the encouragement Brother Andrew has been to me all these years, and for the tremendous team the Lord has placed around us and the Suffering Church in Asia. I am also grateful to God for all our friends in the United States who have supported and prayed for our ministry to the Suffering Church.

The book is not one I planned to write, indeed it very nearly did not happen. Although Brother Andrew and Sven, our Open Doors' International vice-president, consistently asked me for it, I was certain I could not meet their request.

I didn't. It was God Himself who fulfilled that request. Psalm 57:2 says: "I cry to God most high, to God who fulfills His purpose for me." (R.S.V.). The book has truly been *His* doing, as He has gathered around me a team to put it together.

The first to join the team was Marichelle Roque-Lutz, to whom I am very grateful for the six months of research and writing which she put into the first draft.

After that, however, we were to wait twelve months before returning to the task. In the interim, God was very evidently at work in the ministry, and there was to be much more to tell.

At this point He brought an Australian family to the Philippines to join hands with us and the Suffering Church. In that family was the one who would share with me the most in the writing, research and development of this book. Through Sara Bruce, the team, Julie and I were able to share the principles of the ministry and the witness of the Lord at work. Sara and I needed assistance, and so God brought a jolly Englishman to spend many weeks working with us. From the bottom of my heart I want to thank Sara Bruce and Dan Wooding. Without them, we wouldn't have a book.

Of course, the family from Australia were also to become back-up members of the team. While Sara was hard at work for long months, husband Michael and their two little boys gave her untiring and caring support. To them, Julie and I will long be indebted.

Other vital contributors to the team behind the book were the Open Doors Asia staff members. Each one gave time for interviews, research and careful proof-reading of the manuscript. My sincere thanks go to them for finding that time amid their busy schedules.

My grateful thanks go also to Shan Kumar for his editorial assistance and for his fellowship and encouragement from the book's inception – indeed from that of the Asia ministry itself.

To those in the office who have worked so hard on the typing and xeroxing of the manuscript, I want to give my sincere appreciation; Beng Tuazon, Lilith, Adel, Marcie and the rest of the staff. Their corporate attitude can be summed up in the words of one young man who worked on the xerox machine for almost 24 hours straight, yet at the end could still say with a smile: "Thank you, Jesus!"

Behind the scene team-members also included two very special Chinese families whose counsel has been invaluable in the shaping of the ministry to meet the needs of their people in China. Their fellowship, encouragement and love both for us and for one another have been in the true spirit of Jesus Christ. I am grateful to them for welcoming our team as members of their large Chinese family.

Likewise my thanks go to Bill Butler and his great team

at Christian Resource Management for their guidance, support and faithful acts of love.

All of these people have been brought into the ministry by the Lord, and without them we wouldn't have had a story to tell.*

And, of course, particular thanks go to the publishers who have given helpful direction and much wisdom in the completion of the book.

I would like to express special gratitude, however, to the ones who have been my "team-members" from the very beginning. Julie and our children have provided constant support and encouragement, even when it cost them to do so. And through this book Julie has once again given of herself during the long hours I have worked to complete it. In addition, it was Julie who took Sara Bruce across the border bridge at Lo Wu, and introduced her to the People's Republic of China. She also participated in the research and careful proof-reading of the manuscript. Above all I am grateful for her most vital role which caused her to spend many long hours, often far into the night, praying for the outcome of the book.

Finally I offer my heartfelt thanks and praise to the Lord Himself. The book has been His doing, not mine, as He has brought together the necessary people, tools and resources to bring it about.

He indeed is fulfilling His purpose for us and our Chinese friends. The work is going on.

Brother David

---

* Their names, as with almost all those in the book, have been changed to protect their ministry to the Suffering Church. Locations and names of believers inside China have also been changed for their own protection.

FOREWORD BY BROTHER ANDREW

It was fifteen years almost to the day that I stood again on the Great Wall of China, to the north of Peking. Looking down from this impressive fortification which winds snake-like for nearly two thousand miles across the belly of the People's Republic, I was reminded that it was originally for a special reason – to keep the barbarians out; the Mongols who threatened the very lives of the Chinese.

Since it was first built some two thousand years ago, the Chinese have built many more walls; political, military, ideological, always designed to keep people with their beliefs out.

On the first occasion, I had stood amid the crowds of unsmiling Chinese and claimed open doors for China. I had asked in my prayer that the government of Mao Tse-Tung could no longer be able to keep people – God's people – out with their life-changing ideas.

Little did I know at the time that there was also a man outside of China who was praying that same prayer. That man was Brother David, an extraordinary individual whose inspiring and moving story you will read in this book. He was saying, "God give us open doors to reach the people. Give us people through whom You can love China." God is a God who answers prayer, as we have proved time and time again.

God's Smuggler to China will encourage you to ask the biggest things of God and to expect the biggest answers you've ever had through faith and prayer. Why? Because over these fifteen years God did open the doors to China, He did provide people to penetrate the Bamboo Curtain, and He gave a vision to a man so much different from me in many ways, and yet He gave him the same burden, vision and faith.

In reading *God's Smuggler to China*, you will learn the exciting story of how God used my dear friend Brother David to make contact with the remaining believers in China; how He enabled him to find the churches there and to communicate with them; how God miraculously provided the contacts and the people so that they could trust them and us so as to make special request for help.

Now they have asked for and been supplied with thousands of Bibles. Many have replaced those destroyed in the Cultural Revolution, while others have been placed in the hands of those who have never owned a Bible. The ten million believers of China realise that there is no limit with God and have now asked for an initial one million Bibles. We have agreed to trust God for this number because we know those inside can use them as they work to reach all of China with the redeeming message of Jesus Christ.

As you read this book, you will see how God works, you will identify with Brother David and his brave team of people described in these pages. But more than that, you will see that God can do the same with *you*. He can use *you* to open up countries and continents and indeed the whole world for His message of love and salvation.

What God can do through one man, He can surely do through *you*.

Brother Andrew

CHAPTER ONE
Lucky Strike

My brother Chuck spotted him first. A creature was emerging from behind a boulder close to the sea.

"The Japanese have landed!" Chuck's little body trembled as he stammered out his story. "I saw one of them — there!" He pointed to the vast expanse of sand behind him on the beach at Oceanside, California.

"Aw, how can you tell he's Japanese?" I was sceptical. "Have you ever seen one before?"

"N-n-no. But I can tell.

"They have high pitched voices and slit eyes and square mouths filled with big yellow teeth and ..." As another schoolboy "soldier" described his picture-book idea of a Japanese, "it" emerged from a sand slope. A huge figure rose to full height, bearing the Japanese flag of the rising sun and clad in bona fide Japanese uniform. From that distance his protruding teeth seemed to gleam, and the slits of his eyes peered at us through funny round spectacles.

"He *must* be Japanese." We were positive now. "Back into the trench. Hurry!" As the oldest boy in my platoon I felt responsible for our lives.

Our hearts were beating like drums. The ten of us huddled close to each other behind one of the two trenches which we had dug and reinforced with driftwood for our war games. Frightened beyond tears, we waited, our bodies tensed to defend ourselves and our country.

With one blood-curdling yell, he was upon us. Our responses were mechanical: ten wooden guns left our hands and whizzed past their target. Nevertheless, he fell, writhing on the sand like a dying dog. As I stepped towards him, a babble of gibberish came from his lips. And then he lay still. "Slowly now, he might be trying to trick us," I cautioned, although I was sure he was dead.

As I reached his feet, I noticed his body twitch, as if desperately clinging to the last remnants of life. It was a sickening sight. I had never been so close to death before.

Cautiously I raised my eyes to look at his face, almost afraid of what I might see. As I did so, the corpse leapt to his feet and my throat clammed up in terror as this huge man towered over me.

Then all at once, he pulled off his Japanese helmet to reveal a smiling American face. "Hi, Marines! You got me real good."

I watched transfixed as he chuckled heartily at the joke and then dug deep into his pockets to produce candy bars for us all.

"My name's Lucky. I've just returned from Guadalcanal. I got this uniform over there. Do you like it?"

We nodded blankly.

"I've been watching you kids play and I thought I'd see if you were really made of the stuff of Marines. You passed Lucky's test."

Lucky was the biggest Marine I had ever seen. He towered high above us all, and seemed to be twice as broad. He had a square jaw and wide nose. Although he looked rough and tough, he was really the gentlest Marine I had ever met from Camp Pendleton, the massive Marine Base opposite our home.

It was natural enough for us to be playing battle games. Oceanside was a military town and, with the Second World War at its height, each family had an active role to play. My own mother had left her work in a life insurance company to become head of the civilian payroll at the Marine Base. My father was away, training Petty officers in the Navy at San Diego. We saw him only when he could get leave, and found "good-bye's" almost impossible, never knowing when or even whether we would see him again. The tension of it had reached deeply into our young lives so that everything we did or thought was tempered by the war situation.

Lucky became our friend. His blue eyes would twinkle as, day after day, he told us stories about the Japanese. He really brought alive for me the wide, wide world that lay outside our little town; the world that included the teeming millions of Asia.

I vowed to grow like him; tall, square-jawed, and every bit as warm-hearted. Most of all my mind was set. Like Lucky, I would be a Marine. I was going to serve my country.

* * *

But, before I could fulfil that dream, there was another battle I had to fight. At ten years of age, I could neither read nor write.

School had become a constant struggle for me. I had finished third grade, only to be told that my marks were not high enough, and I was to stay behind while all my friends went on into the fourth grade.

As my repeat year began, I sat trying not to look conspicuous in class, watching all the younger boys file in. The fact that I was much bigger even than friends my own age was no help either. On the beach, I was naturally chosen as leader of the troop; here in class I was in the lowest ranks.

* * *

I could never get away from that classroom fast enough. As soon as school was out, I would run all the way home, back to my fox-holes, wooden guns, helmets, canteens, combat packs. Right after cookies and milk, I would "go to battle", with platoon equipment kept up to date by Lucky.

Occasionally I had the chance to come face to face with the human cost of the war. During the day, I often walked by the railway line watching the wounded soldiers return from the front lines. From my mother's office she could see them too, as they were transported onto the base for medical treatment. Mother was always one to show deep concern for any in need, and began visiting the hospital to encourage the wounded. The rare occasions when I was allowed to accompany her left an unforgettable impression on me.

One young man we visited lay out in the sun with his legs bandaged from the knees down. As I looked at him, I realised that those bandages ended in stumps where his feet should have been. Gauze covered the wounds on his head, and yet, in the hot sun, blood was still seeping through. Despite the pain, he smiled at me, and I wanted desperately to say something comforting to him.

"I'm going to be a Marine," was the best I could manage. The young man's eyes lit up. With difficulty he formed the words: "Marines eat their vegetables, especially spinach." Spinach. I hated spinach. But my head nonetheless bobbed up and down with determination.

"Yes, sir."

It was one vegetable I had always rejected. But now that I knew I had to eat it to serve my country, there was no stopping me. Mother used to take me to a restaurant on the base, and I absolutely insisted that spinach always came with the meal.

*　　*　　*

My battle in the classroom was not getting easier. At the end of the third grade, I was put into fourth out of simple kind-heartedness. Yet twelve months later, I flunked again. I had to stay behind a second time while the others went into fifth grade. By now, school was becoming a relentless humiliation for me. By far the largest in the class, I watched the younger boys sitting around me, listening for their names to be called as the class was divided.

Then came the words I was dreading. "David – Group IV – the beginner's books," said my pinch-faced teacher.

"I pity the poor man you marry," I hissed between my teeth.

That night, I returned home in a thick fog that made it impossible for me to go out onto the beach and lead my troops against the "enemy". I felt hopeless. There could be no war games that night. My mother was still at work and my father was away at war.

I always sat at the back of the class, hoping that I wouldn't be noticed there. While the others read their books and seemed to learn so easily, I would draw. The subject of every sketch was the same – the war. There on the page, I would defeat the enemy and win the war once and for all.

On the 2nd September, 1945, I returned home jubilantly from school after our teacher had announced the end of the war with the Japanese. That night Mom took us out for dinner to celebrate. The war was over. Dad would be coming home for good.

*　　*　　*

My father was a well-respected teacher and, after his discharge from the Navy, he was quickly offered a position teaching business administration in Arizona.

The next two years saw us move three times as my father took various jobs around the country. Each time it meant adjustment to new classrooms and teachers for me, and my grades seemed to decline with every new school I attended. At last, the travelling came to a stop and our family settled in Redondo Beach, California.

My parents were both relieved. They believed it was time for the family to settle into a regular routine. They also knew that I needed to concentrate on improving my reading.

I often wondered how parents as talented as mine had produced a son whose class performance was so poor. My father had an excellent academic record, a master's degree in business administration. My mother was very gifted in the field of economics. Yet they never thought badly of me because of my handicap. They simply encouraged me not to give in.

"You can do it, David. Keep trying," my Dad said often in his loving, quiet tone. I don't recall ever hearing him raise his voice, he was too much of a gentleman. However he did command and demand respect, and I was happy to give it to him. My dad was one who faced a problem squarely, came up with a solution, and followed it through to completion. He was quietly determined that my reading problem would not hinder me in life.

My new school also wanted to help. Soon after I arrived, the school principal called for my Dad and quizzed him about the reason for my enrolment in Grade V instead of Grade VII.

"I know it's unusual," Dad told him. "David is much too old for the class. But he seems to have a learning problem which, so far, he has not been able to overcome. We would do anything you suggest to help him." In later years, my father was to diagnose the problem as "dyslexia".

The principal suggested a solution. Realising the embarrassment for an over-sized boy in a class full of younger children, he resolved to move me up two grades – in the hope that the psychological boost would improve my performance.

I was delighted with my father's news. But my classmates were not so pleased. What right did I, a dumb kid from fifth grade, have to join their class without even passing fifth or sixth? They conveyed their judgement in no uncertain terms.

"David is a dummie! David is a dummie!" they chanted as I walked into the playground for lunch.

"Think you're smart, uh Davey-boy?" "You can't even read properly!" "What are you doing with the 'big' kids, huh?"

My beach war training was not in vain. A few days later

I got my chance. Jimmy Hann, one of my classmates, began the usual taunts after school. As we walked across the lawn, he added weight to his words by throwing a punch. I fought back immediately. In the heat of the battle his lunch bucket went flying and landed several feet away on the pavement.

Both of us stopped in our tracks. From enemies at war, we suddenly became two young schoolboys terrified of our mothers' reaction to damaged property. Tentatively, we picked up the lunch bucket and examined the contents. Sure enough, inside were the remains of Jimmy's new thermos bottle, shattered.

"I'll get you for that. You'd better look out, dummie." Blind rage overtook Jimmy as he set out for his vengeance – probably reasoning that if he was going to get it from his mother, I might as well be given a thrashing too.

I too was fighting mad and set to win at any cost. With one determined blow mid-face, I ended the battle. Jimmy sat on the ground clutching his nose. As I walked closer, I saw, to my horror, blood trickling down his cheek and chin.

My elation changed to fear as I watched Jimmy turn off the road home from school. I knew his mother would be waiting for him, and I was scared to the bone when I thought of what she would do. My fears were justified. By the time I had made it down the hill to my house, Mrs Hann had learned the whole story and was already on her way to confront my mother.

Mother listened grim-faced to the story of my misbehaviour and quickly offered to buy a new thermos. However, my mother never let me get away with anything, and the cost was deducted out of my earnings from a paper round. I was only thankful the punishment was no worse. My parents were strict disciplinarians and frequently crossed our backsides with a leather belt, assuring us: "Spare the rod and you spoil the child. We're only doing this for your own good." We were never too convinced.

After my fight with Jimmy Hann, he became one of my best friends. When our classmates heard about what had happened, the name-calling stopped, just as I had hoped. I was becoming one of the boys, and respected, if not for my brain, at least for my brawn.

I was no longer a joke at school.

* * *

In time, my grades began to improve, although school remained a struggle. But when I reached ninth grade a new challenge entered my life which gave me more fulfilment and satisfaction than I'd ever dreamed possible – American grid-iron football. At Redondo Union High School, clad in new shoes, helmet, shoulder and hip pads, I fell in love with the sport. Somehow, after all the struggles I'd endured in class, the rough and rugged game seemed easy.

I seized every opportunity to play the game and glowed with pleasure when I was placed on the school's official team. I began with the BeaHawks, the B-team, and later graduated to their A-team, the SeaHawks. Out on the field I had to knock heads with older guys that seemed twice as big as me, but I wouldn't have missed one minute of it.

It was during my eleventh grade, while playing on the team, that there came the day and the game which were to point my education in a new direction.

Our team had been scheduled to play Santa Monica High School, or "Sammo Hi", as we knew them. It was a vital game since they were almost our neighbouring school, just fourteen miles up the coast. They were also the number one senior school team in the entire state. Everybody, but everybody, was predicting a trouncing for us and rightfully so. Our team was nowhere near their class.

Although we didn't stand a chance that evening, that knowledge somehow motivated us more than ever to get on the field and fight like crazy. If we were going to be murdered by them, it would be a glorious death.

8

The night of the game was balmy, with a cool moistness in the air. Yet for me there was also an excitement that brought the whole place alive with electricity. Our supporters had travelled down from Redondo to cheer us on and we were all the more encouraged to know that three thousand of them were out in the stands.

We did lose that night, but we gave Sammo Hi a much tougher battle than they expected. For all of us, it meant playing better than we had ever played before. I recall one moment of wonder when my name was chanted over and over in pride by our three thousand supporters. Despite our defeat, therefore, we felt elated by the game, a feeling I had never experienced in class.

We left the field covered in the dust and sweat of the brutal clash. As we ran off, I watched Sammo's coach coming down to congratulate his team. He had been a long-time hero of mine, a former pro-player with the Los Angeles Rams – whom I had watched many times from a crowd of a hundred thousand or more. He had even played the same position as me, and I'd have given my eye teeth to meet the man.

To my surprise, after he had spoken to his own team, he came over to three of our best players, and stopped with a word of respect and encouragement for each. But then, instead of returning to his team, the coach kept on walking ... in my direction. It was impossible. I was one of the younger members on the team. He simply could not be coming to speak to me. A moment later, he stood right beside me, warmly shaking my hand.

"Excellent playing, David. I really enjoyed watching you tonight. I'm going to be on the lookout for you again in next year's match. Keep it up – you're doing great."

As he walked back to his own team, I felt ten feet tall. All my life I'd wanted to meet a professional player, and this one had been a favourite of mine. Now, I had not only met one, but been congratulated by him.

I was sure that nothing could have made me happier,

9

but I was wrong. The best was still to come through the words of my own coach some minutes after.

"David, I was real proud of you tonight."

I smiled my thanks at him, as he too shook my sweaty hand.

"Say, did you know the scouts were here for the game?"

These talent spotters were representatives from all the major universities. They attended key football games "scouting" for players to whom they could award scholarships. Anybody fortunate enough to receive one got free education at the university, along, of course, with membership in the institution's prestigious football team.

"Sure, coach, I knew they were here. They're on the lookout for guys graduating this year."

'That's right, Dave. They are. But, I'll tell you something more."

His face broke into a big smile.

"After tonight, they'll be watching you, too. If you can keep up that standard, you might find that when you leave us you walk right into the waiting arms of one of the best universities in the country."

He chuckled, and walked off to see someone else. But I remained right where I was, too shell-shocked to do anything. I could hardly begin to believe what the coach had said. All these years I'd been struggling in the classroom and university was the option farthest from all my plans or even dreams. What was the point? No university was going to be interested in a guy who could hardly read.

When graduation came, therefore, I stood in disbelief with eleven other students from Redondo High, winners of scholarships to college or university. I caught my parents' smile of pride as the names were announced. Ten scholarships had been awarded for academic achievement, and two for football.

The game I loved so much had enabled me to touch down for an education at university.

CHAPTER TWO

The Great Pretender

I was sitting at a corner table in the Students' Union at the University of Denver. It was late afternoon and classes had finished for the day. I leaned back lazily in my chair, and took another sip of soda pop.

Life was good here on campus. I had enjoyed the games our football team, the "Pioneers", had played and often won. I liked the side benefits too; the company of pretty girls, the long drinking bouts with the guys and the never-ending round of parties lasting far into the night. And it felt good to know I had been accepted by such a prestigious institution.

Only one problem clouded the picture – the one I'd carried all my life, that of learning. It was like a nagging headache that simply refused to go away. I was managing to cope in most of my subjects, but my reading was slower than I would have liked it, and now I was doing miserably in maths as well.

In fact, a dozen of us on the football team shared the same difficulty. None of us could master logarithms. Our coach had called in a tutor and was paying him 125 dollars per week to push us all through our exams. If I didn't pass, my days at Denver would be cut short.

"Hey, man." A voice broke into my thoughts. "Have you got a chick for the drive-in tonight?" Ted Mitchell was one of the crowd with whom I often spent many late hours.

"Sure." I was confident. "I'll just bring Barbara along as usual."

Ted frowned. "I'm sorry, old buddy. I heard Steve say he was taking Barbara out tonight."

Steve Burnett was a well-built blond-headed student with a brilliant scholastic record. He knew only too well about my learning problems, and seemed to delight in taunting me.

Lately, just to annoy me, he had also taken to dating my girls. He was getting under my skin. But there was no way I would let Ted know how I felt.

"Oh," I said carefully. "Then I'll take one of the others. Jean will do nicely." I glanced out the window in an effort to look suitably nonchalant.

That night at the drive-in, I couldn't stop thinking of Burnett with Barbara. The resentment was building up inside me; no doubt just as he wanted it to.

A few days later, Burnett struck again. He knew how much pride I took in dressing well. One night he saw one of my best shirts hanging ready to wear the following morning. While I slept, he removed the shirt and managed, of all things, to rub it in some dung before bringing it back and replacing it on the hanger.

Next day I overslept, and hurriedly pulled it on before dashing into class. Suddenly those around me began to whisper and soon a ripple of laughter was spreading throughout the room.

"Hey, David. What happened to your shirt?" Ted leaned across to me in concern. "You sure stink!"

"What do you mean?" I was on the defensive.

"Man you smell like what makes the grass grow green! Take a look at your shoulder."

As realisation hit me, I knew in a flash it could only have been Burnett.

I strode from the class, angrily ripping off the shirt, and headed straight for his room. When I confronted him, he admitted doing the dirty trick but instead of apologising, sneered all the more at my protests. What was a creep like me complaining for? I shouldn't be at college anyway.

"Hey, man, I've got something else to show you." He stood up and took a stick from one corner of the room. Tied around it was a bunch of papers. It looked like somebody's mail.

12

"Did you know I'd been accepted for the Olympics? I'm the lucky torch bearer."

With that, he struck a match. "See the pretty mail light up into a big torch," he laughed as he set fire to it.

Suddenly I understood whose mail he was burning. Blood rushed to my face as I grabbed my burning letters, ripped open his shirt, and jabbed the fire out on his stomach. The pain sent him screaming and cursing.

"Louder, Burnett, louder. I can't hear you," I jeered, cupping my hand around my right ear which I lowered to the level of his chest. In this stooping position, I clenched my right fist and with all my force shot myself up, body, fist, and all, straight under his jaw.

The impact opened his lip up to his nose. The cut alone would mean thirty stitches in the hospital. Not satisfied with that, I picked him up from where he had fallen groaning and moaning and slammed my fists into his face and chest against the wall. I could have killed him, had his screams not sent two students flying into his room in time to grab me and shake sense back into me.

Suddenly, I realised what I had done. I was shocked by my behaviour.

"Dear God. How could I do that?" I was so stunned by my action, I found myself almost involuntarily praying.

I wasn't proud of that day. The more I thought of it the more ashamed I became. Yet at the same time, I was beginning to understand that something inside of me longed for recognition, for dignity. I'd had enough of being put down.

From that time on, I was seen as something of a monster by many of the male students. "Here comes Denver's Rocky Marciano," they would scoff. The girls, however, suddenly had a new respect for no-nonsense Dave.

* * *

13

After eighteen months at university, it still didn't add up for me to be there. And *that*, literally, was my problem. Logarithms continued to drag down my grades in mathematics. Coupled with my reading slowness, my studies remained an up-hill battle. Finally, my coach took me aside. "I would suggest you take a semester off, David. Go home and attend a junior college where you can concentrate on your grades. Come back to us in the autumn for the football season."

Still at the back of my mind was the memory of the encounter with Burnett, and I was quite happy to act on the coach's advice.

But even when I got home, the lure of the football field kept tugging at me. Twelve hours after my arrival, the phone was ringing with invitations from three other colleges asking me to join their teams.

My father overheard the conversations. As he came quietly into the room, he asked: "Well, son, what's it to be?"

"Dad, I'm here to improve my grades, so I can get back to Denver."

My father's expression was sympathetic. "And is that what you want to do, son?"

That was Dad. Never one to push for his own way, he nonetheless could probe to the very heart of a problem. Sometimes it seemed he knew me better than I knew myself.

"I'm not sure. I don't know if I can make it," I told him.

Dad did not say what he thought about that. Instead he said simply, "Before you can begin at our local college there'll be several weeks of waiting. I heard recently of a vacancy in a lithographer's, downtown. Would you be interested?"

Neither of us actually said what was at the back of our minds, but we both knew that it would be difficult for me to succeed in the academic field.

14

I took the job gratefully and never returned to university again.

One further truth remained unsaid between us. This job would make me confront the problem that football could never help me with. If I was going to work as a lithographer, I would have to come to terms with my reading difficulty.

*   *   *

Each day in my new job brought me face to face with the business of getting words onto paper, and getting them right. I was no walking lexicon, but through the work new words were added to my vocabulary and old words were etched into my mind. Any mis-spelt word that made it to the proof reading stage would mean a rap over the knuckles.

As the weeks passed, I became familiar with my new world. And at the same time, my work-mates acquainted me with a second world as well – one which had formerly been outside my province. They introduced me to the gambling den, and I quickly came to love the games of chance. First of all it was fun. Secondly, it was always accompanied by plenty of drink, and plenty of girls. And thirdly, I decided it gave me the right kind of image. I was not a kid any longer. In fact I was quite proud of myself. I was now a real man of the world.

There was only one place where I did not feel so proud – my home. Somehow, as I looked into my father's face and read the integrity etched into every line, I made very sure he was not aware of my extra-curricular activities. I was equally careful with my mother, well aware of her determination to live life "as God meant us to live it, David ..."

I agreed with her in a way, and with my father when he expressed his faith in God. But I could not get involved in the little church nearby as my parents had. Sunday service was not enough for them. They had to attend prayer meetings every week, teach in Sunday School, and sing in the local choir.

15

That was definitely not my scene. "But you must attend worship, David – every week." My parents would not give up. And for many years I complied with them, until the evening when I resolved never to darken a church door again.

The trouble started with Jayne Mansfield. She was to be married in a nearby town and I had the opportunity to watch. I was excited, and counting off the days until the big one when I would actually get to see the film-star with my own eyes.

When at last the day arrived, however, my father told me he had other plans for my activities that evening.

"The church has a special meeting, son, and I think you ought to be there."

"But Father," I started to protest, "tonight is the night when ..."

"David?" He looked gravely at me. "I'm not asking you to go. I'm telling you!"

The evening turned out to be a complete disaster. The church had called its members to gather support for a new building fund and the organisers made it very clear that they were expecting big things from me.

"You see, David, we know that you are now fortunate enough to be in a well-paid job. Why, your income must be in excess of five thousand dollars per year!"

One of the men smiled in a patronising way. "We have done a mental calculation on that income, and we have come up with a figure which we think you could comfortably afford each month. How about it?"

When at last I returned home, I was ready to burst with fury. I had missed seeing the one and only Jayne Mansfield for this? How dare they suggest I give them my hard-earned money? There was no way I would donate a single dollar, not even a cent.

"Dad? Mom?" I shouted loudly enough for the whole neighbourhood to hear. "You listen, and you listen good! I've had it with that church of yours. I've had it up to here." By now I had lost all control and let forth a torrent

16

of anger. "As far as I'm concerned, you can take your church and go to hell!"

I had gone too far. I knew it as soon as the words were out. My parents knew it too. And if I had thought the days of my beltings were over, I was quickly proved wrong. My mother seized a nearby leather strap and proceeded to ensure, once and for all, that I would never speak that way to them again.

One fact remained unchanged, however. Wild horses would not drag me back inside a church again. On that issue I stood firm. As far as I was concerned, my church-going days had come to an end – permanently.

＊　　＊　　＊

Several months after I started in the lithographer's, Uncle Sam pointed his finger at me. My boss arrived one morning to announce that I was about to be drafted. Rather than wait for the government's choice of service, I immediately volunteered for the branch of the military I had loved in my boyhood – the Marine Corps.

The family was delighted. Marine Corps spirit ran high in our home. Before long I was on my way South for the first leg of my training.

At two hundred and fifty pounds, I was one of the largest men in that platoon of sixty-five nervous teenagers who arrived at the Marine bootcamp in San Diego. I never guessed what was ahead for me as the service set out to turn me into one tough, rough, determined U.S. Marine.

The treatment I endured was to make my time at Denver University seem like kindergarten, yet I knew that I must not allow my volatile temper to defeat me. I was prepared to overlook all possible heckling.

Sgt Hall, head drill instructor, a man with a bull neck and a matching temper, honoured Platoon 150 with his first visit. He went through our barracks and inspected our beds.

Even his crew-cut quivered as he delivered his verdict on our efforts.

"You are a bunch of babies. You do not know how to make a bed properly. You do not understand yet that in the U.S. Marine Corps men make beds that will put chambermaids of the Hilton Hotel to shame."

Either he was joking, I thought, or he's crazy. The beds looked fine to me.

Outside our barracks, sixty-five of us stood at stiff, tense attention. He had condescended to watch us as we marched past him and now stood in straight lines before him.

"Surely, he can't complain now," I muttered to myself. He could.

"You pathetic lot do not know how to march properly. You do not know how to stand without looking like girls. You do not know that in the U.S. Marine Corps men are trained to march like one harmonious symphony. And clowns become men of discipline."

At this point, Sgt Peters, another drill instructor, handed him a cup of coffee. Sgt Hall began pacing up and down our ranks, sipping the coffee and sauntering about. Now and then, one of us received his closer scrutiny. He snickered openly as though recalling a private joke.

Then he was in front of me. I pulled in my stomach and held my breath. He made a big production of slowly inspecting me from head to toe.

While his eyes peeled me open, my eyes held their focus on the neck of the black recruit in front of me.

Suddenly, without warning, he threw the cup of steaming coffee straight at my chest. It was so unexpected that I flinched and stepped back in reflex. My skin stung where the hot coffee had driven through my fatigue uniform. The tips of my ears tingled as adrenalin shot into my bloodstream. "No, Dave!" I commanded myself. I gritted my teeth and forced my anger down, the picture of my calm, disciplined father in my mind. When he saw my

reaction, the seconds of agitation followed by the battle with
my temper, Sgt Hall's smirk changed into an amused grin.

"Clown, why don't you pick up that cup?" He pointed
to the now empty cup that lay at my feet.

"I'm at attention," I answered. I saw him stiffen.

"I'm at attention WHO?" His voice hissed for a strike.
"Sir, I'm at attention." I corrected my mistake. The snake
recoiled, but was still watchful.

"Why didn't you catch my cup of coffee, butterball?" I
racked my brain for the right answer. "Sir, because I'm
sloppy, sir." The answer pleased him. "You're g—d—
right you're sloppy. All dumbbells are." He sauntered
away. He was through with me.

But he was not through with us. Back and forth he went,
in that lazy, arrogant stance he affected. And then, the
smirk continuously playing about his lips, he delivered his
parting speech.

"I like you boys. You have the nerve to appear before
the U.S. Marine Corps command looking like a bunch of
girls and believing, actually believing, that the U.S. Marine
Corps can make men out of you! Such gall. Well, you're
g—d— right we're going to change you into men, if it
kills you. This is the Marine Corps of the United States.
We make men. We break clowns, sissies, and slobs. That
just about covers all of you here.

"Boy, you're the sorriest-looking batch I've ever encountered in all my years in San Diego. Nerve, that's what
you've got ..."

At this point, the Sergeant's voice and posture changed.
He finally stopped acting and his impressive baritone rang
out for the first time that day: "Well d— it. You want
to change into Marines, we *will* change you into Marines.
It won't be easy. Not on your part, not on ours. I'm
warning you, before we're through with you, or you're
through with us, many of you will wish you'd never signed
up. Many of you will be squealing 'wee, wee' all the way

home to your mothers. But for those among you who can survive thirteen weeks of hell in bootcamp, you will have the singular honour, the prestige, of being called – no, of being – a U.S. MARINE!"

* * *

Sgt Hall was not exaggerating. The initial weeks of obstacle courses were just the beginning of a physical, mental and emotional nightmare that was intended to build or break a man's body and spirit. We were insulted, physically and mentally assaulted, and every way driven past the breaking point.

I was determined not to give in. I was committed to turning myself into a good Marine. Then, as I saw it, I would be one of America's finest class of men. A man who would die for what he believed in.

At the end of one particularly harrowing day, when most of us could hardly drag one foot behind the other, Sergeant Hall decided to spring one extra honour on us. We were to climb a thick hemp rope without using our feet.

When my turn came, Sgt Hall announced loudly: "Oh, here's our big girl. Let's see what big girls who can't catch cups of coffee can do." I sat on the ground and resolved to make it further up that rope than anybody else in the platoon. At that moment, I felt my whole future in the Marine Corps depended on it. I loathed being called "big girl". I was determined to live that down, even if it took all my will-power and strength to do it. Seventy-five percent of the platoon could not lift their bodies from where they sat on the ground and up that rope without the aid of their feet. A farm boy from Pennsylvania managed. An amateur boxer went even higher. A weight-lifter finished fifteen feet off the ground.

In my concentration and determination to lift my body up the rope, I became oblivious to everything else. The next thing I knew I was twenty feet in the air. Below me the platoon was looking up at my big hulk, awe written on their faces. With consciousness came the pains – of bleeding hands, strained arms, shoulders and chest. It was worth it. The feat earned, if not the immediate approval of my drill instructors, their respect. Though the taunts continued, I found out that they were part of the training which went into the making of a U.S. Marine.

* * *

After the early weeks, the "babies", "sissies", "girls", etc. in our platoon began to look more like Marines. The thin ones were filling out with solid muscles; the fat ones were melting down into hard sinew and tissue. After some months nobody recognised us. Our bodies had hardened into bullets.

Our minds, our spirit, our characters had also become as tough and concentrated as our bodies. The Marine Corps had just one goal: to change us into Marines willing to kill and to die in defence of our country.

One day, Sgt Hall asked me why I had joined the Marines.

"Sir, I joined the Marine Corps because when I was a little boy, I saw the Marines going off to war where I lived at Camp Pendleton's main gate. I've wanted to be a Marine ever since."

"I think you've made it," he smiled.

"Yes sir!" I replied.

That evening, I recalled the scene. When I considered my answer, I realised the reply to his question had been mechanical. I had given the same reply ever since I was a child. I thought about the question once more. Why, indeed, did I join the Marines? I rattled off all the possible reasons. For love of country? Because I wanted to belong to what I considered America's finest class of men? For love of action, and a challenge? To fulfil my childhood dream? To prove a point? Yes, any of these or all of them combined. But was I satisfied?

21

In the dark, I lifted up my hands. I could not see them, but I could feel how big and muscled they had become. "Thanks to the Marine training I now have a killer's instincts," I thought proudly.

As soon as I said that, I knew I had lied. I had no killer's instincts at all. My once foul temper had mellowed under the unremitting discipline of the Marine Corps. Paradoxically, as I mastered the art of killing, I had lost all desire to fight.

At the end of my service, I left the Corps to resume my job as a lithographer. My parents welcomed their new Marine with open arms, and even my usually reserved Mom let down her guard to beam at the green uniform with pride.

It didn't take me long to settle down again in my old job. I liked being back and I enjoyed even more the company of the others who worked there. Every day, after work, we went to a gambling club in Gardenia, the only town in California where it was legalised. We could afford to go there so frequently because the club management had brought the cost of drink and food down to a minimum to lure people in to gamble.

In the gloom of the cocktail lounge, each of us downed drink after drink in rapid succession. I always made sure I drank just as much as the others. I had an image to project.

Of course, the bar was crowded with well-painted "dolls" who, at the start of the evening, we would hardly have considered candidates for a beauty contest. However, as the night wore on, and we swallowed round upon round, their beauty increased correspondingly. Sitting around the curve of the bar, we would swap stories of our "chicks", each boast gaining in the telling. I was up there with the best of them, telling stories and sprinkling them liberally with the colourful language I had picked up in the Marines.

Often, I heard the resident band play the Platters hit, "The Great Pretender". If I allowed myself to think about

22

it, the lyrics would begin to bother me.

I'd never honestly liked drinking, even from the beginning. I'd seen the dignity stripped from any man who had drunk himself stupid. I didn't want to be a part of that. But I'd had enough of being different from everyone, and now I had my chance to show them I wasn't second-rate any longer.

Even as I swallowed another measure of whisky, and eyed one of the nearby girls, the theme of the song still nagged me. I reassured myself that I had as many girls as the others. But somehow even that was not enough. I had a gnawing suspicion that what we were into was second-rate. There was no beauty in it, no satisfaction. Something vital seemed to be missing. Had the others found it? I didn't think so, because they all needed to talk about it so much – almost as though we were trying to reassure each other. The louder my jokes and boasts became, the more hollow they sounded.

Whenever these thoughts threatened to disturb my sense of well-being, I would push them down as deep as I could get them. The drink helped to lull me into a state of oblivion. I was really living now. I had girls, my drink, my friends, and I was accepted. I didn't care about anything else.

At least, that's what I told myself, but really, deep down, I knew I *did* care. That was just the trouble.

* * *

Julie Porter. When I met her, I knew there was nothing tawdry, nothing of the common about this girl. Her beauty was not just skin-deep.

I had first seen her four years earlier, at the nearby church my parents had insisted that I attend in those days. A group of us were sitting in a pew, listening to the pastor's sermon, when one of my friends dug me in the ribs.

"Hey buddy, take a look down the row."

23

I did. A couple of young girls were bent over a note-book, smothering giggles and glancing occasionally at the pastor in the hope that he wouldn't notice.

The one who was writing particularly caught my eye. She was a winner. Long shiny golden hair, flawless rose-petal complexion, grey-blue eyes, and something about her expression that was soft, gentle. She was only fourteen, but already she was the sort of girl you looked at twice – three times ...

Intrigued, my companion decided to find out what they were up to, and, winking at another friend to distract the pair, managed to get hold of the little book.

"Wow, David. Look what it says, man."

All thoughts of the sermon long since forgotten, I read what she had written.

'I'm going to be David's wife ...'

I glanced up in surprise. What on earth had made her write that? The poor girl squirmed under my gaze, blush-ing as she realised I had read those words, intended only for her girlfriend's eyes.

Yet, even the blush itself only succeeded in making her the prettier ...

"She's got a crush on you," my friend whispered loudly.

I smiled. "Well," I thought, "a guy could certainly do a whole lot worse." But with that smile I caught myself. I was eighteen years old after all, unquestionably a man of the world, and this girl was a mere fourteen.

Four years later, I was driving past the church on a Sunday afternoon when I noticed a stunning blonde stepping into the sanctuary. Slowing the car down for a closer look, I immediately recognised her as that "silly" girl who had scribbled in her notebook. I decided to visit the church to see more of her. Now I was the one to feel silly. Could I really get such a girl to be interested in me?

But, after just two weeks, we were both smitten, and with each other during every spare moment. I never let

24

a single day go by without seeing her. We laughed together, drove together, took in the sights, ran on the beach. No matter how much time we shared, it was never enough.

Every night I had to travel across town for classes to improve my reading and writing. Then, right after college, I would be at Julie's house – ten p.m. sharp. She would serve us Coke and potato chips, and we would sit side by side till the early hours, laughing and talking about anything and everything. I told her about my class, and my reading problem, and Julie seemed to understand immediately. Frequently she went through my homework with me, offering her gentle encouragement. I, in turn, loved to listen as she unburdened herself of the worries and problems that had come with her day.

There was only one topic where we had a difference of opinion. Like my parents, Julie was serious about her religion. She had made a commitment to Jesus Christ twelve months before. But she never talked about my own beliefs. She said very little in fact. It was her life that spoke volumes.

One night I watched Julie looking after her eighty-year-old grandmother, who lived with the family. This gracious lady had become seriously ill in her latter years, and could do very little for herself. I looked on as Julie fed her, washed her face and hands, cleaned her room and fluffed up her pillows. When all was in order, she sat down beside her grandmother listening as the old lady reminisced, all the while patting Julie's hand.

This girl knew what it was to care.

Once I had met Julie, I could not be bothered with the other girls any more. She had a depth which was new to me. She stood for something – and whatever it was it rang true. It seemed that the girls I had known previously were mere carbon-copies compared to her. Julie was real, and I was head-over-heels in love.

In time, our talks at night began to include new topics. The two of us started to discuss our wedding, our marriage, the life we would share together. We planned on three children – each of them twenty months apart. We even gave them their names.

I presented Julie with a ring, and she blushed again as I proudly placed it on her finger. We belonged together – for ever.

But two months later, the bombshell landed. Julie broke off our engagement. She was overwhelmed at the extensive preparation for our coming wedding. It was to be a big, lavish affair, consistent with my father's position – and Julie felt it would all be too much for her.

My fingers trembled around the ring as she returned it to me. I was broken. This girl had become everything to me, and now I was afraid I was going to lose her.

A few days later, I managed to persuade her to come for a drive to talk it out. On Easter Sunday, I took her up the winding road leading to Palos Verdes Estates. We parked the car on top of a cliff with a two-hundred-foot drop down to the Pacific Ocean. It was a bright, windy afternoon. Facing Santa Catalina Island, the sea, and the wind, we talked.

"I'm sorry, David – really sorry. But our backgrounds are just too different," she began falteringly. "Your family has a position in society. Your Dad is a well-known figure."

She paused, fighting back tears.

"Julie," I reached across to take her hand. She pulled it away.

"No, David. I'd never do. I wouldn't fit into that kind of lifestyle. It's not just the matter of the wedding itself, it's a whole future with a family so different from me."

"Honey." This time I did manage to capture that hand. "I love you, Julie. And I want to tell you something. It's not my family you're marrying. It's me."

By now I had caught her in my arms. "Julie, do you love me?"

"You know I do."

"Well I love you too. What's more, I believe we belong

26

together. And if you try to leave, to get away from me, I'll chase you anywhere around the world."

Those grey-blue eyes looked up into mine, and held their gaze, as I wiped away the tears.

"What do you say, Julie?"

"I do want to be your wife, David," she replied, her voice trembling.

By this time, the sun was a huge red and yellow ball low on the horizon. Its rays were flung far across the water – pinks, purples, oranges and golds, bouncing off the surface like a pebble skipping the waves. I cuddled Julie in my arms and kissed her gently.

"Then, honey, if you really mean that, when will you marry me?" I whispered against her lips.

"Tomorrow," she whispered back. She meant it.

*　　*　　*

Next day, we headed south of the border to the Mexican town of Tijuana. We were eloping. We told no one except my boss at work, and two friends who came along as witnesses.

Julie and I sat in the back of the car as we whizzed towards the Mexican border.

The tiny wedding chapel had seen many weddings like ours, and the dark-skinned attorney who shuffled into the room to conduct the ceremony looked as worn out as the plastic flowers adorning the chapel.

But, to us, all that mattered was to hear him say the magic words: "I now pronounce you husband and wife." I kissed Julie and led her proudly from the building.

As we headed back over the border, the American immigration officer looked at both of us holding hands in the back of the car. "What have you been doing in Mexico?"

"Eloping," I smiled. "Look, here's my wife's ring."

The officer leaned a little further into the car, and fixed

his expression on Julie. "How old is your wife?" he asked.

"She's eighteen," I replied.

He stared at the band of silver, looked again at the pair of us and said: "Young man, you ought to be ashamed of yourself."

I smiled. I wasn't. It was a border crossing that I would never forget.

CHAPTER THREE

The First Step

Just one week after the wedding, we were back in Torrance, California – setting up house. Together we went out to buy pots, pans, appliances, china and linen. But as Julie unpacked her own things, I realised for the first time how frugal she had always been in buying clothes for herself. This girl definitely deserved a treat, I decided. She was going to have a new wardrobe.

The next free morning, I drove her to Los Angeles. "Honey, this is your special day. And I want you to buy everything you need – and I mean absolutely *everything.*"

We spent the whole day shopping, going from store to store in search of every item. Julie's eyes glowed with pleasure. And with each new purchase, they seemed to get brighter. She bought skirts, blouses, slacks, sweaters, dresses – and in every piece she chose, she looked beautiful. At the close of the day, she was too thrilled to say a single word. Instead, she placed all her parcels carefully on the ground beside her, and threw herself into my arms. I looked at her with pride, my heart positively dancing at the sight. This girl was so special. And she was mine.

I loved loving Julie. If, beforehand, I had expected marriage with her to be good – now that it had come about, I realised it was the best thing that had ever happened to me.

It took Julie's parents no time at all to accept the fact of our marriage. "You can do no wrong in my mother's eyes," said my brand new wife, after her phone call to break the news. "As long as it's you I've eloped with, she is happy. She says I'm very lucky to get you," she added with a twinkle.

29

"Well that makes two of us," I replied, reaching out to give her a hug.

With my parents, however, the adjustment took a little longer. When first we told them what we had done, the two were stunned, and I suspect, a little hurt. And understandably so. Gone were their plans for a beautiful wedding, complete with tiered cake and bridesmaids. The wedding invitations, printed and ready for postage, sat waiting on my parents' coffee table. It was some time before they could bring themselves to throw them out.

Within a few weeks, however, they became used to the idea. One night as we sat at supper, a large package was delivered to our door. Inside we found a magnificent stereo set "from Dad and Mom with love – for your future together". We knew we had been forgiven.

In time, as planned, we had our three babies. All of them bouncing with health under Julie's gentle care, all of them just twenty months apart, and all of them gorgeous. We gave them the names we had chosen so long before; Deanne, Dawn, and David – our three "D's".

But, as they grew, Julie became concerned about one aspect of their upbringing which was missing.

"Dave, the children really need to go to Sunday School."

I looked at her. It was the first time the difference in our beliefs had disturbed the placid sea of our marriage.

"Honey, you know how I feel about church."

She did. For many years I had kept to my resolution never to worship again. Since meeting Julie, I had attended a few times – but only for her sake. In church I always felt like a fish out of water. I didn't belong with the holy Joes gathered in those buildings. All of them always tried to save me – what from I wasn't sure. I only knew I would have been much happier if they had just tried to get to know me instead.

"But David, it's very important for the children."

"Well that's okay. If they need to go, they can. But not me, honey."

On the weekends, I much preferred my old acquaintance, the gambling tables, to that of the local church. Often we would visit Las Vegas to see Julie's family on a Saturday morning, then I always visited "the Mint", one of the city's biggest gambling houses, in the afternoon and evening. Julie's stepfather was himself a dealer at a crap table, and he taught me all the tricks in the system. When we arrived home the following night, I would unwind in front of the television, a glass of Brew 102 in one hand, and Julie curled up on the couch beside me.

Julie's patience was incredible. She never tried to nag me into changing my ways, nor into allowing her to go to church. Instead, while I was at work during the week she would listen to her Christian programmes on Station KGER and study a Bible correspondence course they were conducting.

The kids started Sunday School and our life went on as before. I was more than content with the way it was going. We were happy. I was doing well at the job. Our bank balance was looking healthy. Life was everything I wanted.

But one day, a tragedy took place which was to shatter my feeling of well being.

A friend, Larry, was employed as a fence builder for the world-famous Barnum and Bailey circus troupe which was playing Vegas at the time. He was a small, wiry man, full of laughter, and fond of drinking and gambling. On one Saturday evening, we had been together at the card tables for fourteen straight hours. It was the first time in our gambling experience that both of us lost. We parted that evening with the promise to meet the following night to recover our losses.

I never saw him again. On Sunday morning, he went swimming with some of his firemen friends. He had a few drinks. Recklessly, he climbed to the second storey window of the club house overlooking the swimming pool and hurled himself towards the pool. The first two times he hit the water. He was a performer. He loved the applause that

31

greeted him after each successful dive.

"Have another drink," offered one admirer as he prepared himself for his third dive. He took a large swig of bourbon and then confidently rushed up the clubhouse stairs, two at a time.

Larry did not hear the horrified screams of his friends and the spectators as he hit the hot concrete with a sickening thud. He died instantly. My first thought when I heard of his death was, "Oh, Larry did not know Jesus."

Jesus! That name was always tied in my mind with sickness, weakness, now death. Larry's death was my first exposure to it. It frightened me. It made me think for the first time about life having an end. I did not enjoy the thought.

Two weeks later I was beginning to settle down again. I had successfully pushed Larry's death to the back of my mind, when I was forced to face up to the unavoidable reality a second time.

Art Malone was an army sergeant, a man who had won medals fighting in the Philippines during World War Two when I was still a little boy dreaming of the war overseas. I had met him through my work, and we hit it off instantly. It had become Art's habit to drop off after work for some drinking and kidding around or a game of checkers with me and the boys.

On a typical afternoon, we had enjoyed a couple of rum and Cokes in the office and had exchanged dirty jokes. At about six p.m., we went down to our cars, waved good-bye to each other, and started for home. Art drove down Normandy Boulevard towards Los Angeles, while I went the opposite direction to Redondo Beach. Twenty minutes later, on the corner of Normandy and Manchester, he collided with a truck. He died instantly.

"Jesus!" I groaned when I read about the accident in next morning's papers. "Jesus!" It was the first time I uttered that name with meaning. Julie found me in tears. She put her arms around me. I was trembling. She thought my tears and emotions were for Art, but I knew better. I

32

was crying and trembling for myself.

For the second time in my healthy life, death had shown its horrible skull to me – and I did not know how to cope.

* * *

"Dave, I have a question for you."

"Uh uh?" I was digging hungrily into one of Julie's delicious meals, keeping one eye on the plates of the little girls beside me, watchful for any cups of milk that might be headed for the floor.

"Your parents rang today." Julie's hand shook a little as she reached out to pick up David's bottle.

"Good. Nothing wrong, was there?" I looked up at her, wondering why she seemed so hesitant.

"No, nothing. In fact, they just wanted to invite us out."

"Fine." Living so near my parents, it was common for the four of us to get together frequently. We loved each other's company, and both grandparents doted on the three D's. "Where are we going this time?"

Julie took a deep breath. "They wondered if we would like to hear Billy Graham."

I put down my knife and fork with a clatter. "They did, did they?"

She gulped. "Yes. Honey, they say he is very good ..." her voice trailed off as our eyes met.

"Julie, you know how I feel about ..."

"Yes, I know." The poor girl was doing her best. "I just thought that this might be – you know – different."

"Well, I'm sorry. But I don't think it is. Anyway, our vacation is coming up, and you know I want to renovate the house."

Our home needed only a few more improvements before we'd be able to sell it. Both my father and I had poured long hours into the building, and it was expected to fetch a good price. After that, Julie and I hoped to take a step up the ladder into something better.

33

"I have ordered all sorts of building materials. I'll be working overtime to get it all done. There'll be no time for a trip to Los Angeles." The evangelist was to be speaking in the L.A. Coliseum.

"Then I'll tell them no?"

"Definitely." Subject dismissed, I leaned over to help the girls cut their meat.

But my parents did not give up easily. And Julie, out of her concern, could not leave it at that either. Throughout the following two weeks, the three repeatedly brought up the subject of the Billy Graham Crusade, until on the third week I said I would go.

And I did – not just once, but twice. However, at the suggestion of a third, I put my foot down. Instead I gave all my attention to the house renovations until, on the final day of my vacation, I finished everything.

I sat outside after lunch surveying my work with a glass of my favourite brew.

With the thought of a better home to follow the sale of this one, I was pleased with myself. I was making my way in the world, I was really getting somewhere.

I leaned back in my easy chair allowing the waves of euphoria to wash over me. But right in the middle of my fourth can of beer, a nagging question rose from my subconscious. Oh no. Since the death of my friends I had been having too many disturbing thoughts. "Is it worth it, David; is your life worth it? Money can't do anything for Larry and Art any more, can it? You are trying so hard to make it, but where will it get you in the long run?" It was like a record caught in a groove. To shut it off, I parried, "Well, I'm a decent guy. There's not much wrong with my values." During the last few weeks I had even made the grand concession to accompany Julie and the kids to church.

But there again, my thoughts disturbed me. I recalled that the last evening we heard him, Billy Graham had said something about people who went to church. "There may be many of you out there who have been to church all your lives," he said. "Many of you call yourselves 'Christians'. My address of Wednesday night will be specially directed towards Christians."

Wednesday. That was tonight. If I endured another trip back to that Coliseum, would it set my mind at rest once and for all? All this drinking was driving me crazy. I tossed my sixth empty beer can to one side and stood up.

"Julie," I called, feeling rather sheepish, "I'm prepared to go hear that preacher again, if you can find a baby sitter." Julie was on the phone faster than I could say Billy Graham. Within minutes, she had organised a baby sitter and was waiting enthusiastically at our front door.

It does not usually rain in southern California in September. It did on 4th September, 1963. As a consequence, only twenty thousand people attended the Crusade that evening. The Coliseum was barely a fifth full.

Billy Graham came to the microphone. He was just a speck in the distance, but I heard every word. "Okay Billy," I thought, "you said you were going to speak to Christians tonight. Well, here I am."

Almost as though he was accepting my challenge, the evangelist's first words hit home. "Many of you out there have heard about Jesus all your life. Maybe you've even been to church every now and again. What I want to ask you tonight is – have you ever met Jesus personally?"

That point, I was prepared to concede. I did not know Jesus in the same way Julie and those on the platform seemed to know Him.

His next words hit me with a jolt. He quoted from John 4:24: "God is spirit, and those who worship Him must worship in spirit and in truth."

Truth. Did I know anything about truth? Those aggravating doubts surfaced again and somewhere inside there seemed to be a voice that drove the point home. "You're not living the truth, David. You're out there proving yourself to everybody; the success story, the self-made

35

man earning his way in the world with the things that matter. But *are* they the things that matter? You can't even explain death within your definition of life."

What's got into me? I wondered. These aren't the thoughts of a U.S. Marine. They must be due to the six cans of beer I drank before I left home. But despite my attempts to explain it away, the questioning persisted.

"Even the booze, David, the bars, the gambling, the blue stories you always have up your sleeve, they are not giving you what you want, are they?"

And for the first time, I was prepared to admit the truth.

I had sold out to a lie and had been conned by it.

I looked at Julie. She knew what I had seen in her was something different. Or was it *Someone* different? That night, in the meeting, it seemed a magnetic force was pulling me towards God. The preacher continued.

"You know, if you want to meet Jesus Christ, you've got to be prepared to let Him deal with sin in your life. He wants to save you from all that."

"Okay," I thought, "if sin is the same as the lie I have been living, I've had enough of it anyway."

"And," he continued in his flowing Southern accent, "you have to let Jesus become the boss of your life, the Lord of your life."

As the evangelist gave his invitation, I saw people all around me stepping out from their seats and going down to stand in front of the platform.

If I did the same, it would mean once again I'd have to be different from the circle of friends with whom I was at last finding acceptance. On the other hand, I would be throwing off the counterfeit for the true. I'd be living the life God had intended me to live all along. *That* was the real issue.

The seemingly magnetic force pulled stronger as Billy Graham's voice again reached me. "I assure you that unless you change and become like little children, you will never enter the kingdom of heaven. This is verse 3 of Matthew,

36

Chapter 18. God is speaking to someone tonight in his late twenties. God is telling that person to be converted and humble himself like a little child. A little child does not have to understand all, yet he believes. So should this man believe ..."

We had been sitting sixty rows up in the mighty arena, but the voice of the dynamic speaker reached me as though he were speaking only a few feet away. And he *was* speaking to me.

"When you stand up and take the first step, Jesus will meet you and He'll walk with you down here and for the rest of your life ..."

By now the powerful force I had sensed all evening had a grip on me. I was convicted. I had been wrong and I knew I wanted to start again. I stood up and moved past Julie, pausing to murmur as I went, "Honey, I'm going to get myself right with God tonight." She didn't need to say anything, her thoughts were written all over her face as she looked at me, her pretty eyes brimming.

Even so, I felt daunted at the prospect of the long walk to the front and edged my way tentatively towards the end of the row. But when I reached the first step of the aisle down, an extraordinary thing happened. It was as though Someone did indeed meet me just as the evangelist had said. I couldn't explain it, but when I got to the front, I recognised this Someone as the Jesus to whom Billy Graham was calling for commitment. As the preacher prayed on our behalf, I quietly repeated the words after him, handing my life over to Jesus in that instant. When I raised my head again, I found a smiling snowy-haired man beside me, sporting a lapel-button which read "Counsellor". He gave me reading material and spent time talking quietly – or rather, listening. I was struck by the warmth in his immediate understanding of me.

Some minutes later, I turned to take the long walk back to Julie knowing that my life, too, was turning, never to be the same again. That same presence which had accompanied

37

me all the way to the front remained beside me as I climbed those hundred and twenty steps to my seat.

He has never left me since.

* * *

The next morning, I greeted my colleagues at work with such warmth that one of the girls commented: "Someone I know made a killing in Vegas!"

"No way. You're right off. And you'll never guess it, so I'm going to tell you. I accepted the Lord. I'm saved." The phrases which had previously made me retch now flowed naturally from my lips.

"Quit putting me on!" I couldn't blame her for not believing me. Dave — return from vacation talking about God and religion? Impossible.

Within a week they believed. The staff watched agog as I tore down the Playboy centrefolds which had papered the wall near my desk. My buddies showed visible consternation when they found I had obviously lost interest in our gambling haunt.

"You don't even talk the same, man," they announced. It was true. The cussing which had been a part of every second sentence for me since the Marines, had abruptly and completely stopped.

The contrast was so marked that I was astonished. I knew that it had nothing to do with my own will-power or self-discipline. Neither was I strong enough for me to achieve this kind of change. No, it was as though Jesus had literally lifted the old interests from me. I loved Him for it.

The crap tables, the centrefolds which well-meaning buddies continued to bring to my desk, and the invitations to join them in drinking myself blind, had lost their pull. The scene which I had revelled in before seemed tawdry and cheap. It had all the appeal of a week-old loaf of bread. For the first time I felt really free.

38

Now that I had met Jesus I couldn't get to know Him quickly enough. I approached the Bible with the hunger of a starving man, and no amount of reading seemed to satisfy my appetite.

Little David's night feedings gave me the perfect opportunity. At three months of age, he needed a bottle in the early hours to see him through till morning. While Julie slept to get her much needed rest, I stayed up, reading my Bible until he woke for his bottle.

Within six weeks I had completed the study course given to me by old Mr Roy, the white-haired man from the Crusade. He faithfully rang me several times a week, and often came to our home for Sunday lunch. His loving concern was felt by every one of us, and before long he was an established member of the family.

His gentle direction gave me the basic principles of growth in the new life I had begun.

"Are you attending your local church, David? Are you playing an active part there?" he would ask.

"You need fellowship, David," Mr Roy would insist. "You need the support of others and you need the teaching."

I battled inwardly. I had attended church for so many years in my childhood. And I knew that the lives of some who claimed to be Christians didn't match up with their words. They were a bunch of hypocrites, I had decided. And the unforgettable night of Jayne Mansfield's wedding was still vivid in my memory.

"David, I know the church is made up of human beings, and that they make mistakes." Mr Roy was always understanding. "But you're a human being too," he added gently, "so am I. Why do you think Jesus died for us? And there's a way you can get your eyes off human failing and back on the One you're there for."

"What's that?"

"Service, son. Find a way to serve others."

I did. Julie heard of a church nearby which needed some

39

printing assistance. "You'd be the ideal one to help, David," she said pleadingly.

We started to attend regularly and play an active role in its work. And I came to be very grateful we did. The pastor, Kelly Walberg, was a clear and uncompromising teacher from the Word of God – the book I had come to love so much. For the first time in my life I began to sit through sermons without fidgeting or glancing at my watch.

Not always, though, was the teaching to my liking. One morning I returned home from church very thoughtful. His sermon had touched on the Christian's use of money, and I knew I was about to have a battle with myself. Julie and I were having trouble making ends meet. There was little need for overtime at work, and my basic wage was stretched to accommodate the needs of the family. How could we possibly spare money to give away?

On the other hand, if our lives belonged to Jesus, that money belonged to Him too. And, we decided, He loved us too much to allow us to starve.

We began to tithe – and within a few days I was called upon to do overtime work. Immediately our income increased to the point where, despite the amount we were giving away, we had more than enough for our needs.

As the weeks passed, we became happier than we had ever been before – except for one thing. At first I could not put my finger on it but slowly a feeling of unrest was growing within me. I felt unsure about the job I was doing. I had a feeling that while I was busy in one place, I should actually be at work in another.

I didn't know quite how to explain it, nor what to do about it. At the end of my course with the Billy Graham Association, I sent in my final answer sheet along with a request. "Would you please pray for me?" I asked. "I am not sure what the Lord means me to be doing with my career."

Their reply came quickly. In essence, it said: "We are praying for you, David. Wait patiently. The Lord will show you in time. Meanwhile concentrate on four areas: prayer, reading God's Word, fellowship and witness."

It was the last one that touched a sensitive nerve. Telling others about Jesus was something I found difficult. Somehow I didn't know where to start or what to say, so I said very little. I was sure I would not be able to witness if anybody asked me to. Now people were. It was not only the Graham Association, but Pastor Walberg and, of course, Mr Roy as well.

"David?" Another phone call. "You won't grow yourself unless you share your faith with other people."

A couple of my friends had become very concerned for the teenagers in the Watts area, a nearby area where the population was largely black. "The kids aren't too keen on thinking about Jesus yet, but they do enjoy football. And maybe afterwards, they would like to hear about Him. Would you be interested, Dave?"

I chuckled to myself. How like this Lord I was getting to know, to ease me into making a start in the area of witnessing. I was always interested in a game of football ...

I gave my friends their answer. "Okay, I'll join you. But on one condition only. You'll have to teach me first how I am supposed to talk about my faith. I don't want to blow it."

Their instructions seemed straightforward. I was to befriend the kids we would meet. I should pray for them. And I must memorise the appropriate verses of Scripture so that it would be easy to quote God's Word.

And that was it? Would I then be able to speak to these six-foot, well-built, black teenagers for Jesus?

"The Lord will do the rest," one of my buddies assured me.

He was right. After the first game we played, the boys were more than keen to hear about Jesus Christ. As we talked that day, the Lord brought five of them to Himself.

The following week, two more followed their example. And soon twenty hot and sweaty new believers were

41

meeting together after an afternoon on the football field.

With Pastor Walberg's encouragement, Julie and I began a group for teenagers in our own church too. Yet, although we were very happy, the feeling of restlessness had not left me. If anything, it had grown stronger. What exactly did Jesus want to do with my life, and my training as a lithographer?

My first inkling came a few weeks later, during one of my continuing nights of Bible Study. That evening, a verse in Mark struck me for the first time. Mark 13 : 10, "And the Gospel must first be published among all nations." Published! That was my line of work. All night long the verse remained in my mind. Even as I slept it would not go away.

The next night, another line from the Bible leapt out. I was reading the last chapter of Matthew and came to the place where Jesus told His disciples to go into all the world and preach the Gospel. I read it again. The idea struck a chord.

Pastor Walberg was one with a deep interest in missionary work. Every Sunday, at one of the three services, a missionary gave the sermon. The pastor himself was on twenty-six missionary boards. But until that evening, I had never asked myself about my own response to the Great Commission. What if God ever called me to become a missionary? Would I be willing?

The answer had to be no. I was a brand new Christian. What on earth was I doing even contemplating such questions?

A few days later, my Bible reading confronted me again. Psalm 68 : 11, "The Lord gave the Word: great was the company of those that PUBLISHED it."

Was it possible, just possible, that there was direction for me in all of this?

I put the idea to Julie. "Honey, you don't suppose the Lord could be calling us to some place in the world where there's a need for Bibles to be printed?"

Her blue-grey eyes blinked in surprise. "Well I – I – what makes you ask?"

I explained about the verses and she began to nod with understanding. "Perhaps Pastor Walberg is the best one to advise us," she suggested. After so many months of praying, neither of us wanted to miss the Lord's leading.

The pastor too was sympathetic. "As a matter of fact, David, the speaker at our fellowship meeting this week is from the Far East Broadcasting Company. Why don't you come to hear him?"

I already knew of FEBC, and the reports I had heard were excellent. Their broadcasts were beamed to countries throughout South East Asia – particularly those under Communist or restricted government. China was the focus of their work.

I listened closely as their speaker described the ministry and its needs. At that time, they were looking for an assistant in one specific area – literature. They were printing Scriptures for distribution among the countries of their region.

It was an unexpected need for a broadcasting company. I had thought they might want people for broadcasting, script-writing, or translation work – not literature.

Yet it dovetailed exactly with the verses I had been given the week before.

Still it seemed unlikely, if not crazy, that I should consider going out as a missionary. Together Julie and I put it before the Lord. "Father, you know how this looks to us – impossible! Yet if, somehow, this is your leading and your plan, we don't want to get in your way. Show us Lord ..."

Despite the prayer time I still had many doubts. I listed them all to Julie. "You know me, honey. I don't have any formal training at a Bible College. And you know what I'm like at studies anyway." The doubts which had haunted me from my school days returned to me. "I don't have what it takes to be a missionary."

43

She turned to look at me. "David," she said quietly, "if the Lord is taking us out to work for Him, He will be the one to do it, not you."

A few days later, the speaker and his wife came to dinner and told us more about the need. After the meal, they showed us slides of their base in the Philippines, at the same time warning me that sixteen others had also applied for the job. Every one had been rejected. But I was welcome to apply.

I looked across at Julie as if to say: "I told you so. If they have been turned down, what chance do I have?" But she just gave a slight shake of her head, and smiled her encouragement.

The following Sunday, during the service, Pastor Walberg surprised the congregation with an announcement: "I want you all to be praying for a young couple in our church, David and Julie. Will you two stand up for the congregation, please?"

Our faces were as red as beetroot. It was the first time we had stood up in church like that. Who was I to be standing before all these people, I thought. I was only nine months old in the Lord. I stammered and stuttered our thanks and sat down as soon as was politely possible.

* * *

Yet in time, I had to admit even I couldn't deny the facts. We had asked God for a leading and all the signs seemed to point in the same direction. I began to believe we were to go after all.

The same conviction seemed to have been given to the deacons of our local church. Without our knowledge, two days after we'd stood up in church, they had approved a resolution to support Julie and me for the first term of our literature ministry with FEBC.

It only remained for us to await FEBC's reply. I was at work when it came. As I answered Julie's phone call, the office secretary warned me she appeared to be crying. But surely the news she brought could not be bad ...

"Julie?"

"Honey," she sobbed. "They don't want us. It's a rejection. I'm so sorry ..."

CHAPTER FOUR
"If China Opens Up . . ."

I was sure there had been a mistake. That evening, Julie and I prayed as we had never prayed before. We recalled the verses that God had given me about *publishing* His Word abroad.

As we knelt by the side of our bed, I asked, "Lord, if we have understood you correctly, could you please talk to the Far East Broadcasting people also?"

He did.

The next day at work I received another phone call from Julie.

"I have just heard from FEBC," she said trying to contain the excitement in her voice. "The man told me that if we'd received the letter saying they could not use us, we should disregard it. He was recommending to the FEBC Board that they accept us as missionary candidates."

The Lord had done it. Now we really knew we were following His direction.

Two weeks later, FEBC called again, and I asked what had caused them to change their minds.

"Didn't you know that your church board members had committed themselves to you? We received their letter after we had written back to you," he said.

"We realised the Lord was telling us we had made a mistake."

*   *   *

The following months flew by as we organised our household for the coming move and began a never-ending series of good-byes to our friends. It was hard to leave them; Pastor Walberg, old Mr Roy, the black kids in the Watts district, the teenagers in the group Julie and I had started, the other couples at church, my buddies at work. The list went on and on. Hardest of all was the wrench from our families, as we stepped out into a future which was, in many ways, unknown.

During our final days of packing, however, we had an unforgettable reminder of the One who would be going with us, and His ability to look after His children.

I had been up most of the night, preparing our household goods for shipment to Manila. First of all we had transported our belongings to an enormous warehouse, a full block long, and then I had stayed behind to construct a wooden crate around them. At midnight I returned home for a few hours sleep, but was back on the job before dawn to get it completed.

At six a.m. I finally left the building, blinking in the sunlight. I reached thankfully into my pocket for the car keys, only to discover they were not there. Instead, my fingers located a large hole through which the keys had no doubt fallen.

I looked at the warehouse hopelessly. I had walked the full length of that place more times than I cared to remember to pick up materials for the crate's construction. Somewhere along that well-trodden path were my keys. Somewhere.

But where? Not only was I tired, I was also in a hurry to make another appointment that morning. Our church had a working bee for the men, and I had promised to be there. I had no time to lose.

Starting at one end, I trudged slowly up and down the building for a full hour, trying to cover the steps I had taken previously. There was no sign of the keys. After that I decided to hunt specifically around the crate itself, where I had spent the majority of my time. On hands and knees, I checked out every nook and cranny, but was still without success. And then, quite unexpectedly, I had a strong conviction that the Lord was speaking to me.

47

"Son," He seemed to be saying, "you're in the right position, but you're doing the wrong thing."

What did He mean? What position? I looked down, and all at once, realised I was on my knees ... His voice seemed to continue. "I could have told you all along where they are. But you didn't ask me."

"Dear Father, forgive me," I said. "I never even thought to pray about those wretched keys." It suddenly seemed so simple that I wondered how I could have come so far in my search without consulting Him. "But Father," I concluded, "I do ask you now. In Jesus' strong Name, I ask you."

At that I opened my eyes, and there, four feet from where I knelt, was the shining gleam of metal.

'Thank you, Father," I almost shouted, as I ran joyfully to the car.

I reached the church a few minutes later and ran into the church grounds. Absent-mindedly I had put my keys back into the pocket with the hole, and as I ran past the hedge I heard with dismay a loud clink. The keys had fallen on the pathway, and ricocheted into the greenery.

Groaning at my carelessness I turned to begin a second hunt for them. But the foliage was very dense, and a feeling of defeat came over me as I searched in vain. This time it seemed I had lost them for sure. I dropped to the ground, crouching on my knees as I continued my search. And then, just as surely as the first time, I sensed the Lord's voice again. "Son, haven't you learned your lesson yet?"

I hadn't. I was down on my knees again: in the right position, but doing the wrong thing. "Dear God, I am sorry. Don't lose patience with me yet!" I told Him. "Please, where are they now?"

Unbelievably, as before, I opened my eyes, reached into the branches and, without even seeing them, placed my hands right onto the keys.

The lesson seemed too incredible for words. And yet – maybe it was not so. It seemed the Lord wanted to reassure

us in the most unmistakable way that He could take care
of our family whatever the future held, right down to the
smallest detail.

*   *   *

When finally we reached the Philippines itself, He had
another surprise in store.

Our final good-bye to our friends and family in the States
had been a tearful one. We knew it would be some years
before we would see any of them again, and we couldn't
help feeling alone as our plane took off for a country where
we knew almost no one, and had no family.

Hanging outside our house at the FEBC compound was
a huge sign welcoming every member of the family. And
shortly after we had put down our suitcases, we were
presented with a book of introduction to the team. In it
was a photograph of every family on the compound with
a caption describing the roles of the parents and the ages
and interests of their children. The book was ours to keep.
It had been specially prepared in our honour.

That evening, as Julie and I prepared the three D's for
bed, we glanced at each other over the top of their curly
heads, already resting wearily on their pillows. Jesus had
proved faithful again. We *did* have family here in the Philippines – His family.

We knew at once there would be no chance of loneliness
at FEBC.

*   *   *

There were more lessons to learn.

Although I knew without a doubt that the Lord had
brought us to FEBC, I still felt inadequate to fulfil the
role of missionary. Being so young in Him, I wondered
how in the world I would have the wherewithal to minister

49

to others. Before long, it became obvious that God had that in hand too. He was going to train me on the job, and each of the lessons was going to be painful.

Item number one on His list must have been the task of making me face myself honestly; to work out where my true values lay. My first morning on the job, I was enthusiasm itself as I fronted up bright and early for work.

"David, it's good to have you here. We'd like you to begin in the bindery," I was told. "You'll be assisting Joe."

My spirits soared as I walked towards the machines. But then, as I realised the task they had in store for me, my excitement quickly turned to dismay.

"You'll be doing the stapling, Brother David," said Joe, the Filipino foreman.

"And what else?" I asked.

"Oh, that's all for the moment; you needn't worry about any other work, yet."

He had to be joking. A nearby press was churning out thousands of copies of the Gospel of John, all of them requiring someone laboriously to staple them together by hand. Was this to be my job for the next days, weeks, who knew how long? Was this why I had been called to the mission field? Surely not.

"Thank you, I'll get to it right away," I said as politely as I could.

I walked to the table and began to work. Hour after hour that day, I sweated in the debilitating humidity.

The next day was the same, and the next, until the long days turned into equally long weeks. Why had I trained all these years as a lithographer? It took no skill at all to do this assignment. It took no brains either. It took nothing but time. In the States I had held a far more responsible position. My daily routine included the clinching of deals which would bring in thousands of dollars for the business.

Each day, as I stapled the Gospels, the contrast loomed before my eyes. And the struggle continued for several weeks until at last the Lord gave me a thought that struck with all the force of a sledge hammer.

What do you want, David? To go out and get rich? Or to follow Me?

That morning, I viewed my work through new eyes. It was slow, yes, and neither I nor the organisation was making much money. But the books we were producing were tools that God could use to change people's lives.

*　　*　　*

In the months that followed, I began to see the full breadth of FEBC's ministry. Its twenty-three broadcasting stations were beaming out programmes every day: ten of them to destinations within the Philippines, the rest to other countries in South East Asia, particularly the People's Republic of China.

After my "apprenticeship" with the stapling machine, I became involved in the installation of new equipment and later began to assist in the production management. Julie had become busy too. She took on a part-time role in the radio section of the work, editing tapes before they went to air.

We did not have much spare time. But what little I could find, I channelled into yet another ministry to young people. Robert Foster, also from FEBC, worked with me among the teenagers on the streets of downtown Manila.

Twelve months after our arrival, we had begun to feel very settled in our lives at FEBC when, unexpectedly, we received a call from home.

"David?" It was my mother.

"Mom – how are you?"

She paused for a second. "I've got good news for you." Her voice, however, sounded strained. "It'll be hard, David, but it's good."

"What is it Mom? What's happened?"

"Your Dad is with the Lord, son. He's gone home."

I sat down, numb with shock. Dad had been in perfect

51

health before we left, without even a trace of illness. My mother's voice continued.

"God was good. He had no pain, no pain at all. It was all so sudden ..." She was obviously fighting tears and I had a sense of helplessness being physically so far from her.

Almost as though reading my thoughts, she pulled herself up and said, with just a hint of her usual strength of character, "Now I'm sure you're thinking you should come home. Well, don't. Your father would not have wanted that. He'd have wanted you there, where God means you to be. He would have wanted you to go on serving Jesus."

Julie was as shocked as I when she heard the news. After the phone call I had run home to share it with her, and both of us had found it impossible to check the tears. The two of us felt strangely bereft. We could not accept the fact that Dad, the wise, thoughtful soul whom nothing could ruffle, would no longer be available to talk through problems. He would not see his grandchildren grow up. Mother's house would be strangely silent without his presence and the steady stream of young people who always came to our home seeking his counsel.

We battled our grief through the remainder of the morning, until an understanding friend knocked at our front door. He stayed to pray with us and, in the quiet of that moment, I came to comprehend more clearly than ever before that to be absent from the body was to be present with the Lord.

I was at peace when at last I left the house to walk slowly back to work.

*　　*　　*

The literature production began to expand as FEBC took on contract work for other organisations. We were producing thousands of tracts for different groups, and distributing Gospels of John throughout the length and breadth of the Philippines. After we had sent out a million Gospels, however, our team sat down for some serious thought. These islands were receiving masses of literature telling of Jesus Christ. But there were other countries who were getting little or none at all. Wasn't it time we investigated their need for Scriptures as well?

For me, this was the start of frequent trips to assess the situation in some of our neighbouring countries. Indo-China was the main one on the list, and in time, a second million Gospels of John was produced for that land.

War-torn Vietnam was a particular focus for my travels. I regularly visited the missionaries who had chosen to stay there during the Tet Offensive. Surrounded by troops, gunfire and shelling, these brave men and women were determined to remain as long as they were allowed. Some of their colleagues had already been killed.

In time the trips brought orders from many groups: Wycliffe Bible Translators, The Bible Society, Christian and Missionary Alliance, the Southern Baptists and many more. At the same time we had maintained our regular production for literature required in the Philippines.

Each one of these experiences taught me so much that it was as though I was back in school again, although this time with a very different curriculum. My "Teacher" had a great deal to show me about what it meant to follow Him into situations where I knew I couldn't cope in my own strength.

One of those involved taking care of my family. For me, security had always been inextricably bound up with the mighty dollar. At FEBC, there were periods when our financial support would be held up due to any one of several obstacles, particularly the erratic nature of the postal system. At one stretch, it was sixty days between checks and, for the entire period, we had only forty dollars to our name.

During that time, there were evenings when we sat down at the supper table and gave thanks to God for empty plates. After praying, we spent the meal hour just enjoying one another's company. Later, we went to bed committing ourselves once again into the Lord's care, trusting Him for the following day.

The Lord did not allow our hunger to last long. Although our principle was never to tell anybody but *Him* of our need, somehow, just at the right time, bundles of food would "arrive" in our kitchen. Sometimes when we, as a family, had gone out for a walk on the compound, we would return to find some other FEBC family had left a sack of provisions inside our back door. Opening the sack we would find eggs, meat, canned food, vegetables, fruit – all the basics. To this day, we have never known which families put them there.

One morning Julie was preparing Deanne for school, and doing her best to thank the Lord although she knew she had no lunch to pack. "Father, I am trusting you," she whispered quietly, "I know we are here in Your will. And You will not allow any need to go unmet." She reached into the cupboard for a paper bag in which to place the non-existent lunch and at the moment heard a tap on the window.

"Can I come in for a minute?" It was Leila, our neighbour. "I've made one too many sandwiches this morning. Would Deanne like an extra one?"

Other times, Julie would have the basic lunch ready, when again the knock would come – this time with simply an extra cookie or cake which would brighten up Deanne's meal break. It was just that additional touch from the Lord showing He cared even about the little things.

Finally, we had only five dollars left. One steamy Sunday afternoon Julie and the children were sleeping through the siesta hour upstairs in our semi on the compound. The air seemed to hang still, thick with the crushing humidity of the tropics. Downstairs, in the kitchen, I was trying to cool myself with iced water in one hand and a fan in the other.

"Excuse me, sir," a little girl's voice broke the oppressive silence. "Please, I need help."

54

I opened the door cautiously. "Help" usually meant money. We had almost none left. "Hello. What can I do for you?" I asked.

Her face had a look of embarrassment. "It's my father. He is waiting at the gate. Would you be the one to help him, sir?"

I followed the poorly-dressed mite to the entrance. There I was greeted by a frail-looking man, his clothes no better than his daughter's. Gaping sores covered his legs.

"You are very kind to come, sir. I need help."

"What for?" I asked.

"I have leprosy, sir. I have been told of a place where I can go to be cured. But I do not have the bus fare." It was obviously an effort for him to ask for money, and he looked at the dust in shame.

"What is your occupation?" I said, stalling for time in an effort to avoid giving any of our depleted funds away. Why us, of all people, at that particular time?

"I'm a pastor," he replied. "I hope to come back to my church when I'm cured."

"How much do you need?"

"Twenty pesos, sir."

Twenty pesos. At that time, the exchange rate was four pesos to one U.S. dollar. He was asking for exactly five dollars – all that we had left in the world.

"Surely not, Lord," I protested silently. "Do you really mean me to give it all away?" Even before I'd finished the prayer I knew the answer. He did.

"I have twenty pesos with me," I told the man, and reached reluctantly into my back pocket. "Here, take it. God bless you." I meant it – at least, I tried hard to.

Together, the three of us prayed and then I turned to walk slowly back to our home.

I sat once again in the kitchen and laid it all before the Lord. "Father, I've done my best to obey You. You have led us out here and we believe we have been following You. We left everything we had built up in America, and now we have nothing left here either. You have asked for everything and we have given it."

Then it was too much for me. Marine or no Marine, I bowed my head and cried, my whole body shaking with emotion. How could I tell my wife that now we had nothing? And how could the children be expected to understand?

Even as I wept, a sensation of reassurance began to creep over me; a feeling of calm, of peace. My tears subsided and at last, I found myself telling the Lord that I trusted Him, and loved Him. And I knew He was taking care of us no matter what.

The following day, Julie went to the mail box, collected our correspondence and brought it back to the house to read. One letter bore the postmark of Redondo Beach, California. Inside was a cheque written out in our names.

Our home church had sent us a thousand dollars.

* * *

The orders from overseas, coupled with local needs, had ensured plenty of activity for us at FEBC. Nearly every machine was faithfully churning out reams of Christian material; all, that is, but one. The largest of them all, a Fairchild ColorKing press, stood idle in the corner. It had been donated by an American businessman and could produce twenty thousand Gospels of John in a single hour. It didn't make sense that God would lead someone to make such a gift, and then not allow it to be used.

"Why did You give us that press?" I asked Him. "Satan is laughing to see it lying there dormant."

The answer came a few weeks later – although in a form which at first I found difficult to recognise.

Because of tiredness from work, Julie had persuaded me to take an afternoon off and join her and our family at one of Manila's swimming pools. As soon as I jumped into its aquamarine waters, I was glad Julie had twisted my arm. I was all set for an afternoon of just drifting and relaxing, not thinking of the work at all. But Peter Jones, a friend with a ministry among the Chinese, changed all that.

"Hello," a roguish voice flew into my right ear the moment my head surfaced. A bronzed Jones, sporting a huge grin, trod water to my right, only a foot away from me.

What do friends talk about while floating in a pool on a warm April day? Everything light and summery and idle, surely. I don't know why Jones and I had to discuss our work. He could not stop himself from speaking of the Chinese he worked with, and I could not keep away from the topic of printing.

"China and the printing of Gospels ... hmmmm," he remarked.

"What about them?" I asked idly. My eyes were closed while I allowed the water to cool my perspiring body. Peter was floating somewhere on my left.

"Are you prepared to get Scriptures into China if it opens up?"

Was he serious? Everyone knew that Mao Tse-Tung had locked the country tighter than a drum. Even at that moment, the Great Helmsman was ruthlessly trying to eradicate all traces of pre-Communist economy, religions and culture and to re-mould the nation according to the concepts of Marxism.

Mao's Cultural Revolution had begun in 1966 and, led by the teenage "Red Guards", had left in its wake three years of unparalleled chaos and suffering. Thousands were in prisons or re-education camps, thousands more dead.

"You've got to be crazy," I told him. "China's never going to open up. Anyway, we're busy with Vietnam right now."

He turned to me. "David, don't say 'never'. Czechoslovakia was once considered closed to the world. But it opened up for a short time. When that happened, what did the missionaries do about it? Do you know?"

57

I didn't know. I'd never really thought about it. It was only much later that I was to learn of one missionary who did take action. On the very day the Soviet tanks were rumbling into Prague to crush the liberal regime of Aleksander Dubcek, a slender Dutchman had also entered the city. He had loaded up his station-wagon with tracts and Bibles, and had deliberately driven right in amongst the massive tanks, to make the most of the last opportunity to distribute the Word of God freely among the Czechoslovak and Russian people. His name was Brother Andrew.

Peter was insistent. "You see, David, we have to be prepared. Let me put the question again. If, someday, China does open up again, will you be ready?"

I already knew the answer. Of course, I wasn't. To my knowledge, nobody was. The last of the missionaries had fled China by the early fifties. I hadn't met one since who believed China would open again. It seemed too incredible for words.

But in the days that followed, that question would not leave me alone. Until then I had believed the only way to get the Gospel beyond China's Great Wall was by radio. And yet I also knew the Psalms promised that with God's help a person could leap over walls. God was going to have to teach me a great deal before I could really believe that promise for the impenetrable country of China.

The question of China opening continued to bother me, however, until at last I decided it simply had to be answered. I shared it with a colleague at FEBC, and the two of us resolved to get down on our knees and wait on God for His reply. So a May evening in 1969 found us kneeling together in prayer.

We had two questions to put to God regarding China. Was the country going to open up? And if so, should we already be getting Scriptures prepared?

I agonised on my knees as we prayed, "Lord, please speak to us through your Word, and please, would you tell us within the next fifteen days? If you don't let us know

58

in that time, we will completely forget the whole crazy idea."

A few days later, I woke at two-thirty a.m. with a strangely disturbed feeling. At first, I tried to go back to sleep, but it seemed as though I was being prompted to stay awake. More than that, something, or Someone, appeared to be telling me to go down to the printshop.

I'd begun to recognise when the still small voice of the Lord was instructing me to do things, and this time I felt sure I was hearing it once again. The last thing I wanted was a visit to my place of work at that hour. But protest as I might, the Lord was not giving me any option.

Somehow, I knew that God was going to give me an answer about China that night. "Great," I thought, "I'm going to get a big red light saying 'stop', and I'll be able to go back to bed and sleep peacefully."

I crept quietly out of bed, to avoid waking Julie, dressed, grabbed my glasses and tiptoed out the door. When I arrived, I was still unsure what God intended me to do. I sat at my desk and decided the best place to start was in the Word.

At that time, I had been studying the Psalms daily, so I turned up the one which was next in line: Psalm 37.

I started at the beginning. "*Fret not yourself because of the wicked, be not envious of wrongdoers! For they will soon fade like the grass, and wither like the green herb. Trust in the LORD, and do good; so you will dwell in the land, and enjoy security. Take delight in the LORD, and he will give you the desires of your heart. Commit your way to the LORD; trust in him, and he will act.*" (R.S.V.)

As I read, it hit me. "My goodness, Lord, I am not supposed to 'fret' about 'evildoers'. 'They shall soon be cut down like the grass.' Are you telling me that Chairman Mao and these other 'evil' guys are going to fall? Lin Piao, Chou en-Lai, the lot?"

With an unquestionable conviction in my mind, I picked up a pen and wrote at the side of the Psalm, "Mao falls."

Then I added the year in which God had told me, 1969. As I read on about dwelling in the land, it became clear to me that when Mao died, God was going to open up China.

Next morning, I shared my findings with my prayer partner, and then with Rip Carlson, the business manager of the printshop. "I believe God has given me His answer to my first question. I truly believe China will open up, but not until Mao has fallen."

Rip listened, as always, with understanding. "I agree. That also sounds like God's voice to me. But what about your second question?"

"I don't know. I have no leading on that at all."

"David," he leaned across the desk, "read Acts 26. You'll get it there."

"Why Acts 26?" I asked.

"The Lord will show you why. Just read it."

I knew Rip. He was a man who walked very closely to the Lord, I had too much respect for him to argue. I opened the chapter, and verse sixteen certainly came alive for me.

> But rise and stand upon your feet, for I have appeared to you . . . to serve and bear witness to the things in which you have seen me and to those in which I will appear to you. (R.S.V.)

Was I being called to witness to the "things which I had seen" last night? I read on to verses 17, 18.

> Delivering you from the people and from the Gentiles – to whom I send you to open their eyes, that they may turn from darkness to light and from the power of Satan to God, that they may receive forgiveness of sins and a place among those who are sanctified by faith in me. (R.S.V.)

Yes, I could see that the people of China lived in darkness – Mao's darkness. But what could I do to open their eyes? My mind flashed quickly over my life, looking again at the academic failure I'd experienced.

Despite these thoughts, I returned to the present to finish my extraordinary Bible Study – verse nineteen.

> *So then, King Agrippa, I was not disobedient to the vision from heaven ...* (R.S.V.)

There it was. It wasn't my place to question my own qualifications or ability. All I had to do was make sure I was not disobedient to the "vision" put before me.

God would do the rest.

* * *

That day I "bore witness" to that "vision" with several other colleagues. Together, we signed a letter addressed to Bob Bowman, the FEBC president in the United States, outlining what we felt about China.

His return letter was one of enthusiastic encouragement to go ahead. With this endorsement, we immediately went to work. We put out a newsletter entitled, "China will Open Soon, Are you Ready?", copies of which were circulated to the Chinese community of Manila. While funds were generated for the printing of the Gospels, our little group pooled our savings to enable me to make a research trip to the Chinese borders.

The journey was timed to coincide with my next liaison trip to Vietnam. But in that September of 1969, I took additional trips to Laos, Burma, Cambodia and Hong Kong. I wanted to seek out what we termed "depositories": people who would store Bibles for the future, when it would be possible to take them into China.

On my trip I looked upon Burma as a key country because of its important route into China through an isolated mountain range. We suspected that pathway might be ideal for Bible couriers. At the time, however, Westerners could only enter Burma for twenty-four hours.

After the country had received its independence from

Britain in 1948 it had soon closed up with the Marxist-tinted Burmese version of socialism. In 1965, that government was toppled in a military coup. I knew the present government was atheistic, yet afraid of the religious leaning of the people.

The twenty-four hour restriction, however, left me very little time to search out both depositories and mountain passes. I wondered how I would manage to achieve my goals, little suspecting that the same Lord who had proved faithful so many times previously had this problem in hand too.

I applied for my visa in the Burmese Embassy of another country, shortly before my planned visit. The girl behind the counter checked my documents closely, and then, looking up at me with a smile, asked casually: "Would you like a visa for seventy-two hours?"

I did a double take. "Is that possible?" I said, trying to restrain my excitement.

"Yes sir, we have a new policy for foreign visitors. You can now stay for up to three days."

Seventy-two hours. That was more than enough to accomplish all my plans.

"When did your government introduce this new law?" I asked her.

"Yesterday," she smiled. "You're the first foreigner to make use of it. Will it be seventy-two then?"

I nodded absently, all the while wondering at this God whose caring provision I was only just beginning to discover.

* * *

As we had hoped, Rangoon did indeed provide me with key Christian contacts, willing to store Bibles for future delivery to China. And, as also hoped, they confirmed the fact that the mountain route would be perfect for the transportation of Bibles.

On that first night in Burma, I remember looking out of the bedroom window in the Christian home where I was staying. I stared at the impressive building opposite, sporting a red flag with five golden stars. The cool breeze of that Rangoon night caused it to flutter slightly.

My heart fluttered a little too. It was the Embassy of the People's Republic of China.

CHAPTER FIVE
Dutch Courage

Julie thrust a paperback into my hands. "Honey, you've just got to read this. It's the story of a guy who's done everything you're talking about."

I wasn't too keen. Because of my reading problems, working slowly through a book at a snail's pace was hard for me. And when I saw it was in small type and more than two hundred pages, I winced.

"That'll take me ages to read. Are you sure I would enjoy it?" I said.

"I'm sure. Go ahead – read it."

The title was promising: *God's Smuggler*. I scanned the blurb. Interesting. I devoured the book in four days which, for me, was a record. The story inspired me. The chapter about the author's trip to China thrilled me. Julie was right. This man, in his work in Europe, had done all that I longed to do in China.

Then, shortly after my trip to China's borders, a letter arrived in my mailbox. Julie suspected it was important, and rang me at work. "Honey, there's an airmail letter here, and it's from Holland. There's no name on the back, but it does say P.O. Box 47, Ermelo. Does that address ring a bell for you?"

I couldn't recall it, but she was convinced.

"I don't know where I've seen it before, but I'm positive I know it from somewhere. Mind if I open it?"

That was fine with me. I knew of no one in Holland likely to be writing to me anyway.

But at the end of the phone, I sat up very sharply when I heard what it had to say.

Dear Brother David,

Whilst passing through Saigon and Bangkok recently, I heard your name in connection with your recent trip to Burma. As you can imagine, I was deeply interested and very much wanted to see you ...

She read on to the final paragraph.

Please continue the good work, and let us pray that we can meet soon and discuss the work of getting Scriptures into Red China.

"Hey David," she exclaimed, "it's signed, 'Yours in the wonderful battle, Brother Andrew.' Wasn't he the guy whose story we've just read?"

I couldn't believe it. I had only just put that book down, and here was the very same man encouraging me. For some time I sat trying to take it in, wondering how on earth Brother Andrew had even heard of my vision for China. I later discovered what had happened. He had been travelling with Corrie ten Boom, the author of *The Hiding Place*, whose book described her World War Two work for the protection of Jews. The two had passed through the same countries I had just visited. They were moving, as it happened, in the opposite direction. And during the trip, some Wycliffe missionaries with whom I had made contact had shared my burden to get Bibles into China.

*   *   *

Money was the problem. Julie and I were both in agreement that I should accept Brother Andrew's invitation to Holland. But we knew there was no way we had the financial resources to pay for the ticket.

FEBC didn't have the money either. Julie and I had decided that our furlough in the States, later the same year, was the ideal time for the journey. But when I visited FEBC headquarters in California, Bob Bowman found it impossible for the organisation to fund the trip.

"I'm sorry, David. The idea is great. But we just don't have the cash to send you."

"But sir," I replied, "my wife and I truly believe it is God who has been leading me there."

His face showed empathy. "I can understand that, but there simply isn't any money, David."

He tried to make up for my disappointment. "You can still go to the Christian Literature Conference as we planned in Chicago. That far we can afford to send you, but no farther."

I did my best to thank him politely, but could not resist sharing once more why I believed it was the Lord's will to go to Holland.

"I, too, can see God may be in this, David," our president said. "I'll tell you what. If the Lord brings the money to you, you have my permission to go. But He must be the one to supply it. You're not to ask anyone."

"Thank you, sir." I grinned broadly. "I'll let you know what happens."

He shook my hand. "Meanwhile, enjoy yourself in Chicago."

*　　*　　*

The conference was attended by gifted men and women who had travelled from around the world. They were at the top of their fields in Christian literature work within their respective organisations. I had been sent to represent FEBC, but I felt out of my depth before that august group. Gathered in the place were some of the top brains in this ministry.

Yet, at the same time, I knew it wasn't me, but God, who had brought me into this situation. And I knew I had to put before the group the burden which by now was weighing heavily on my heart.

So that, when my turn came to address the conference,

I included our plans for China in my report on FEBC's current work. Until the moment I mentioned China, the heads of those before me had been nodding approvingly. But our vision for Bible distribution inside the People's Republic went over like a lead balloon. I watched as a cloud of disbelief and doubt descended on the faces of the participants.

I couldn't blame them. At that time, China was at the zenith of the Cultural Revolution. Violent persecution was "purging" the nation of all dissident elements. Mao's Little Red Book was daily studied with a vehemence and enthusiasm hardly to be found even among Christians in Bible Study.

No one present seemed to consider China a mission field any more, and without logic or data to table, I could not convince them of the possibility of Scripture distribution there. "China is closed," I was told. "Where is the sense in spending time, effort and money on China at the moment? Someday, perhaps, when it opens up, when the climate shifts ..."

I agreed. It did seem impossible, even crazy, to be looking towards China at such a time. I couldn't see how God was going to open the way for such a ministry either. But at that moment, one of old Mr Roy's favourite sayings came back to me with renewed force. "We're not called to 'see', son. We are called to obey the voice of the Lord. Paul says ours is a walk of faith, not sight."

Whether or not it made sense from a human perspective, a conviction within me left not the shadow of a doubt that the China work was a task God had set before me. And I had to get on with it.

*   *   *

That same voice of conviction was also urging me to trust for the trip to visit Brother Andrew. Again, if I looked at things logically, it made no sense at all. I had only enough money to take me to New York, with a mere fifty dollars over. And fifty dollars would not fly me very far across the Atlantic.

But if this was indeed the urging of the Lord Himself, He would provide the rest of the money.

For reassurance, I frequently reminded myself of another of Mr Roy's verses, John 15:7: *"If you abide in me, and my words abide in you, ask whatever you will, and it shall be done for you."* I decided to proceed with the trip as planned.

Before my flight to Holland, I had allowed several days to spend with two old friends on the East Coast. The first was Neil MacKinnon, a Scots-born WEC missionary who had previously worked in the Philippines.

I told him about the changes in the direction of the FEBC press. I shared the China vision. Neil was sympathetic. I explained that I was on my way to meet Brother Andrew in Holland.

"How are you getting there, David? Who is paying the bill?"

"The Lord is taking me there," I said, quoting that verse again. "I'm not allowed to ask for help from anybody. So it has to be God who meets the cost."

"And how close are you to taking the trip?" Neil asked.

"Well, I have thirty-five dollars in my pocket." Fifteen dollars had already gone in living expenses. "After seeing you, I'm going back to New York to visit other friends, the Olsen family. From there I'm flying back to L.A. to see Julie and the three D's. And ..." I stopped. Even though I already had a ticket for Los Angeles, the prospect of lasting out the week in Washington and New York on thirty-five dollars was dismal, let alone making that trip to Holland.

Neil grinned widely and shook his head. "Dave, you're incurable," he said.

"You don't believe in miracles?" I asked.

Neil chuckled.

68

"Sure I believe. What do you think I'm grinning about? Listen to this. Someone has gone and booked you for four days at the Washington Hilton, all expenses paid, to attend a fellowship conference with me before you leave."

"You're kidding."

"I'm not. Keep your thirty-five dollars, man. It might take you to Holland yet." Neil and I never found out who it was that shouldered my expenses.

* * *

On the third morning of the conference, I was on my way down for breakfast when the elevator stopped on the floor beneath to admit two ladies. The older of the two gave a start as soon as she set eyes on me. I was not sure if I knew her from way back, but to play safe, I said hello. She did not reply nor did she stop staring. It was getting uncomfortable. Finally, like one awakened from a deep sleep, she opened her purse, rummaged through it thoroughly and brought out some bills.

"Excuse me, sir," she said, "we don't know each other but the Spirit of the Lord is telling me right now to give you all the money in my purse. Here it is." She handed me twelve dollars.

Somewhat taken aback, it took me a moment to find my tongue, and then stammer out my thanks. That lady has regularly supported the church in China to this day.

On the fourth evening of the conference, I went to a crowded late-night prayer meeting. Towards the end, an old black woman in her eighties stood up and said: "The Lord is speaking to me and telling me to pass messages on to some of you here."

The grey-haired lady, her black face radiant, moved around the room ministering to the people. When she got to Neil she said, "Brother, the Lord is telling me that He has called you into a ministry with young people." Besides me, Neil had told no one that he had been praying about

69

returning to the United Kingdom to engage in youth work there.

Later, she moved in my direction. I was feeling rather embarrassed about this kind of meeting, and at one time even contemplated leaving the room. I'd never seen anything like it, and found the whole scene somewhat disconcerting.

She stood in front of me, and I wondered what she could possibly say, knowing that she and the others had no idea about my burden for the People's Republic. "Young man, I have something to say to you, too. The Lord is telling me that you're to be involved in a ministry to China."

I was still a long way short of my trip to Holland, let alone Bible distribution behind the Bamboo Curtain. But this old lady's encouragement was confirmation that I *was* headed in the right direction.

* * *

After the conference I left Washington, twelve dollars richer, and headed for New York City to see the other friends I had on my itinerary, the Olsens. I had come to know this family five years earlier when I had been sent to New York for training in the use of some specialised equipment for FEBC.

At that time I had gone in faith, knowing that I did not have enough money to cover an extended stay in a hotel. I'd met the Olsens on my first Sunday, standing on the snow-covered pavement outside the church where I had worshipped. Although I had not mentioned anything about my needs, they had invited me to stay with their family for the time of my training. They had a special "missionary room" reserved in their house, specifically for these kinds of occasions.

Later, I discovered this Godly family of Eastern European immigrants had been featured in David Wilkerson's story, *The Cross and the Switchblade*, though, at the time,

I had never even heard of the book. They too were working with young people in his Teen Challenge rehabilitation programme among the teenage slum dwellers of New York.

Every night of my stay with them I saw one moving scene consistently repeated. As soon as dinner was over and the cleaning up completed, Mother Olsen would kneel beside an old leather chair near the homemade fireplace. Hour after hour, she would pray, interceding in turn for each one of her eight children. Afterwards, she would pray also for God's work in the United States and around the world. It could be as many as five hours before she would stand up again. Later, many of her children went into full-time work for the Lord and one of them, Amo, began a ministry among Jewish people – "Bless Israel Today".

The day arrived for me to visit them again and I approached with enthusiasm the stone house they had built in Bethpage. My knock at the door was answered by one of their daughters, Marie.

"David!" she shrieked. I took a step forward, expecting a warm greeting and an invitation inside, when all of a sudden she did an about-turn and left me standing there. I shivered in the cold, wondering what could be the reason for her disappearance. Then, just as mysteriously, she returned and handed me an envelope.

"Open it," she urged with a secret smile. The envelope was addressed to me. I opened it. Inside was three hundred dollars.

I stood on the doorstep unable to speak or to tear my eyes away from the money. It was all that I needed to get across the Atlantic and back.

Marie's happy laughter pealed out. "Well, don't just stand there. Thank the Lord."

"Thank you, Lord!" I exclaimed fervently, and then threw back my head to laugh in sheer joy. From various parts of the house, I heard the other Olsens running to greet me. My boisterous joy had announced my arrival.

Later, over coffee and sandwiches, Marie told me God

71

had directed her to save part of her tithe for me ever since the day we had left for Manila. She was not sure how much she was going to give me. "But you will step in one day, and whatever sum is in the envelope on that day is the right sum for you." It was the right sum indeed. Hello Holland and Brother Andrew!

There was no trace of doubt about it. I knew without question that the Lord was leading me to Holland, and His faithful provision was taking me every inch of the way.

* * *

On 2 March, 1970, I stepped out of the plane on to Dutch soil, right on schedule. George, one of Brother Andrew's staff, was there to meet me. I had expected to be driven from Schipol Airport straight to Brother Andrew's home and office in Ermelo, about fifty miles away. Instead, George drove me south of Amsterdam to his friend's house in a village near the coast. "We're treating you to dinner. Dutch treat," George explained, but caught himself. "No, I mean this is on us, but the treat is typically Dutch."

I was intrigued, little realising I was in for a stomach-turning surprise.

"Ah! We've been expecting you, David. Come in!" Three gentlemen greeted me at the door. The spokesman for the group continued, "I am Peter van Dyke, your host for the day. The gentleman with curly hair is Kees, and that one with the moustache is Frits." He led me inside as he chatted. "We're Brother Andrew's welcoming committee. But you must be famished. Come. Dinner's been waiting for the past thirty minutes."

Mr van Dyke said grace as we gathered around the beautiful dining table, taking in its magnificent setting of bone china, crystal, and silverware – even tulips.

"Lord," my host prayed, "thank you for our brother's safe trip and this chance of fellowship with him tonight. Thank you also for this wonderful Dutch dinner of raw

herring and raw onions. May it nourish his body as well as
it has nourished our Dutch bodies since the birth of the
Dutch nation, in Jesus' Name we pray, Amen."

My ears twitched. Raw herring and what? Alarmed, I
opened my eyes. Right in front of me was a crystal platter
brimming with raw herring and raw onion rings.

"Amen," I gulped audibly. I watched them cut off the tail
and debone the herring. Then they laid the raw clammy fish
on a piece of rye and slapped two thick onion rings over
it. I meekly accepted one of these from my host and watched
as the other men hungrily devoured their servings. I opened
my mouth to follow suit – and pray. With each bite I prayed
harder.

The four Dutchmen watched me casually. One of them
caught my eye and smiled. A nervous grin distorted my
features until carefully, deliberately, I had swallowed every
bit down. Instantly, four Dutchmen rose as one to give me
a standing ovation. "Congratulations. Marvellous!"

Mr van Dyke scratched his head. "You're something.
You're the first non-Dutchman who did it. I thought Americans hated raw fish and raw onions!"

"You better believe it. We hate it. I did it for you. If you
want to know the truth, I asked the Lord to help me through
every last mouthful." All five of us bellowed with laughter.
It was a test, from beginning to end, confound them. "Now
our American brother deserves to eat the rest of the dinner,"
Mr van Dyke announced, and the cook brought in a hot
thick soup and a juicy pot roast. It was delicious.

*   *   *

"I hear you've already had one of our herrings," Brother
Andrew said as he stepped into the office. I looked up into
the face of a man you knew smiled easily. The laugh lines
around his eyes and mouth had become a permanent fix-
ture. I rose from the sofa to clasp his proffered hand.

This was the "smuggler" of God whose life and achievements for the Lord have become a bestseller; a slim, neatly dressed man, not in the least prepossessing. How humble he looked, how gentle. Yet his inner strength and courage overwhelmed me. In his presence, I was tongue-tied.

Brother Andrew misconstrued my silence for fatigue. "You must be exhausted. That was a long journey." We chatted for just a few minutes and then, after leading us in prayer, my Dutch host took me to the warmed room his thoughtful wife Corrie had prepared for my arrival.

Over the days we spent together, I felt very much at home with this concerned Dutchman. I showed him the Psalms which I had marked in my Bible. He saw "Call to China" written in the margin beside Chapter 26 of Acts. I explained my vision for getting Scriptures into the hands of the Chinese. After the doubts and scepticism that had greeted me elsewhere, my spirits soared as he nodded in agreement, his face reflecting a light of understanding.

I described to him the way I had visited countries on the border of China, and found people willing to store Bibles. I expected him to be delighted with the news.

"Brother David, that's not enough," he said earnestly. "You need to go yourself."

He couldn't be serious. How could I, an American, enter the land whose leaders so loathed us and had taught their people to despise the "Paper Tiger" of the United States? I opened my mouth to speak and then shut it again, suddenly recalling that *God's Smuggler* told of the way the Lord had done the impossible by taking Brother Andrew into China in 1965.

"I had American and Taiwanese visas in my passport and still I got in," said Brother Andrew. "If God wants you in, He'll open the door for you to go through."

"And brother," he added, eyes twinkling, "I believe the door is already open."

Brother Andrew shared with me his longing to make contact with the remnant of the Chinese church. To find out whether it had survived, how it had survived, and what could be done to help and encourage it.

"While I was in Shanghai, I actually found a Bible book-shop that was still trying to sell Bibles, but could hardly find anyone interested," he told me sadly.

"The government allowed this funny little place to sell what it considered antiques because it represented no danger. No one cared.

"I tried to hand out Bibles to people but no one would take them. I had offered the first one to my interpreter in Canton. She handed it back. She had no time for reading, she said.

"I tried next leaving several 'accidentally', behind me in hotel rooms as I checked out. I never succeeded. Always, before I left the floor, the chambermaid would run after me, Bible in hand, and return it to me.

"In desperation, I tried giving Bibles away on the street. My guides made no objection. They seemed in fact to feel sorry for me when person after person stopped to see what I was offering, then gave me the book back."

The one church he had been able to locate in Peking discouraged him almost as much as the indifference on the streets. In the barren little building, he had seen just a tiny group gathered for worship, all of them very old Chinese. And at the point where their equally elderly pastor delivered his message, all had nodded off to sleep.

"If this was representative of Chinese Christianity, I realised their government could stamp it out overnight if it wanted to."

So was the church in China dead?

Certainly, to the outside world, it seemed that public religious activity – Christian, Muslim, or Buddhist – had all but disappeared in China since the Cultural Revolution. Churches, mosques, monasteries, temples had everywhere been looted and then closed. Many became factories, warehouses, movie theatres, meeting halls; others were simply locked and left derelict.

"David, I believe the Lord would have you go and seek

out the church in China. In fact, you need to go on what I like to term a 'seek and save' mission."

After the gloomy description he had given me of the China situation, the suggestion sounded pretty daunting. "What do you mean – a 'seek and save' mission?" I asked.

His face clouded. "On last year's trip, when we were flying into Vietnam, I read an article in an American newspaper which disturbed me deeply. It was one of those reports on the war in Vietnam that used a military expression I had not heard before – 'search and destroy'. It got such a hold of me I felt like weeping. Corrie ten Boom was travelling with me, and she read the article too. Afterwards she quoted the very words I had been thinking of.

" 'Search and destroy'," Corrie mused. "It's just the opposite of what Jesus said." Then she cited Jesus' description of the reason for His coming. " 'I am come to seek and to save that which was lost.' "

Brother Andrew concluded, "In that war-like situation, where 'search and destroy' had become a watchword, our job was to 'seek and save', and do what Jesus did.

"It's the same in Red China today. They may not be at war with another country, but there are many people within their own country who are out to 'search and destroy' the others.

"Brother David, I believe you should find the church in China. Locate it. Help it. Encourage it. Feed it. Love it."

* * *

In the cold crisp mornings before I went down for breakfast, I often sat at the little window of my room and watched Brother Andrew's family at work in the garden. I could see the famous "Bible smuggler" in his gardening clothes tending his vegetable plot: beans, potatoes, tomatoes, cucumbers, cabbages.

At the same time, he would help his five children in the care of their animals. The young girls were busy looking after their family of rabbits, and the boys the chickens and goats.

As I watched this laughing, loving family doing their various tasks, they would occasionally glance at my window with a wave and a grin. It became obvious to me that the famous "smuggler" enjoyed nothing more than to be with his wife and children.

Looking at the scene, I marvelled at the amount we shared in common. Both of us loved to be at home with our families. Both of us shared the same burden for the church in China. Even our childhoods had been similar, both grounded as they had been in the Second World War.

I felt a God-given bond with him as we prepared to link up in an alliance to fight a *spiritual* battle – to declare war on Satan in those atheistic countries where he had established a stranglehold.

Indeed, not only had the devil established a grip on these nations, it seemed that he had set up a counterfeit religion as well.

One afternoon, I sat fascinated, listening as Brother Andrew explained his view of Communism – the religion.

"At the end of my trip to China," he said, " I was seated beside an English woman on the flight out of the country.

"Almost the first thing she said to me was, 'How can any nation survive without faith in God, without an object of worship?'

" 'But they do have one,' I told her, 'they have Mao.'

"That set me thinking. How many elements of religion is Communism emulating on a world-wide basis?

"In every Communist country I can think of, they have an object of worship. Even in Moscow, they have the mausoleum in Red Square. I have seen with my own eyes the extreme devotion of the people lining up to pay homage to Lenin.

"But that's not all. Communism takes other religious guises as well. For example, it often finds an enemy. You must know what you stand against in religion, and China's substitute for that right now is America – the Paper Tiger. When there is no visible enemy on the outside, they create one on the inside, and I believe that is part of the reason for the Cultural Revolution. That's why there are continuous purges in Communism, and of course that fits their basic concept of continuous struggle and continuous revolution.

"Another major element they copy is the need for a holy book. In Europe, it is of course the Communist Manifesto, and in China, Mao's own Little Red Book.

"The fourth aspect is more subtle than these. All around the world, religions have a martyr figure, and no doubt the Communists see Jesus in just such a role. Of course that isn't fair. Martyrs are men who die for a cause – and stay dead. Jesus has overcome death for all time. He is the Resurrection and the Life! But all the same, they like to copy.

"So many Communists make a big deal of their countrymen who have died 'for the cause', and set them up as heroes for their people."

His final point was that Communism, like all religions, had its own promise for the future.

"They don't proclaim the life hereafter, but they look to the 'heaven on earth' their philosophy will bring. That's why no country in the world claims to be Communist. They all say, 'We are Socialist', which is a stepping stone to Communism. Communism can only be realised when the new man has emerged out of the new society. That is the great hope for the future – the goal of their efforts."

"So that makes Communism a religion," I said, as he finished.

"Sure," he replied. "Communists are no fools. They know man is looking for something greater than himself. That's why they try to feed their people this way to keep them quiet."

"No wonder they are so frightened of Christianity," I mused.

"Yes. And no wonder so many people living under Communism are looking for something more. Do you know, Brother David, there are strong elements of Christian revival in Russia today?"

"You've got to be joking."

"Not at all. The people are fed up with a counterfeit religion. Now they are after the real thing." His voice was earnest. "I just pray that will soon be the case in China too, as the people have time to become disenchanted with what their government is offering them.

"I believe it is possible, David. More than that, I am sure it will happen. It has to."

He paused for a moment, deep in thought.

"And do you know the craziest part of all?" he continued in a subdued tone.

"What's that?"

"These so-called world powers think they are masterminding the whole operation. But even they are being deceived. There is another power working behind them, whose purposes they don't even realise they are fulfilling."

He laughed. "Satan *is* stupid! He is trying hard to win the battle himself, yet the very system he is propagating is leaving the people so hungry they are turning back to the Lord in greater numbers than ever!"

* * *

During our time together, we spent hours talking, praying and sharing the Scriptures. Towards the end, I showed him Mark 13:10, where I had been challenged to *publish* abroad the Gospel.

"David, what are you really thinking about in terms of Bibles?" Brother Andrew asked.

I paused, and then launched into my burden. "I'm praying with my friends in Manila for ten million Scriptures for China."

I had said it.

Now I waited to see whether this man, so much more

experienced than I, was going to laugh at such an idea. I wouldn't have blamed him if he did. Many others had already assured me it was crazy. For a moment, I almost wished I hadn't told him.

"Well, from our perspective that may sound like a lot of Bibles," he began. "But I'm sure in God's eyes it's not so many. Anyway – it's only a quarter of one percent of the Chinese population."

His eyes were bright with enthusiasm as they held mine. "If we can't trust the Lord for such a tiny proportion, we can't trust Him for anything.

"I stand with you in that vision, Brother."

* * *

"How then can we work together?" I asked Brother Andrew.

I told him that within FEBC I could work the presses, just as we had for so many other organisations. His role would be to share his experiences of crossing Communist borders in Eastern Europe.

"You are the one who can show us how to get into closed countries," I said.

"No, you're wrong, David. China is *not* closed. No country is closed. The Bible says, 'I have set before you an open door which no man can shut.' All we have to do is obey the Lord, go, and He will show where that open door is."

* * *

I left Holland excited. Somewhere there was a way to get Bibles inside China. It was time for us to find it. And the sooner, the better.

CHAPTER SIX

Mushrooms, Peanuts and Watermelons

On my return to Los Angeles, I recounted enthusiastically all that had happened with Brother Andrew, and our mutual conviction that a Bible ministry inside the People's Republic was possible.

I began to look around for a place to start the China ministry, and to my dismay, promptly discovered that I was not to start anywhere at all right then.

The organisation had already decided which task I should tackle on my return. I was to organise an evangelistic campaign for young people in our home town, much as Robert Foster and I had done in Manila.

It was the last thing I had expected to be doing, but trying hard to be patient about my plans for China, I went into it as enthusiastically as I could.

God blessed that campaign. Ralph Bell, from the Billy Graham team, had the audience's riveted attention as he spoke. Andrae Crouch, with "Love Song", backed up his message powerfully in music. We gave thanks to God as one thousand, five hundred people came to Jesus. It was a good time – a great time.

But it wasn't China. That country continued to tug at my heartstrings.

"Perhaps now, Lord," I prayed as we headed home after the final meeting. "Will I be able to do something for China now?"

No. My next task with FEBC was to work on equipment at Station KGER in San Matao. The need was urgent, and they required immediate assistance.

"I'll be gone only a week, honey," I assured Julie, doing my best to put on a brave front. But inwardly I was resenting the job. I'd already spent weeks without making any

81

move towards the needs of China – and I was becoming frustrated and angry.

The "week" in San Matao became a month, and the first month was followed by a second. After three months, Julie and the kids came to live with me. The end of the job was nowhere in sight. Neither was the People's Republic of China.

By now resentment had almost taken me over completely. Not only had this task nothing to do with China, but in addition, many well-meaning friends were advising me to drop my "pipe-dreams" for that country. I became bitter, resenting both the job at hand, and those who had given it to me.

Another six months dragged slowly, relentlessly by, and I knew I had allowed myself to become captive to my frustration. Despite Julie's gentle encouragement to hand it over to the Lord and allow Him to solve the problem, I couldn't. Or rather, I wouldn't.

My spiritual life was at an all-time low. I had no joy, no enthusiasm, no goal to work towards, nothing.

The drought finally broke quite unexpectedly on a Sunday morning. I had half-heartedly turned on the television, and caught Rex Humbard's programme from his "Cathedral of Tomorrow", in Akron, Ohio. As he spoke, I might as well have been looking into a mirror as a television screen. I was seeing myself as I really was.

"Some of you have been harbouring bitterness and resentment in your heart. You may not know it has been there, but now's the time to take an honest look and acknowledge it. Only God can do that for you." The more he spoke, the better his description fitted me. "As long as you allow those feelings to dominate your life, they will prevent you from living out God's perfect plan for you."

The preacher looked straight into the lens of the camera. "Even now, in your home, if God is speaking to you, why don't you bring your resentment out into the open – lay all that bitterness before Him. Ask His forgiveness and begin life anew."

I knew I had to pray that prayer. And, as I did so, I slowly began to unwind. For the first time in months, I found myself able to relax as my frustration and anguish seemed to release their grip on me.

I awoke next morning with a new tranquillity, and headed off to work for what I expected to be a normal day. Half-way through the morning, however, I was called to the office of one of the FEBC administrators.

"David," he told me, "we have a new job for you. We'd like to send you to Sacramento to work with one of our men, Jack Hill. You will be taking down five radio towers we have bought there."

"Where will they be going?" I asked.

"Once you've got them down, we will ship them to an island in South Korea. From there, we will use them to beam Gospel programmes into Red China."

As soon as the resentment left my soul, the Lord had allowed me to work for China again.

* * *

My job was to drill five thousand, eight hundred holes into the dismantled towers to prepare them for galvanisation. It was one of the most dreary assignments I could imagine; to stand sweating in the hot sun of California's capital city, drilling hole upon hole for three long weeks. Yet it was for the Chinese that we were working – and my spirits soared in that knowledge.

"Lord Jesus," I would pray each time I drilled, "for this hole I am going to trust you for a thousand souls in China."

I repeated the prayer five thousand, eight hundred times, during the three weeks it took to complete my task. I was literally drilling for China.

* * *

Step number two towards China followed a few days later. It began with a little red light on the phone at my

Sacramento hotel, following a hard day's drilling.

"Your wife wants you to call her immediately," the operator informed me.

Wondering what was up, I called Julie in San Matao and she explained that Brother Andrew had been trying to make contact with me again. "He is concerned because he hasn't heard anything for so many months."

I knew why Brother Andrew hadn't heard anything. Up until the last two weeks there had been nothing to report. My bitterness and resentment had brought our plans to a standstill.

Brother Andrew sent me a ticket to meet him for a one-day stopover at JFK Airport in New York. As I told him what had happened, he listened sympathetically. "I had no idea all this was going on, David. I thought you had just been too busy to write."

The past behind us, we spent that twenty-four hours looking to the future. We prayed together, planned together, discussed our goals for Bibles to penetrate China.

Again and again we came up against one brick wall. Even when the "smuggler" himself had managed to get Bibles into China, nobody there would accept them. Why? The reason was simple. The only reading allowed in China at that time was Mao's Little Red Book – or a narrow selection of other writings, equally political in style. It was impossible for the people to accept anything looking like a Bible.

We prayed on together until the Lord finally broke through our frustration. Why couldn't we print our New Testaments to look precisely like Mao's famous book?

"I can see it now," Brother Andrew enthused. "Everyone carrying them up and down the streets looking like dedicated supporters of the Revolution. In fact, they will be holding the Word of God."

I was equally excited. "I can easily get hold of one of Mao's books – and we will copy it down to the final detail.

84

Our New Testament will be the same size, same colour, with an identical cover."

I left Brother Andrew that day with an order for twenty-five thousand of the most unusual New Testaments we were ever to print at FEBC.

*   *   *

The *Hong Kong Bear*, a cargo freighter which had accepted us as passengers, quietly entered the waters of Manila Bay. Julie, the children and I sat on the deck, savouring the warmth of a tropical August afternoon. I was happy and content. I was returning to the city that I have learned to consider my second home. As I watched the orange sun slowly sinking behind the mountains of Bataan, I understood why the Filipinos were proud of their sunsets. I was proud with them.

Our furlough in America over, we were returning eagerly to our work in the Philippine base of FEBC. Top of the list was the order that had been placed by Brother Andrew for twenty-five thousand New Testaments. There was only one machine which was adequate to handle this particular order – the Fairchild ColorKing, the one I had asked the Lord about that night more than two years before.

The next few months were very busy. I had a new peace as I bustled about the press, doing the work which I knew God wanted us to do. We were printing Bibles; we were ministering to China. The two were united now, and would be united for a long time at FEBC.

Inside, I could still feel an inner tugging to follow the China ministry even further, yet I could not see what the next step should be. It seemed I had come as far as possible, and for the moment I was to concentrate on my other responsibilities at FEBC.

It was only later that I realised another reason why my pull towards China had come to a temporary halt. The Lord had one more step of preparation for me to take –

another lesson for me to learn. Without it, I would never have been in a position to trust Him for a mission field as large as the People's Republic of China.

That lesson came through an exciting scheme for an FEBC multi-media project, dreamed up by Pablo, one of my friends there, along with Todd Martin, our communications man, and my old drilling companion, Jack Hill.

Out on the field for FEBC, Pablo and Todd had undertaken a research programme to locate the listening audience of FEBC's Manila market. They had discovered that the vast proportion of the city's population was under the age of thirty. These young people, as with millions around the world, had a major drug problem.

With Jack Hill they made plans for a multi-media approach to the problem. In the early seventies, such a strategy was not common and when they shared their plans with me, the idea at first sounded a little far-fetched.

In order to reach into the young people's market, they were going to begin a top-forty programme which would be broadcast from a commercial rock station, not a Christian one. The broadcast would be the central hub of the plan, heavily supported by other media. A tabloid newspaper would be prepared, presenting the message of Jesus in a readable format for teenagers. They also hoped to import a good quality Christian film for screening in a commercial theatre, and a top Christian music group for live performances. Their goal was to use all four media to put Jesus Christ before the young people, right where they were, in the market place.

In time, I too caught their vision. With my assignment for Brother Andrew well underway, I accepted their invitation to get involved. We decided to begin with the radio show. Every night, the four of us came together to pray about it. We needed to pray hard, because, if this scheme were not of the Lord, it had no chance of success.

Already, questions were being raised by many Christian friends about the wisdom of the undertaking. Gradually those questions turned into outright criticisms. How could we honestly hope to do anything worthwhile on a commercial rock station? The show we were to follow was open in its promotion of drugs, telling how, when and where listeners could get hold of them. Announcers on the programme also took the opportunity to set up dates with girls ringing on the phone-in line – and made it quite plain to them the kind of night they had in mind. The studio itself was filled with obscene posters, and clouds of smoke – whether from regular cigarettes or others we weren't sure.

Night after night, as we waited on God in prayer, we would also discuss our plans for mounting the programme. The costs involved were enormous – to our minds anyway. None of us had a cent or a peso to spare, yet we would have to pay fifteen thousand American dollars to get the show on the air. Where would that kind of money come from?

"Sponsors!" I had come up with what I thought was the perfect solution. "We can get a couple of multi-national companies behind us. They will never miss a mere fifteen thousand dollars!"

There were a few minutes' silence as my suggestion was digested. Jack spoke up first. "It's a great idea, Dave. But they will want to know what's in it for them. What do they stand to gain out of promoting a Christian programme?"

I hadn't thought as far ahead as that. But Todd, with typical quick-thinking, had an answer at the ready.

"I suppose we could simply tell them that by financing us they would be helping to overcome the drug problem here in Manila."

"Okay," agreed Jack. "I'll buy that – I just hope they will too. The question is, who's going to approach them?"

Three sets of eyes turned in my direction. I realised I was elected.

Within a few days I had an appointment with two major companies and put the idea before them.

"And what are you planning to offer these young people who listen?" I was asked, after outlining our plans.

"Jesus, sir. We believe the answer to their need lies in knowing Him."

That night I had good news for the others. "As far as they're concerned, it's okay. They just have to get the nod from their headquarters in the States."

All of us were excited that evening. Our hopes were pinned on the return phone call from the companies which was to follow a few days later.

When it finally came, it was put through to me at work.

"David?" The voice sounded rather stiff and formal.

"Speaking," I replied. "What's the news?"

"It's not good, I'm afraid."

I waited for him to continue, holding my breath.

"Our U.S. base has turned the project down."

"I see," I said, not seeing at all. "But, sir, didn't you say ...?"

"I said the answer was 'yes' as far as I was concerned. But the U.S. thought differently."

"May I ask why, sir? What was the reason?"

The man hesitated for a moment. "Well, to be quite frank, their actual words were: 'These people are offering us a peanut, and asking for a watermelon in return!'"

*   *   *

Our meeting was very different that night.

"Do we call it a halt?" asked Pablo, gloomily.

All of us were thinking the same thing. Was this an indication that we should stop the whole project? How could we go ahead without the sponsors' backing? It was impossible.

As we fell to prayer yet again, we begged the Lord to show us what came next. "Father, you know these young people. You know that they have no understanding of what it means to follow You, to believe in You. They're headed for a grave with no future, Lord. And, for some of them at least, that grave is not far away, the way they are going. Please, Lord, show us."

"I've got it!" The prayer time over, we had been sitting around wondering what we should do, when Jack Hill suddenly straightened up with enthusiasm. "I can see it all now. We've got ourselves trapped. Our problem is that our eyes have been on the sponsors. We keep talking about the things we'll be able to do if only we can get the sponsors' backing."

He thumped the coffee table with his fist. "It's not the sponsors' backing we need, it's the Lord's! I believe He allowed us to miss out on these two companies just so we would get our eyes back on Him again."

We glanced around the room reading a common conviction on one another's faces. It was true. Although we had kept the Lord's Name on our lips, our real trust had lain in those big companies. Once again we got back on our knees, and asked the Lord for forgiveness – telling Him that if He still wanted this project to go ahead, we were willing to follow. This time we would rely on Him alone.

All at once things began to change. Within a few days, the Lord had actually provided us with another pair of sponsors, and our programme, "Maranatha", began transmission from station DZMB. Its time-slot had been rated number six among the stations when we began, but within two months it rose to number one. Hundreds upon hundreds of kids were regularly phoning in their requests, or far better, their need for counselling – for which we would refer them to an over-worked team of Navigators waiting on another line. Every few minutes, we interrupted our programme "to bring a special message ..." These were counters to the drug-peddling of the preceding programme – often just a single line such as: "Hey Babe – Mary Jane is a bad date." Mary Jane was a local term for marijuana. Often a young Filipino who had found Jesus would let the audience know briefly just how much of a difference the Lord had made to his life.

Soon, the film medium came into its own as well. We brought the film *The Cross and the Switchblade* to Manila, and a total of a quarter of a million people came out to see it. After the show, Christian teenagers handed out the tabloid newspapers we had produced inviting audience members to have for themselves the experience of Nicky and Rosa in the film. More than fourteen thousand replies came from the newspapers – all of them people who wanted to give their lives to Jesus.

"This whole thing's blowing my mind," I said at one of our nightly prayer times. "In my wildest dreams I never dared hope it would get so big."

"You know when this all started?" asked Todd, "when the show really began to get on the road?"

"When?"

"The moment we realised it was crazy to put our hopes on anything but God. That was the turning point."

"It's like a mushroom cloud," mused Pablo. "The whole thing started out so small, and just expanded from that little bit of faith we had to begin with."

None of us could have had the faith to expect such growth in the venture. We had never anticipated such a massive listening audience for the radio programme, nor the quarter of a million who had turned out for the movie. We had just trusted God to work out His purpose, and He had taken us all by surprise.

"You know what else it is like?" I asked with a chuckle, "It's as though we gave the Lord a 'peanut' of faith, and He gave us back a whole *field* full of watermelons."

* * *

The show was not over yet. "Love Song", the renowned Gospel group of that era, had accepted our invitation to come to Manila, along with their manager Mike Mac-

Intosh, a former drug addict. They were to hold a massive
outdoor concert for young people throughout the city. To
accommodate the fourteen of them, we needed hotel rooms,
and, as ever, did not have enough money to pay.

I decided to approach some hotels with Billy Wee, a
Chinese friend I had met on the FEBC compound. Billy
was a businessman, but he helped out with the radio broadcasts into mainland China. He was deeply concerned for
his people.

Together we went to one of the hotels in downtown
Manila and asked to speak to their sales and promotions
manager. Beng Tuazon was her name, and from her description she did not seem the kind of person who would
deal sympathetically with our requests for concession rates.

We were told to wait outside her office until she could
see us. "Please Lord," we prayed – "You know our needs."

After twenty minutes a baritone voice belted across the
room. "What can I do for you?" The voice belonged to
the creature who had just entered. Judging by that voice,
the cigarette dangling on the lower lip, and the drink in
one hand, it had to be a man. Judging by the miniskirt,
black stockings, low neckline, hoop earrings and long red
fingernails, it had to be a woman. We stood up. It was
Miss Beng Tuazon.

"We ... we're in need of an exchange deal with your
hotel," I managed to blurt out through my confusion.

"An exchange deal ... Go on!" She was impatient.

Billy continued with my help. It wasn't easy, talking to
a person whose face was hidden behind a layer of make-up
and eyes thickly screened by false eyelashes.

"When and where are they performing?" she said. Her
baritone matched her personality – too strong for sheltered
missionaries like us.

"On Valentine's Day at the Rizal Stadium," I said.

"You can't do that." What did she mean by that? "I'm
sorry, gentlemen. On Valentine's Day, I'm planning a show
in my hotel's supper club. You'll be competing with them

and I can't accommodate my show's competitors in this hotel." She stubbed out her cigarette and quickly lit another. I objected weakly. "Oh, they're not really competitors ..." She ignored me.

"Unless ..." she took a sip from her cocktail, "you consent to perform in our supper club upstairs as part of the barter."

I should have shouted, "Right on! You've got yourself a deal," but I couldn't do it. Instead I almost protested. "We'd like that, Miss Tuazon, but this group is not like anything you have in mind. They're ex-drug addicts and they don't just entertain, they also deliver a message. Jesus loves Manila's youth. Jesus will deliver them from any burden, including drug addiction."

I caught sight of Billy desperately signalling with his eyes for me to shut up. I had already said all the wrong things, and mentally I kicked myself for being such a simpleton. I stood up and was about to thank Miss Tuazon for her time when she interjected: "My God, that's what we need! Filipinos need Jesus to deliver us like that." Her baritone changed to alto in her excitement. The volley of smoke thickly spouted from her red mouth as she continued: "Here's what I'll do. I'll give you seven rooms, a banquet for three hundred people, a press conference, a TV appearance. In exchange, your group performs for thirty minutes upstairs in our supper club after their performance in the stadium. Fair?"

Fair! She was giving us more than we had dared hope for. We could hardly believe our ears.

To allow "Love Song" to perform, Beng had to take a stand against her manager's wishes. He had planned to continue with a series of enormously successful lingerie fashion shows – strictly for adult viewing only. They were a far cry from "Love Song" ... Nonetheless, the group performed at the hotel as promised, and although the manager complained about the message, their audience remained seated quietly until the end of the show.

The main concerts in the stadium, however, took us all by surprise. President Marcos had now declared martial law and no public gatherings of any size were allowed in Manila. But the "Love Song" concert proved the exception. It was the very first public meeting held at that time. Crowds of young people turned up; some smoking pot, others drinking beer, all of them paying for their tickets to hear Christian music. Eighty-five percent of the audience there were not Christians, and anything looking less like a crusade couldn't have been imagined. But on the third night – when Mike MacIntosh followed the songs with his account of the way Jesus had delivered him from drugs and restored his marriage – five thousand, out of the fifteen thousand gathered, came forward to receive Christ.

* * *

When the venture was over, I turned to Robert Foster, and gave vent to my feelings.

"I don't believe it, Robert. None of us ever imagined the youth ministry would bring results like these." It was the "Mushroom Principle" from start to finish. Just one small step of faith, and God had done the rest ...

Robert, throughout my years at FEBC, had been my prayer partner – and could always surprise me with a question that was unexpected.

"Praise the Lord," he agreed. "But tell me, David. Now that it's completed, what will you do next? Where do you go from here?"

My reply came easily. "China," I said. "China is the next step." I opened my mouth to continue, and then shut it again. Where on earth had those words come from? What did I mean by that?

For several days, I thought about my reply.

My assignment for Brother Andrew had been completed. Twenty-five thousand New Testaments had been printed and moved to the borders of China. The six-month youth project was over. Our books for FEBC were filled to capacity for the next half-year, leaving me little to do.

Was now the time for me to be doing even more for that "impenetrable" country? Was this why the Lord had been teaching me the "Mushroom Principle"? That with one small step of faith, taken in obedience, God could be relied upon to do the impossible ... Had He been preparing me so that now I would be able to trust Him for something much bigger again? For China?

Finally, a few nights later, I could stand the questioning no longer.

"Honey," I asked Julie, "I need to do some solid praying tonight. You go ahead and get some rest, I won't be ready to sleep for a while. I want to pray through this issue until I know for sure what God wants us to do."

It was old Mr Roy who had taught me how to get down on my knees with the Scriptures when I wanted to draw close to God. I put his method into practice that night, and knelt on our wooden floor for seven long hours. I had been studying Isaiah, and spent the time reading through several chapters, in between times of searching prayer.

"Lord, what do you want me to do?" I asked, as I agonised over the decision. Somehow, I just knew we were at a crossroads, but I didn't know which road was right for me.

"I'll follow you, Lord, but please show me."

And then, as I stopped to read on in the Scriptures, the words in Isaiah 42 came booming off the pages.

> *I am the Lord, I have called you in righteousness,*
> *I have taken you by the hand and kept you,*
> *I have given you as a covenant to the people, a light*
> *to the nations, to open the eyes that are blind, to bring*
> *out the prisoners from the dungeon, from the prison*
> *those who sit in darkness. (R.S.V.)*

In essence, I knew this was a prophetic passage pointing to the coming Messiah. But in the context of that evening, and the decision which I had put before the Lord, it came alive for me in a second sense as well. These verses could have precisely described a ministry to China. Could this be it? Was this what God had to say to me?

"Please Lord," I whispered, "I want to know for sure." I loved being at FEBC. We had very good friends on the compound, and I had no wish to step out of the warmth of that security into the coldness of the unknown.

Besides, full-time work for China would be hard. "Lord, You know I don't have all the learning and skills to cope with a job of this complexity. If You want me to take it on, You'll have to do it for me. Do You? Do You want me to leave FEBC?"

I prayed a little longer, then I looked down again to pursue my readings in Isaiah.

And there, immediately, I took in the words of verse 9.

> Behold, the former things have come to pass, and new things I now declare; before they spring forth I tell you of them. (R.S.V.)

I got the message. I was not to cling on to the former things, but be prepared to accept the "new".

The struggle was over. I knew what the Lord was telling me to do, and with that knowledge came a sense of quiet peace.

* * *

Julie was waiting for me as I walked into the living room. She had not been asleep after all, but had stayed up to pray for me as I battled through the decision with the Lord.

"Well?" she asked eagerly, "what did He tell you?"

"To leave FEBC, and go full-time into the China work."

Julie gave a little smile as she prepared me some tea

95

and cookies in the kitchen. "To be honest, I've been expecting this, Dave, ever since you met with Brother Andrew last year. I guessed it then."

"Guessed what?" This girl still had surprises to spring, after fourteen years of marriage.

"That you might leave FEBC to start the China ministry full-time."

"Why didn't you tell me?"

"Honey, it wasn't for me to tell. It had to be the Lord who should lead you in this."

Next day, I went to see Rip Carlson, the man who had given me the verse in Acts 26 in 1969. He was sympathetic when he heard what I had to say.

"I think you should work with Brother Andrew," he suggested. "After all he did visit the States some time ago, asking FEBC for your services. You knew that, didn't you?"

I had been told, but I had forgotten about it. Now I praised the Lord.

Later that day I discussed the idea with Julie. "I don't know whether or not I should approach Brother Andrew over this. I had thought we would be doing the work on our own, but Rip's idea does make sense."

As always, Julie was down to earth. "Perhaps you could write to him, honey. Let his reply be confirmation about whether the Lord means you to do it alone, or with Brother Andrew."

I penned a letter to Holland the following day. It had all kinds of spelling mistakes and the Dutchman could not have been under any illusion about my academic qualification for the work. Its basic message was simple.

"May I ask you to please pray asking the Lord if it is His will for Julie and me to join with you in the area of the China work ..."

It was only a few weeks before the reply came. Julie brought me an envelope with a Dutch postmark, and we sat together to open it.

Inside was a warm letter of shared conviction that this was the road ahead. Brother Andrew outlined the steps we should take to get the ministry up and running.

At the end, almost as a postscript, he had added: "Welcome to the ministry!"

CHAPTER SEVEN
On the Edge of the World

Where should I begin? I had no staff, no secretary, no office, nothing. Just Julie and me – and the Lord.

But that was enough. He had the rest in hand.

"David?" Julie was calling me one morning in April, just four weeks later. "Remember Beng Tuazon? She's on the phone."

"Beng – How's everything?" I hollered. We had become friends. Beng had turned out to be a very lonely girl searching for herself and desperately in need of true friends.

"Tell me what's with you first," she insisted. I told her.

"Wonderful. Now listen to this. I got into a fight with one of the girls in the hotel. No, don't feel bad. It's the nicest thing that happened to me. That was the old me fighting my old life. Now I'm new. David ... I've accepted Jesus Christ." Only after she said that did I notice the change in her voice. Her happiness had raised the key of her baritone voice and now she actually sounded like a girl.

"Why, Beng, praise the Lord! How'd it happen?"

" 'Love Song' did it for me. You may not know it – a lot of young Filipinos were changed by 'Love Song'. I've been seeing them. Only last week I attended a Christian Youth Conference in the mountains." She paused for a breath. "Say – listen to this. I know of Brother Andrew. They showed slides of his work at the conference. I even read his book up there. Do you know, David, I've got a marvellous idea."

She spoke all the more quickly as her excitement rose.

"I think I should join your new ministry. You will need someone to help with all the office work, won't you? I'm sure it is God's timing that I rang right now!"

I wasn't as sure as she. How could I allow Beng to join me when all I needed was a secretary? I did not have the money to pay her. But she refused to listen to my excuses. She was prepared to live by faith and "don't you dare refuse God's grace". I didn't.

The change in this lady was dramatic. The new Beng Tuazon who uncomplainingly worked long hours without overtime pay had nothing in common with the cigarette-smoking, cocktail-guzzling girl Billy and I first saw in her office barely four months ago.

*   *   *

Before long, the Lord had also provided us with an office and equipment. We were ready, but we still needed to find a way to send someone into China; to make direct contact with the church inside, to find out its needs, and to deliver some copies of God's Word.

I flew to Hong Kong to begin research among the Christians there. Many of them had come from the mainland, and still had relatives living inside. Since FEBC also had a branch in the Crown Colony, I decided to contact its staff during my stay.

I arrived enthusiastically at their office, only to find, to my astonishment, that they were no longer there. Instead I was standing on the premises of another Christian organisation — one with a major ministry of world-wide evangelism.

Their secretary blinked at me in surprise and I hastily explained my mistake. We chatted for a short time, and then, since this organisation also has a ministry among Chinese people, she ushered me into the director's office.

Shan Kumar welcomed me with an outstretched hand and invited me to take a seat. The visit was not long, just enough to share our ideas about reaching out to the Chinese. Shan, originally of Eastern origin, had worked in America with his organisation before moving to Hong Kong. He was obviously a very well-educated man, with a deep under-standing of a wide range of issues, and an equally deep love for God.

I liked him at once. I knew I had met someone to whom we would be able to turn for counsel in the future course of the ministry.

The time of research in Hong Kong was fruitful, but we simply had to find some Chinese Christians whom we could work alongside. Only when East and West were working hand in hand could we truly know how best to serve the church in China.

Within a few weeks, I was to meet the pair I had been praying for. Joseph Lee and his Uncle Liu had just returned from a trip to the mainland where they had tried to witness to their relatives about Jesus Christ.

I first came across the pair at a party given by Billy Wee and his brother James. I was struck at once by the glow in their expressions, as though the two lived very close to their Lord. When we spoke of the need for the Gospel in China, a wistful, far-off look of longing came over them, and I knew that both found this a heavy burden.

We met within a week. We prayed together, listened to the way that God had led us, talked of China, of Bibles and of our plans for the next few months.

Finally we agreed to begin a four-month project together. They would spend three months in Hong Kong, asking the Christians there for contacts inside China to whom they could take Bibles. The final month would be a trip to the mainland itself. (At that time, there was no problem for overseas Chinese in gaining a visa to their homeland – although for American "foreign devils" like myself it had so far proved impossible.)

Their decision was a costly one. Either man could have been busy carving out a lucrative career in their family's business. But both had chosen a course which not only would pay them little in terms of salary, but could place their very freedom on the line, once they had entered the People's Republic with Bibles.

* * *

While they sought for routes into China through its front door, I was searching out other openings through its back and side entrances. I began travelling to each of the borders of China's neighbours.

My arrival in Kabul, Afghanistan, could not have been timed at a more tense moment. It was September, 1973, just after a coup which placed the country under martial law. As soon as the stairs were propped up to the exit and we stepped out of the plane, armed soldiers herded all the passengers into customs for a thorough search. They wanted to make sure that no bombs or guns were being smuggled into the country.

During the customs check, each passenger was surrounded by three soldiers, armed with machine guns. Every item in our suitcases was emptied out on to the table, picked up, examined slowly, and then, if the guards were satisfied, finally replaced in the bags.

I had been told of one road leading from Afghanistan to Tibet. Since Tibet was now part of China, this could be a critical route for Bible deliveries.

On the third day of my stay I visited the little town closest to this route – Qala Panja, perched eleven thousand feet up on the Hindu Kush ranges.

The town looked like a set from a biblical film epic with its tents, camels and nomads blending closely with the brown of the earth. Time must have stood still for the past two thousand years in this remote part of the world. Along the wayside, clusters of magnificent green grapes hung from their vines, begging to be picked. I did not know which smelled more exquisite : the pure, thin mountain air or the mouthwatering aroma from the strange confections for sale in the market place.

My guide from the hotel probably thought I had come on this excursion simply to take in the beauty of the mountains and the town. With deliberate casualness I asked him about the little trail I had seen during a drive we took just outside the town. The trail was no wider than

101

a finger, and pointed northeast along the thin arm of Afghanistan.

"That is Baroghil Pass," my companion informed me. I inquired what lay at the end of it. "Sinkiang province, China. It is seven day's ride by horse," he replied. I asked if there were Afghan traders going into China or Chinese coming out into Afghanistan.

"No, very far, very hard. Nomads go sometimes," he answered.

Now I had found a back door route into China, all I needed was a nomad to take Bibles and contacts to take them to.

* * *

Quite unexpectedly I was to receive confirmation about the possibility of using this route shortly after, while waiting for a plane in Pakistan. The flight had been delayed for at least twenty-four hours, and no one knew when to expect it.

A young journalist, clad in well-worn blue jeans and Eastern shirt, was impatient to get a story back to his editor's desk.

"It's a scoop, man. It's mind-blowing," he said desperately. "I've got to get a plane out of here."

With a scrutinising glance to make sure I was not a rival journalist, he poured out his story.

"I was up in the mountains doing a feature story when I heard rumours of a stockade beyond Afghanistan. The intellectuals who were arrested during the Cultural Revolution were supposed to be there."

He, his wife and a friend disguised themselves as nomads and travelled with genuine nomads for seven days along a tiny trail – the very road I spotted from Qala Panja. It wasn't a rumour. Once inside China they saw them – hundreds of intellectuals herded like animals and looking like animals. Five times a day they were being brainwashed with Communist doctrine.

I tried hard to digest this information. Now I knew for sure that it was possible for outsiders to travel the route to China – but I also knew so much more. In the past I had heard just a little of Chairman Mao's treatment of intellectuals, but in its worst excesses I had not realised it would take this appalling form.

I tried to imagine how the men and women were living in that place. They were probably more dead than alive under the shocking conditions. Once again I found myself crying out to God that we might find a way to get the message of His love into that stricken land.

* * *

In Lahore I discovered that some of the labourers on the Karakuram Highway, then under construction between China and Pakistan, were professing Christians. The Lord enabled me to make contact with a printer who agreed to pass them Bibles for delivery to the mainland. Elsewhere, too, Bibles began trickling their way into China; from remote countries which seemed to me to be on the very edge of the world. The twenty-five thousand that FEBC had printed for Brother Andrew were slowly making their way over the country's boundaries. Nomads on mules or on foot would load their packs with as many Scriptures as they could carry, then travel enormous distances to get them to their destinations. It was back-breaking work through dense jungles or over mountains in Burma, Nepal, Afghanistan, Pakistan, every frontier possible which would provide an avenue into China.

* * *

Pastor Ling, a Chinese pastor who had been driven from his homeland, was another who risked his life constantly in his work to get Bibles to his people.

I had first met him during a visit to Vientiane, Laos, and that day was etched deeply into my memory.

A number of Christians in the country had organised a strategy meeting with key believers, to discuss ways to transport Bibles across their border with China. When I arrived, the little group was waiting to meet me at the airport, and were quick to introduce me to Pastor Ling.

I looked at the old man's face and saw there a terrible scar disfiguring the skin. This believer had obviously suffered heavily for his faith.

Mechanically, I extended my right arm to shake his hand. He offered his left. Then I understand why. His right arm ended in a stump at his elbow. I embraced him, hating myself for being so unobservant.

"Did you know how long it took Pastor Ling to come here, Brother David?" asked one of the others.

I shook my head. "How long?"

"Twenty days. He and three of his friends have walked all that time just to be with us."

I looked with amazement at the old man, only to find his eyes were sparkling. "Of course I wanted to be here. We're going to get Bibles to my people! Right, David?"

And he did. From that first meeting he was tireless in his commitment to organise Bible deliveries across the border. The pastor had personally been responsible for quite a proportion of the 25,000 which had been moved in.

He didn't speak often of the persecution he had undergone in the past, he was too busy speaking of his Lord. But during one morning before I left Vientiane he shared his story.

Pastor Ling had been trained in the China Inland Mission School in Hunan province and soon after had taken up a position as a young pastor. "After the Communists took control," he explained, "the missionaries were forced to leave, and I worked on my own with our 'flock'.

"But in 1952, the Communists arrived to inform me they didn't approve of what I was doing and put me in prison."

His face lit up as he continued. "Yet during that time

104

my congregation never ceased to pray for me, and in 1957 I was released." The authorities forbade him to witness to his faith, but undaunted Pastor Ling had returned to his area and continued to preach. Revival began to break out and word of it soon reached the ears of the Communists.

Once again he was dragged off to prison. This time the senior officer came personally to deal with him. He ordered that Pastor Ling be tied against a wall, his arms outstretched in a crucifixion stance. Two soldiers were sent to torture him, shouting angrily, "Fool! You haven't learned your lesson yet. You *must* learn it."

With that, one turned around the rifle he was holding and brought the butt down right across the prisoner's face from his nose to his jaw. The skin was peeled open, as though cut with a surgeon's knife, and began to bleed terribly. Then the soldiers released him – by cutting off one of his arms at the elbow.

"I was put in prison again," he concluded, "for just a few more years. Now I can only do my work here from Laos. But at least, I can get the Word in to continue 'feeding my sheep' that way."

I looked at him for a moment, disturbing thoughts passing through my mind. "You really are laying out your life on the altar for Jesus every day," I began shamefacedly, "You're right out on the front lines."

"I am not. I just make a short trip and then go back home again. I'm not up here with the Communists like you."

"How do you feel about the danger? How do you cope with it?"

His eyes had a distant look, as he gently smiled. "If the Lord should call for me to give my life for my people," he said softly, "I am ready."

I knew he meant it. Once again, I dwelt on his scar, and the stump of his arm. I wanted to echo his words. But I had never been in that position where my very life had been put on the line for my faith. If that day ever came

to me, could I know for sure how I would respond?
Could I be certain I would pay the price?

* * *

Shan Kumar had given me the address of another Chinese
Christian to see while in the border countries. His name
was Yan Chee and he was an evangelist among the Hima-
layans.

The man was originally from Inner Mongolia where his
father had also been an evangelist, until Communist pressure had forced the family to flee in 1949. Yan Chee had
met Shan a few years later when the two had worked
together delivering Bibles into Tibet.

The evangelist was not expecting my visit, but at the
mention of Shan's name he welcomed me warmly into his
little home high in the Himalayas.

His smiling, gracious wife prepared us toast and Dar-
jeeling tea as we exchanged initial greetings. Before any
more could be said, however, Yan Chee leaned forward
in his chair, with a very serious look on his face.

"Brother David, would you allow me to share something
with you? Something which is very close to my heart?"

He told me of his early years in China and his life since,
most of which he had spent ministering to the Himalayan
people. For an hour and a half he spoke, uninterrupted
other than to offer me more tea and toast.

As he drew to a close, he laid his main point before me.

"Brother, I want to start ministering to my own people
again. And I know one way to do it. I believe God is telling
me to start getting His Word to the Chinese across the
border."

My mouth must have fallen open in surprise. So far there
had been no opportunity to explain to Yan Chee the
purpose of my visit. Yet this man was telling me all that
I had planned to tell him.

"How would you get the Bibles inside?" I said at last.

"Oh, I know many ways through the mountains. The Communist government need not know about it. It is physically difficult to cross these mountains," he paused to grin, "and that makes it safe from detection. I know people who will help me."

I could still hardly believe this was happening. It was as though God Himself had been here before me, preparing every word of the conversation.

"Have you delivered any before?" I asked, when I found my tongue.

"Once. A friend gave me some Bibles that were recently deposited here." I knew the friend he meant. We had delivered some of the twenty-five thousand to a European missionary in the area. "Nice ones," he continued, "with red covers. They looked just like Mao's book."

By now I was smiling broadly. "If someone provided you with all the Bibles you wanted, could you get them into China?"

"Certainly."

I reached across to shake his hand. "Yan Chee, I am positive God has brought us together," I said delightedly.

We spent a week together talking, praying, planning strategy. I promised to give him some of the Scriptures that had already been moved to the country. He told me that he had three men who could depart on a delivery immediately.

That was to prove only the start of many long treks for him and his teams.

* * *

While on the borders, I had one other task to fulfil. Brother Andrew had repeatedly stressed the need for me to get inside China myself, and every attempt I had made so far had met with dismal failure. I had been to a number of Chinese Embassies in the border countries, and usually got no farther than the front door. However, on the final leg of my journey I decided to try the embassy in Katmandu as well.

"I'm a friend of the embassy people," I told the guard at the entrance of the building. He opened the door and gestured for me to come inside.

With time to wait, I looked around the reception area and gathered my impressions. Bare, except for the sofa, coffee table, and two armchairs. Grey, except for a few books and pamphlets on the magazine rack. Very quickly, I took some red-jacketed New Testaments from my pocket and slipped them into the magazine rack beside identical Mao books. Just in time. A grey-suited embassy official entered politely, if somewhat warily.

"Yes, what can we do for you?"

I gave my name. "I'm interested in travelling into China," I told him.

"Please have some tea," he offered. We sat quietly for a few moments sipping tea. The officer openly watched me. Since Nixon had made his much-heralded China trip, he seemed not at all surprised that an American wanted to go to China, too.

"You are a friend of our country?" he asked, after some time.

"Oh yes, your country is a favourite of mine. I love it," I replied. "I have many Chinese friends."

He smiled and we took another sip of the tea. It was my turn to take the initiative. "And how is the Revolution coming along?" I asked for openers. He gave me a selection of pamphlets to enlighten me on the country's progress. The official was very eager to chat. He told me that the embassy received very few guests and almost no foreign ones at all. The afternoon wore on with small talk.

The time for me to leave arrived and still he had not told me how I could get to China.

"Please come for tea tomorrow?" It was a sincere invitation.

"Thank you, I shall be very happy to come back," I

said, and I meant it. He smiled warmly and accompanied me to the door.

When I returned the following day, I was again taken to wait in the reception room. I glanced quickly at the magazine rack, and seeing that the New Testaments had been taken already, re-stocked the supply as soon as I was left alone.

My visa to China did not appear that visit. The official was very apologetic over tea as he explained it was still not possible for me to go to his country.

Yet I did not leave disappointed.

For the first time I'd been able to sit alongside a Chinese Communist and relate to him as an everyday person. The man was not just a cog in the giant machinery of the party, he was a human being with feelings. He had responded to friendship – even betraying a hint of loneliness in the isolation of his position.

With so much talk at that time of "Commie B ..... s" and the dreaded Red Peril, it had become easy for us in the West either to hate or fear these people.

Jesus had not called us to do either. He had died for them just as He had for us – and He was calling us to love them, for His sake.

CHAPTER EIGHT
"Don't Go to China"

The Star Ferry threw its engine noisily into reverse and pulled slowly into the terminal. A sea of hurrying passengers poured up the passageway and out into the streets of Hong Kong. Among the crowd was Joseph, borne along with the current.

"Hey Joseph. Wait!" At the sound of his name he turned and saw a friend from one of Hong Kong's Bible colleges. It was difficult to stand still in the face of the oncoming tide, and Joseph had to dodge right and left as he waited for the man to catch up.

"What brings you here to Hong Kong?" he asked breathlessly when he reached Joseph's side. The two began to walk together with the crowd.

"Well," Joseph replied quietly, "my uncle and I are going to China."

The man looked at Joseph in disbelief. Then quickly he grasped Joseph's arm and pulled him to one side of the street, away from the flow of the crowd.

"I must warn you," he began urgently, "listen to me, Joseph." He pushed his spectacles to the end of his nose, tightened the grip on his arm and locked his eyes on Joseph's. 'Don't go to China. It's dangerous!'"

Joseph held his friend's eyes. Here he was, an inexperienced young man searching for contacts inside the People's Republic and more than aware of the dangers involved. He had hoped to find help and encouragement from a man like this Bible scholar who knew so much more about the situation than he.

But as the man's face looked up into his, all Joseph could read was concern and fear.

The warning continued to ring in Joseph's ears as he

threaded his way through the noisy congestion of Hong Kong traffic. Suddenly his thoughts brought him to a standstill.

"I must be crazy wanting to go into China. I may not even be able to get out again."

His mind went back to his father and mother. Was it fair on their family to take this risk? Was it sensible to enter a hostile land in search of a people who legally were not supposed to exist?

*   *   *

The Bible scholar's advice was not the first of its kind that Joseph and Uncle Liu had encountered in Hong Kong. Despite the weeks they had already spent there, they had received very little encouragement for their coming trip. They had not been able to find any Hong Kong Christians willing to divulge the names of believers on the mainland whom they could visit. Every meeting they attended brought them up against a wall of silence.

The story was always the same. One of the pair would preach or lead Bible study and share their burden to support the believers behind the Bamboo Curtain.

After the talk, they would look with longing and expectation for the congregation's reaction. Always they were met with a frozen stare. Nobody knew of anyone inside, or if they did, they were not about to give away the contact.

Despite their disappointment, Joseph and Uncle Liu could understand the people's reticence.

Since the start of the Cultural Revolution in 1966, the "Great Helmsman" Chairman Mao had begun a vicious purge of dissident elements in China, including the Christian church. In fact, the suffering of believers in China dated back almost as far as the Communist take-over in 1949. The newly established Communist government began its regime with a "honeymoon" period during which the worst evils of the old society disappeared in the bright promise of the new. For two short years Christians had been able to continue worshipping much as before, and many missionaries had even remained to carry on with their work.

By 1951, however, the Three-Self Movement had been organised. It was dedicated to the principles of self-government, self-support, and self-propagation, ironically enough the principles to which many missionary organisations were working for the Christian church in China before "Liberation". The origins of the new Three-Self Movement lay in a meeting between the "Church of Christ" and Chou en-Lai held the previous year. From that conference emerged the "Christian Manifesto" – a required admission that the church had been used as a tool of imperialism in China, and a pledge of allegiance to the People's Government and the Communist Party.

Gradually, under the aegis of the Three-Self Movement, independent Protestant churches of an evangelistic bent were forced to close, and only those cooperating with the government allowed to remain open. By the mid-50s, some outstanding Christian leaders had come under severe pressure, as had those who associated with them, and many were imprisoned at this time.

In 1958, during the "Great Leap Forward", a severe crackdown on all church activity began particularly in the countryside. Open expression of faith became much more difficult. This period led into a time of economic privation and natural disasters which reduced the living standards of all China to an extreme low. The church suffered particularly, as believers, in common with those in other restricted countries, are always singled out for criticism and "struggle" during times of national difficulty.

1966 marked the beginning of a cataclysmic period in modern Chinese history, the Great Proletarian Cultural Revolution. It touched everything and everyone in Chinese society. Christians bore a major brunt of the radical attacks on "the old", "the bourgeois" and "the imperialist".

Thousands of Christians not already in prison were brutally attacked and ridiculed. Those in detention were subjected to further pressures, mental and physical. Hundreds renounced the faith and betrayed other believers. Fellowship and trust grew rare, and the scars of this terrible trial remain with the purified Body today.

In the 1970s, the harsh repression of all open Christian activities continued, although the fierce personal attacks, the mob trials and physical torments at the height of the Cultural Revolution frenzy had ceased.

Joseph and his uncle had heard of many instances of persecution. They knew that, in the audiences they addressed, there were those whose relatives inside China had been imprisoned for as many as twenty years. Others had families there where the father had been arrested and sent to labour camp. Little had been heard of these believers for many years, other than the knowledge of extreme persecution, both physical and psychological.

How could Hong Kong Chinese risk endangering these loved ones further by giving their names to complete strangers? Especially when they could not be sure how this information would be used?

Joseph and Uncle Liu were touched by their love for the believers inside, and realised that they could not be expected to understand that the two of them shared that love. The pair were further moved to realise that the Christians were also worried about them.

"You know that once you get inside they may not let you leave the country again."

"You have the rest of your lives ahead of you. Why place your future at risk?"

"We see your love for the Lord. Why don't you let Him use you in some other work?"

Over and over these responses would be given, as Joseph and Uncle Liu struggled with their three months of searching in Hong Kong.

113

Their first encouragement took place at a meeting held in a Bible school. During the gathering, Uncle Liu addressed the students and noticed that sitting quietly amongst the fresh-faced group was an elderly lady, listening intently to Uncle Liu's challenge for students to become burdened for mainland China.

After the meeting the little woman introduced herself as Miss Woo and invited the pair to her home for coffee.

As they walked behind the fragile figure, dressed in her black trousers and pastel blouse, they could have had no conception they were following someone who would eventually become one of our chief links with the church in China.

Sister Woo made them very welcome in her large home, but during their coffee and crackers she seemed thoughtful. After they had eaten, she turned to Joseph and came straight to the point in her direct way. "I wonder if you and your uncle would pray for me? I am suffering from a haemorrhage and I know I will not have long to live unless God intervenes."

Although surprised with such a direct request, they immediately prayed with her, believing that she would be delivered from her illness.

The next day, Joseph received a phone call from Miss Woo.

"Praise God, I've been healed," she told him excitedly. "As you prayed, I felt something happen inside of me and now I am completely well.

"Please, I want you to come and be my guests during your stay in Hong Kong."

The pair shortly moved in with Miss Woo, who quickly became a mother to them both.

*   *   *

During Joseph and Uncle Liu's weeks of searching, I spent much of my time travelling the borders. When I returned home, however, it was to find that the family too had special needs to be taken care of.

After one of the early trips, I had come home to find Julie and the three D's in the midst of a family conference. The house that we were renting had been put up for sale by the owner. We had to find somewhere else to live.

"Have you done any looking yet?" I asked Julie.

"Yes, but I haven't seen anything." She paused, "at least nothing we could afford anyway."

Her eyes flickered away from mine.

"But you have found something you like a lot?"

She gave a little shrug. "Dave, there's no way we could even contemplate it. The rent is far too high."

"How far?"

"It's double what we are paying now." Double ... and we had been struggling to live within our budget as it was. "Besides," she added miserably, "the landlord wants three months' rent in advance."

I did a quick mental calculation and didn't much like the result.

"But it's really something, eh?" I asked Julie.

Her eyes shone. "Oh, David, it's gorgeous!"

"Then I think we should at least go look at it together," I said. "What do you say, kids?"

"You're on, Daddy!" Deanne needed no second invitation. The other two leapt to their feet to follow suit.

"But David ..." Julie began, placing a restraining hand on my arm.

I grinned. "Come on, honey. Looking won't cost us a cent."

The house was within walking distance, and the five of us set off, hand in hand across the road, to see it.

The children, like Julie, fell immediately in love with the place. It was more roomy than the house we had been living in, and had a very welcoming atmosphere. I watched as the kids explored each of the rooms, chattering excitedly. The light in their eyes was reflected in Julie's, and

I longed to get this place for them.

The family had uncomplainingly put up with all the travelling I had now taken on. At the very least, I thought, they deserved a home where they were truly comfortable during my absences.

"Julie? What's preventing you from taking this house?" I said at last.

"Why – the cost, of course. We don't have the money," she replied.

"No, we don't, I know. But if Jesus wants us to take it, He will have the money, won't He?" I continued. We had already seen Him provide for our office needs – could we now ask Him to do the same for our home? We knew His Word showed His resources were limitless ...

Together we approached the landlord who, to our delight, allowed us to take the place with only one month's advance rent instead of three.

Then we moved in. I still had no idea where the extra money was going to come from, but I was certain the family was in the house God had chosen.

After the move, we watched in amazement as the support we received from the States suddenly began to increase, double, treble. Yet our friends had no idea of the new rent we had to pay – we had retained the policy of not telling anybody when we personally were in need of money.

We were witnessing the loving care of our Heavenly Father who, in His own way, could alert His children in different parts of the world to one another's needs.

* * *

Throughout this time, however, Joseph and Uncle Liu had still been unable to find an opening among the Christians in Hong Kong. The two would spend hours talking and praying about the rightness of the trip. How could God be in it? There was no contact yet and the three months were drawing to a close. Soon they would be crossing the border and still had no one definite to see.

In his heart, Joseph was hoping the trip would not come about. He remembered only too clearly the first China trip he had taken with his uncle a year before.

The two had known that they would stand out because at that time it was normally only old overseas Chinese who went inside to visit relatives. So they were not surprised when their baggage was thoroughly searched. They had not taken Bibles with them, but still the checks were harrowing. If even once they stepped out of line, there was always the danger of arrest and detention.

They also remembered the difficult conditions of their one chance to witness to their relatives. The encounter took place in their far from private living quarters in a large house which they shared with many other families. Joseph's relatives occupied one bedroom and an adjoining "living room" which doubled as a passageway for other families in the building. Private conversation there was clearly impossible.

Joseph was not fluent in the same dialect as his relatives, so to communicate his faith to them he had to become a scribe. Although Chinese is spoken in many different dialects throughout the country, the written form of each is the same.

As they sat around the table, Joseph wrote his testimony on a piece of paper and passed it to the others. The final one to read it would crumple the paper and throw it into the fire. Someone would reply with a further question on paper, and then his answer would come the same way.

And so the "conversation" went, each piece being carefully destroyed once it had been read by all. Writing down their thoughts had the double advantage of ensuring complete privacy, since none of the people in the house were Christians.

Whenever someone from the rest of the building passed by the little group, Joseph and Uncle Liu would notice their relatives stiffen. Their activity would stop immediately and they would pretend to be discussing mundane matters. At that time, it was illegal to propagate one's faith in China. They knew only too well the dire circumstances if the authorities discovered what was happening.

Joseph and his uncle still recalled the tension of the situation and would have been only too glad not to go back into that environment again.

* * *

As well as Joseph and Liu's fears about China itself, there was another problem causing them almost as much concern.

Me.

They were not quite sure what to do with their foreign friend. If they were seen to be associating openly with an American, there would have been little chance of gaining the trust of the Hong Kong Christians.

China regarded America as its number-one enemy at that time. Everywhere large slogans were displayed on the streets of the major cities proclaiming their message of hate.

"People of the world, unite and defeat the U.S. aggressors and all their running dogs!" was particularly popular.

No wonder Joseph and his uncle were careful not to mention anything about an American to those around them. The two themselves were not even completely certain about my motives.

They took particular pains to ensure that Miss Woo did not know anything about me, but the astute old lady soon learnt of my existence and pressed for details.

It was only much later that I found out the full extent of the difficulties Joseph and his uncle were experiencing. But even at that time, I could sense their reticence and their doubt. And, more than anything else, I wanted to love these people. I was learning that it took time to build trust with the Chinese, and I needed that trust if I was to serve them.

As I agonised before the Lord, His love for His Chinese children seemed to grow within me until I felt weighed down with all that they were going through.

I would walk, praying, for hours in the humidity of the heavy tropical evening around the streets where I lived in Manila, oblivious to the constant hooting of horns on the nearby highway. I would talk it all out with God.

"Father, I sure don't like what's happening to China under Communism. I feel sickened at the thousands in prison, the thousands more being tortured in labour camps, not to mention those who have been killed," I said.

"But Lord, You know my life too and yet You love me despite the terrible things I've done to people. If You can love me, then I can look at the people of China the way You look at me. And I can love them too.

"Father, there are eight hundred million Chinese out there. I know You care, because You died for every one of them.

"Show us the way to reach them. Will You trust us with one contact, soon, Lord?"

Nevertheless, trusting Him for that contact was a battle. I had placed Joseph and Liu in Hong Kong and they hadn't found one lead during all these weeks. I found myself wondering whether I was right to have put them through this. Did God even mean them to make this trip and attempt to reach out to the Suffering Church?

Even as I asked these questions, somewhere, deep inside, I knew the answer was yes. As before, the teaching of old Mr Roy came into its own. "Are you going to walk by faith, son? Or by sight? You know which way Paul chose ..."

*   *   *

To our surprise the answer to our prayers had its origin in a dream. One night, before he had even left for Hong Kong, Joseph had seen a map in his dreams. It depicted two southern provinces of China – Kwantung and Fukien.

119

When he woke, he tried to reflect on what he had seen. At first he couldn't understand it. Why had he been shown a map? If anything he might have expected to see the land itself – the blue mountains, the paddy fields speckled with peasants hard at work.

But later, he understood the message. God seemed to be telling him that they were to go to China – to those two areas, Fukien and Kwantung.

* * *

One day, Joseph and Uncle Liu attended a service in the Kowloon YMCA. Afterwards, an elder of the church introduced them to a believer who had just come from China, having undergone severe persecution himself.

From the first, the Christian responded warmly, and turned to the pair with enthusiasm. "Why don't you come to my home for a prayer meeting?"

They trekked through the backstreets of Kowloon to his tiny apartment. The trio had spent more than an hour in determined prayer for China, when the believer suddenly stopped and said: "When you go to China, I'll give you the names of three people in Fukien and they will help you. They are some of the Christian leaders of the province."

Their hearts leapt and they found themselves close to tears of joy. After six long months they had received a breakthrough. And, they realised, as they turned to each other with a smile, this was one of the two provinces in the dream.

But by the time Joseph got home, the smile had left him. He knew he should be rejoicing that with only a few days to go before the start of their trip, God had finally brought them a contact. But he wasn't. Now he knew that the trip was a certainty. He had to go through with it.

Fear gripped Joseph's heart and he began to read in his Bible, Revelation and Daniel.

"These are two books which deal with the end times,"

he told me, "and if they catch me or put me in jail, at least I will know God's Word."

Joseph even contemplated writing his parents a letter, a last farewell. He wanted to assure them of his gratitude for the way they had brought him up and provided for him throughout his life.

The days ticked by and, despite their fear, they booked their tickets, aware that God had already shown He was authorising this journey.

Instead of searching for the next contact, they spent every day in prayer, some days fasting as well. Three days before they were due to leave, they attended a fellowship meeting and afterwards a friend there suggested they go to meet another believer – originally from Shanghai.

When Mrs Ho opened the door to them, one would never have known that they were strangers. Breaking through traditional Chinese reserve, she greeted them with all the warmth normally given to a close relative of many years' standing.

Joseph felt baffled. Although she had not known they were coming, it seemed almost as though she had been expecting them. She was so excited to see them.

"Please come into my lounge and let's share the goodness of the Lord together," she invited them with eyes shining.

Mrs Ho spoke Mandarin with a Shanghai accent, which made it difficult for them to follow all that she was saying. But they gathered that, while she had been praying, God had shown her two men fitting their description who were going to visit her.

"I had a vision that you would come and now you are here," she explained. "You have obviously been sent to me by God, and so I have someone I want you to meet."

With that, she called for a friend to come to the house, a Christian woman who gave them the name and address of a believer they could contact in another province. That province was the second one on the map – Kwantung.

* * *

I flew to Hong Kong to be with the two men before they left. We knew it would be unwise for me to be seen accompanying them to the railway station, so I was to say good-bye the evening preceding their departure.

A passage I had read in Isaiah some weeks before seemed the best possible gift I could leave with them.

> *Thus says the Lord to his anointed, to Cyrus,*
> *whose right hand I have grasped,*
> *to subdue nations before him and ungird the*
> *loins of kings,*
> *to open doors before him*
> *that gates may not be closed:*
> *"I will go before you*
> *and level the mountains,*
> *I will break in pieces the doors of bronze*
> *and cut asunder the bars of iron,*
> *I will give you the treasures of darkness*
> *and the hoards in secret places,*
> *that you may know that it is I, the Lord,*
> *the God of Israel, who call you by your name.*
> *(Isaiah: 45:1–3 R.S.V.)*

We did not know what "treasures" in the spiritual darkness of China they might find. Nor did we know what kind of mountains might need to be levelled before them.

But we did know that the same mighty God of Cyrus would go before Joseph and Uncle Liu. The way the contacts had come about had been confirmation that the hand of God was leading them to make the trip.

Now, they simply had to grasp the hand for strength and guidance as they stepped out to meet those believers who had also put their life on the line for Jesus, inside the People's Republic of China.

CHAPTER NINE
Apples on the Way

The stony-faced customs official, business-like in his dun uniform and black belt, began to open Joseph's suitcase.

As he did so Joseph felt a clamming perspiration in his hands. His eyes darted from a huge picture of Mao, to the red political texts that decorated the customs hall. "Long live the People's Republic of China." "Long live the Great unity of the People of the World."

The pair were crossing at the border post of Macao, a tiny Portuguese possession on the South China coast at the mouth of the Pearl River, forty miles from Hong Kong.

Joseph stood nervously in line with his uncle and scores of other overseas Chinese on tour to the People's Republic to visit relatives there.

Now came the crunch. Joseph had in his case nine Bibles. His eyes returned to the red texts on the wall as he tried to look as casual as possible. But he used that opportunity to call on the Lord for the hundredth time that morning.

"You cannot take this into China." Joseph was rudely jolted back to the fraught situation. Expecting the official to have discovered the Bibles, Joseph's heart dropped. But no. Instead, he fished out part of a Hong Kong newspaper that he had used to wrap up his slippers.

As he rummaged through Joseph's personal belongings, his fingers stopped momentarily and then closed around a book – the Bible. He roughly pulled back the clothes and laid bare the remaining eight Scriptures.

"These are Bibles. You cannot bring these into the People's Republic of China." The officer looked at him closely. "Are you a Christian?"

Joseph didn't have to think twice about his reply. Before leaving, he and his uncle had discussed how they would react to such a question. They knew that an admission of faith could lead to a discussion of the Lord – and this might be construed as propagating the Christian faith, a completely illegal activity in China. Would they then be detained? Might they be refused entry? Whatever happened, they would not deny their Lord. Their Bible taught them that to deny the Lord would lead to the Lord denying them, too, before His Father in heaven.

"Yes," he answered in an unwavering voice. "I am a Christian. I would like to take these books to my relatives."

The customs guard was immovable. "You cannot bring these in."

"But," Joseph said, seeking to identify with his "homeland", "our constitution says that we have freedom of belief. And I am a Christian."

The customs man could not refute Joseph's point. "I'll have to consult my superior," he said, taking the nine Bibles away. While he was gone, Joseph's eyes looked again around the room, registering the watchful eyes of the armed soldiers clad in green trousers and blue Mao coat.

When the man returned, he gave a shrug. "Okay, you can bring one in. The rest you will have to leave here and collect on the way out."

Joseph made one final attempt. "But one is not enough." Yet even as he spoke, he was silently thanking God that he had been able to get even one Bible across the border.

As the guard shook his head, Joseph shut tight his suitcase and walked past, sneaking a look at Uncle Liu. The two did not want it to be obvious that they were together, because they had previously agreed that if one of them was caught, the other would be free to move on.

Uncle Liu was surrounded by three customs officials, all of them in intense conversation. The group was bent over the well-worn table examining something in great detail. Joseph knew this could only be for one reason.

He wanted to support his uncle in this predicament and immediately began praying. He took comfort from the knowledge that right at that moment friends around the world were also doing the same. We had already planned that on the morning of their departure, I was to send out a number of telegrams. All carried the same cryptic message: "Apples on the way."

On the receiving end, Brother Andrew in Holland, the American headquarters in Orange, California and those in other parts of the world could decode it immediately. This was a call to prayer. It told them that the team was on its way and all prayer supporters were to mobilise behind them.

Uncle Liu had also been told that he was allowed one Bible, the Chinese version, but he insisted that he also needed his English-language copy as well.

"I am not very good in Chinese, so I need to bring another one, my English Bible."

The officials looked uneasy. "Why is the Bible so important to you, anyway?" asked one.

Uncle Liu stifled a smile as he silently gave thanks for such an opportunity to speak of his Lord. As Joseph stood praying for him on the other side of that large room, Uncle Liu began to tell his questioners the way Jesus could be known through His Word. For them, it was very likely the first time they had heard such a witness.

Soon, the three became four, as Uncle Liu explained the difference Jesus had made in his life. "Life had been empty for me before I knew Jesus. I had been disillusioned and hurt, and I wanted to die.

"But then," he continued, "my mother told me I could know Jesus Christ. I opened my heart to Him, and what joy came afterwards." Joy – Uncle Liu knew that whatever else they had known under Communism, joy would not have been a part of their experience.

"My sickness of heart became a delight, a burning desire, a love for all people. I wanted to share Jesus with all my Chinese brothers and sisters." A tear began to trickle down Uncle Liu's cheek. "This may be my only opportunity to see these relatives for many years to come."

One officer particularly seemed moved by his words. He leaned across the group to hand Liu the English Bible. "You may take this with you."

Uncle Liu began to gather up his belongings. But at that moment one of the others voiced a final suspicion. "Do you have any other Bibles on your person?" Liu, before going over the border, had placed three Bibles in his pockets. Now he reached in and offered the customs officials one of them. "Yes, here." The man took it and didn't think to ask if he had more.

When Liu joined Joseph by the currency exchange, they swapped stories in whispered tones. "Thank you, Lord," they said almost in unison, and Liu added: "Now we can go to our brethren with Bibles in our hands." He turned to Joseph with a grin. "It's time to break our fast. This calls for a celebration."

Joseph and his uncle had been praying and fasting for twenty-four hours, but now, as they sat in the border post restaurant, the two hungrily tucked into the colourful dishes before them. Their eyes met over the red and white patterned bowls. This was a feast of thanksgiving.

After the meal, the pair boarded an ancient bus for the ninety-mile journey to Canton, the nearest city to the border, sprawling on the banks of the Pearl River.

The bus motored its slow way through the rural scenery. Peasants in the adjacent rice paddies were hard at work, some bent double to plant the seedlings, others wielding heavy wooden farm implements. The fields themselves were coloured with the various stages of the rice cycle; newly planted patches awash with brown muddy water, the young plants in clusters of dark green, and the mature field a bright yellow-green under the sun.

There was a stillness about it all, a charm that made the men feel they had travelled out of one universe and into another. On the edge of the neat paddy fields, groups of buildings nestled close together, in quiet tones of ochre,

cream and brown. It seemed as though they had stood still
for many years, allowing wind and rain to beat mercilessly
upon them. The paint was peeling. Walls were crumbling.
The tiled roofs were breaking away at the corners. Yet the
subtle colours of the buildings, set against the different
greens of the fields and mountains, gave the scene a beauty
all its own.

The pair arrived in Canton late in the afternoon of the
same day and checked into a hotel for overseas Chinese.
Their sparsely furnished room had only a couple of faded
armchairs, a writing table with an old-style lamp and two
large, wooden beds. To combat the far-off heat of summer,
a slightly rusting electric fan stood on a table in the corner.

They both decided to clean away the grime of the dusty
journey, but it had to be a cold bath. Their only source of
hot water was a small thermos given pride of place by the
table lamp.

*   *   *

Next morning, Joseph and Uncle Liu fortified their
bodies with a breakfast of rice porridge mixed with chicken
and spring onions. Both had begun to feel uncertain about
the way they should visit their first contact. They did not
know how to get to her place and could not be sure they
would be welcomed once they found it. It might be difficult
for this Christian to trust them and they could not be sure
if they could trust her either. It was not uncommon for
believers to bow to the pressure of the government and agree
to inform on their Christian brothers and sisters.

Most of all Joseph and Uncle Liu were anxious about the
timing of their visit to the believer. They knew they would
cause her embarrassment and even possible exposure if
they arrived at the wrong time.

After breakfast, they laid their fears before the Lord, and
asked Him to show them when they should move out. Both
felt a certain conviction it should be late afternoon.

Dusk was falling as they hailed a motor tricycle. Liu told the driver the address of their contact. She was the Christian woman whom they had heard of from Mrs Ho's friend in Hong Kong.

The tricycle meandered its way precariously through the sea of cyclists, its noisy engine contrasting with the jangling symphony of bicycle bells.

Joseph and Uncle Liu sensed that their overseas clothes made them the focus of attention on the streets. But as they looked into the faces of the people around them, eyes were quickly averted, or those who returned their gaze did so with a look of suspicion.

The tricycle edged its way towards the district where their "sister" lived, past streets lined with rows of crumbling brick or cement buildings and billboards displaying Maoist slogans in bold red simplified script.

"Be self reliant and work hard."

"Long live the glorious, correct and great Communist party of China."

The driver wanted to please his overseas visitors and desperately tried to find the address. But it soon became obvious that he had no idea where it was. Joseph and Liu became more and more worried as he questioned the locals at every street corner.

Finally, the team felt urgent action had to be taken. "Here is our money. Thank you very much. We are getting out here."

It was night when they began searching for the address on foot. The task was made even more difficult because public as well as private lighting was at a minimum. Often, the darkness was broken only by a naked bulb casting a yellowish hue over the family scene. Through the barred windows, the pair could see the standard furnishings, the grey mosquito net on its wooden frame, a peeling wall which carried the ever present, benign face of Chairman Mao.

Although they asked one man for directions, he could only give them vague instructions. Reluctant to inquire any more, they began to walk in the general area to which he had pointed them. At last they came to a despairing halt and looked down at their scrap of paper bearing the address. As they looked up again they discovered, to their astonishment, they were standing outside the very place they had been looking for.

The joy of finding it, however, quickly gave way to dismay as they realised their "sister" lived in a large building with many apartments. How could they find out which was hers without knocking on every door and once again focusing attention on their visit?

At that moment, they noticed a young girl with pigtails walking towards the building, wheeling a bicycle. To their surprise, as they watched her approach, it was as though there was a line of unspoken communication between them. Joseph and Uncle Liu felt certain she was a believer, and she seemed to sense the same in them. For, as soon as she had leaned her bike against the building, she came directly over to the men.

"Who are you looking for?" she asked quietly.

They gave her the name of the contact, and her face lit up. "She is my mother. Come with me." The timing could not have been more perfect. The three of them were able to move together as if they were old friends and had deliberately met for a pre-arranged visit. It was as God's Word had promised: He had gone before them.

The "apartment" comprised a tiny room with a window at one end. The bed which mother and daughter shared was placed near the window, curtained-off from the rest of the room.

As Joseph and his uncle entered, they bowed in greeting to the mother. "How do you do. We are Chinese Christians from overseas. We have come to greet you in the name of Jesus." The mother remained impassive. "I am sorry. I don't know what you are talking about," she said.

Joseph opened his overnight bag and took out a box of chocolates. He explained that he had been asked to deliver them by her friend in Hong Kong. At that, the well-lined face softened. Then she added almost apologetically, "Oh, thank you. How is she? Times are very difficult now. We have to be very cautious."

Uncle Liu asked her if she owned a Bible. "Yes," she said, "I was very fortunate. I have never let on that I was a Christian and the cadres did not think to search my house." She went inside the curtained-off "bedroom" and brought out a dilapidated New Testament. It obviously had known exhaustive use over the years.

Joseph took out the one Bible he had brought into China and placed it in the mother's hand. She fingered it gently, dwelling particularly on the pages of the Old Testament. She looked up at her visitors with moist eyes. "I haven't seen a whole Bible since 1949."

"Haven't any of your friends a full copy of the Bible either?" Joseph asked her. "Not even your fellowship group?"

As she replied, they could hear the loneliness in her voice. "I am only in touch with one other believer. I have heard meetings are held, but I have never attended one."

"What then do you do for fellowship?" asked Uncle Liu.

"I have my daughter and my radio."

"Radio?"

"We are able to receive a broadcast from your country." The two exchanged glances. "It is from the Far East Broadcasting Company.

"I listen every night," she continued. "I can't have the radio very loud, so I put a blanket over it and put my head inside. That way I can listen in secret."

Joseph smiled at his uncle, knowing how much this discovery would mean to me.

"I wonder if we'll find FEBC is also getting through to the believers on the rest of our trip?"

The woman looked alarmed. "Surely you are not going to contact other believers?" The two nodded their assent and she looked even more concerned. "But that's very dangerous. You could be arrested. Just the other day, I had word of friends from the north who were thrown into prison because of their faith."

Joseph felt a sense of despair returning to him. He had set out that day feeling very nervous to begin with. This lady obviously knew what she was talking about and she was warning them not to go on.

Her voice broke through his thoughts. "Are you sure you want to go through with this?" Joseph paused hesitantly, but Uncle Liu answered for them both. "Yes, sister." His voice was quiet. "We know the Lord is walking before us."

She accompanied them to the door. "Then, my brothers, I will be praying for you – that Almighty God will take care of you ..." Her voice trailed off, and she finished with a whisper, "and keep you safe ..."

* * *

Next morning they again boarded a bus with the tour group and set off for Fukien province. As the vehicle bumped along, Liu seized every opportunity to take photographs. Beside him, Joseph pressed his transistor radio to his ear, constantly turning the dial to see if he could pick up further broadcasts from FEBC, but without success.

In time Joseph became aware that the tour guide was looking at them with considerable interest and nudged his uncle. "I think they are wondering what we're doing," he whispered. The two toned down their activities for the rest of their journey.

Their Hong Kong contacts were with Christian leaders in the city of Foochow. Their precious Bibles were soon distributed and with each one the conversation went the same way.

"Have you need of more Bibles?"

"Our people are starved for the Word of God. We can use all that you can bring."

Yet there was always a "but", often expressed with a sad shake of the head. "I fear it is impossible to bring in many, my brothers. I cannot see how you can do it."

*　　*　　*

By the time they reached Pastor Henry Chai, their final contact in Fukien province, they had no Bibles left to give. Yet the middle-aged pastor received them warmly.

When they arrived at his modest home, they could see a still figure sitting in a chair by the window. In response to their knock, he came to the door.

"Pastor, we have been given your name by a friend in Hong Kong," Joseph began quietly. "We too are believers."

He opened the door wide for them to pass and ushered them into an inner room. "I am so pleased you have come at this time – because our meeting is about to start."

They sat down in some surprise. There were no other members of the "congregation" in the room except for the pastor and his young daughter. An old clock noisily ticked away the minutes as they sat politely, occasionally smiling at the man when they happened to catch his eyes.

After a short time, two people arrived and were introduced to them by Pastor Chai. A little later, one more "drifted in" as if on a social visit. This pattern continued over about twenty minutes until fifteen people crowded into that small room. A few unaccompanied hymns were sung from memory, but in a very subdued tone. Then the pastor asked the team to testify before the group bowed in prayer.

After this came the highlight for the congregation – the sharing of God's Word. Although Pastor Chai owned a copy of the Bible, he never brought it out for worship services. If an outsider were to surprise them, the Bible would immediately identify them and their activity. Instead, while the pastor was preparing the sermon for the week, he carefully memorised the Scripture verses to quote during the service.

Joseph and Uncle Liu watched the faces of the people gathered as they drank in the words. They later learned that this was virtually the congregation's only contact with God's Word through the course of the week.

The two were moved by the pastor's sermon. He was preaching against sin and stressing that one man's sin could affect their whole group. He urged them to greater sanctification and holiness in their living. Knowing what price these believers must have already paid for their faith, the pair were very challenged by his message.

As they looked around the group, they noticed how silent every member was; listening intently and drinking in every word. To anyone outside, it would have seemed there was just a simple visit underway with quiet conversation. Yet inside believers were risking their freedom for the privilege of meeting together for worship.

After the service, the congregation left as it had come, in ones and twos at well-spaced intervals. When they had all gone, Uncle Liu asked the pastor whether the official had ever been aware of his activities.

In response, the man began to reveal what had happened to him during the Cultural Revolution, when persecution had been at its most intense.

Pastor Chai had been subject to many kinds of suffering. On one occasion, he had been arrested at gunpoint and called upon to deny Christ. The Red Guards assured him that, if he would simply deny Jesus, he would be freed. He refused.

For several hours, they continued to harangue him, but he would not meet their demands. Eventually, they took another tack. The fanatics produced a large colour picture of Chairman Mao and began to chant over and over: "Kneel before our great and wise leader." When he would not comply, they roughly grabbed him by his shoulders and tried to force him to his knees. After that failed, they decided to "encourage" him by savagely beating him on his legs with sticks. The attack was so brutal that he collapsed on the floor.

"Brothers," Pastor Chai's face showed concern, "it's not only I, but also my daughter who has suffered. Because of our faith, she will not be permitted to pass her exams at school. Since the authorities know we are Christians, they will not allow her into university. It is the same for all of our friends. Every one of their children has suffered academically for their faith.

"Could you help me to get my daughter out of China?"

The team agreed they would do everything they could to help.

Uncle Liu cut in. "What about you, Pastor? Would you like to leave China yourself?"

"I already have the opportunity to go to Hong Kong, but I have no wish to." There was a look of peace on his face. "My place is here where I can serve the flock the Lord has put in my care."

* * *

Although they had reached the last of the names given them in Hong Kong, the team had many more leaders to visit. Those they had already seen had given them further contacts, and it soon became apparent that there was, even at that time, a network of secret believers in a number of provinces. It extended like the veins of a leaf through at least the central part of China, including the cities of Canton, Shanghai, Peking, Foochow and Amoy. But to meet those outside Fukien province, the team would have to wait for another visit.

One contact led to another and at times they would find themselves in most unusual venues. One of the most surprising was a dental clinic in a little town close to Amoy. The pair had trouble finding it as they worked their way through a labyrinth of narrow streets.

People seemed to be silently watching them as they made their search. The atmosphere was tense. They were reminded that the Communist government had called upon all people in the land to keep close observation on each other and report anyone who was not following the party line.

In time they were able to arrive unnoticed at the clinic and, as they entered through the back door, found themselves in the dentist's reception area. Already gathered were a number of Christian leaders and a middle-aged woman, whose faith could be seen clearly in the expression of her face.

Uncle Liu was called upon to testify to them and he began by expressing his awareness and concern for the suffering they had undergone. As he continued, he explained the way God had led them into China from the outside world.

At that moment, Joseph noticed that the lady sitting next to him began to cry. Tears trickled silently down her line-worn face as she listened intently. Joseph was deeply touched. Never before had he seen anybody so moved by the sheer fact of fellowship. He had no gift to give her. But the woman was not concerned about that.

For this believer, it was simply enough that they had come.

* * *

As the trip drew to an end, the pair left Fukien province to travel by train back to Canton. It happened to be the Chinese New Year when they left and the country had been given two days of public holidays.

Joseph and Uncle Liu found the station swarming with people. As the train pulled in, the crowd surged forward and began to pour inside through every available doorway. Joseph and his uncle saw that they would have little chance of access that way, so they did the next best thing. The two climbed through the nearest window and lowered themselves into the seat beneath.

The journey lasted through the night, and Joseph and Uncle Liu remained seated for its entirety. The train was crammed to capacity, and it was impossible for them to move around.

Next morning they arrived at a little town where they were to change trains for the connecting ride to Canton. The two were stiff-legged after the long night, and took advantage of the break to stroll through the town.

Wandering into a department store, their attention was caught by the radio section in one corner. "May we hear one of these?" Uncle Liu called to the sales clerk, hoping they might catch something of interest to fill in the time before they caught the train for the final leg of the journey to Canton.

"You have come far?" The beaming salesman was only too happy to please his overseas guests. After exchanging pleasantries, he brought over the largest model in the section and placed it carefully on the glass-topped counter. He bent over to switch it on and then went to serve another customer. They waited for it to warm up. Suddenly, booming loud and clear, they heard a message of the love of Jesus Christ. The preacher was speaking Mandarin with a strong Philippines accent.

"It's the Voice of Friendship. That's one of FEBC's programmes." Uncle Liu leaned on the counter and placed his ear closer to the set. Suddenly the glass underneath gave way and shattered beneath his weight. The two jumped back with shock.

The commotion that followed distracted all attention from the nature of the broadcast. The radio was turned off as the pair helped clean up the mess and left money with the bemused salesman to cover the damage.

As they walked back, Uncle Liu nursed his bruised right hand. Despite the pain and their embarrassment, the two were rejoicing. For the first time they had been able to hear

FEBC for themselves. It was absolute confirmation that the ministry was reaching deep into China.

* * *

When they returned to Canton, Uncle Liu and Joseph again visited the "relatives" they had witnessed to in writing the year before. This time, they had practised their Mandarin and, though they were not fluent, could communicate the basics of the Gospel message.

Their relatives listened to them quietly but Joseph felt sure more out of politeness than genuine interest. Before they left, he wrote down the words of John 3:16 on small scraps of paper for each of the families.

> *For God so loved the world that He gave His only son that whoever believes in Him should not perish, but have eternal life.* (R.S.V.)

As he handed out the copies of the verse, Joseph felt a little discouraged. His relatives were too well mannered to refuse them, but he wondered how long they would keep them before they got lost.

It was to be four years before he received his answer.

* * *

When the day came to leave Canton, they boarded a bus for the Macao border. Like all visitors to China they had been told how Mao's thoughts had transformed this country into a paradise on earth. Chairman Mao had created a noble society where people had become better, less selfish. Crime had gone with this new age.

So it was quite a jolt on that final bus trip when Uncle Liu turned to Joseph with a disturbed look on his face.

"What's up Uncle? You look worried."

Liu was, by now, desperately searching through his

137

clothing for his wallet containing all his money and other valuable documents.

"Joseph," he finally said. "You know we heard that Mao's thoughts were supposed to change human nature? Obviously, they didn't do such a good job in Canton."

"Why?"

"Well, I've had my pocket picked."

CHAPTER TEN
China, Let Me Love You

I lay on my back on the creaky bed in a hotel room in Hong Kong. I was feeling excited as I looked again at the cable that had reached me just twenty-four hours before.

"Coming home February 20. Father has been wonderful to us stop Joseph Liu stop."

This was the day that I had been looking forward to for five long weeks. Each day had ticked by at a snail's pace as I asked myself a thousand times what was happening inside. Were they all right? Could they be in any danger? The pair were being exposed to a hostile government from which I knew they had no guarantee of return.

Frequently, too, I found myself asking whether they had made contact with the believers inside. How were the Christians coping with the pressures of the government? Did they need our help? Then a more fundamental question would come into my mind: Was there even a secret church left inside the People's Republic?

Each time a question arose, I would talk it out with the Lord. Many times a day, Julie and I would stop whatever we were doing and lift the dedicated pair up to Him.

It was hard to lie still. One minute, I'd be on my back, the next I'd be pacing the tiny box-like room. The pair knew I would be waiting for them there, and any minute a knock on the door would announce them.

Finally that moment came. In three strides I got to the door and opened it wide. At the sight of their two faces, I flung out my arms to greet them in a giant bear hug.

"Praise God, you're safe." I felt tears well up inside of me. But even as I greeted them, something about their response made me pause.

"You are okay, aren't you?"

139

The two smiled, though I had the feeling it was something of a mask.

"We are fine, Brother David. We are just tired, but we are glad to see you again," Liu reassured me.

"Well, come on, sit down, let's talk." I motioned them to sit down on the faded settee and perched eagerly on the edge of my bed.

"Where do we begin? There have been so many questions I have been dying to ask you guys. Where would you like to start ... ?" I broke off as a look of uncertainty began to cloud their expressions.

Something *was* wrong, but as ever the pair were scrupulously polite.

"We would like to know how you are too, Brother David. How is your wife? Your kids?"

"They are just fine. They send you their love. They've all been praying for this day." I was perplexed as once again their eyes seemed to be avoiding mine in embarrassment.

"Are you quite sure everything's all right?"

As if with his uncle's tacit consent, Joseph leaned forward to speak for them both.

"Yes of course, Brother David, it is just that the trip has been a very long one. If you would excuse us, we feel the need for rest. Perhaps, we can meet again to talk in detail another time."

I helped them downstairs with their suitcases and called for a taxi to take them to Miss Woo's.

Back in the room, I sank slowly back onto the bed. After all my expectations, this response was not the one I had bargained for. I sat perplexed looking out of the unwashed window at the view of the rusting fire escape on the nearby building. Maybe they *were* tired. Maybe, as they said, next time they would be more forthcoming. Or would they?

*   *   *

The following day I invited them for lunch at the Juno Revolving Restaurant, commanding its beautiful view of the Hong Kong skyline. Once again they were typically courteous, but still revealed almost nothing of the trip.

Perhaps they needed to unwind. For two or three days, I concentrated on taking them out to places where they could quietly relax and enjoy themselves. All would go well until I once again mentioned the events of the journey inside. Then, as before, they would go strangely silent. Slowly, I began to sense the problem. It seemed certain they had found what they had been looking for. Their problem was that now they did not feel comfortable sharing it with me.

I thought back to the way the Christians in Hong Kong had been reluctant to give information about their relatives to Joseph and Liu. I realised now that the pair were being every bit as reserved towards me as these people had been towards them.

The information that they had gathered was so precious, they felt the need to guard it carefully. They had heard so much, often whispered to them by one who still bore the scars of the cost of his faith. Could they really trust their findings with an American?

"Lord," I prayed when the problem crystallised for me, "I've got an awful lot to learn about the Chinese. And I want to learn. And the only way I can is for you to give me patience and understanding for these men. Not only these two but their people as well."

I leaned back on the bed and closed my eyes. "China," I thought, almost speaking the words out loud, "let me love you..."

* * *

In time the Lord did answer my prayer. A little at a time, the ice slowly began to thaw as warmth once more was established between us. The picture started to emerge.

I began to see a church which had been purified by fire. A church which had experienced the very pains that Jesus experienced. This church was one that understood Golgotha, to the point of praying drops of blood because of their persecution. As the story unfolded, I felt deeply challenged. I had never known that place.

"And can we stand with them?" I wanted to know. "Do they want our help?"

By way of answer, Joseph recounted a story he and Uncle Liu had been told by a pastor they met in Amoy.

"In 1969, the Red Guards stormed their little group of believers. They confiscated the pastor's Bible, along with those of all the congregation.

"The Bibles were taken out into the streets and burned in one horrific bonfire. Then the pastor was thrown into prison.

"In fact, that wasn't the first time. He had been in prison for nine years before that. His brother was also still in gaol, where he had lain for fourteen years. He had been kept in the darkness of solitary confinement for so long that he could no longer see. And he could not walk because of the torture and malnutrition.

"His brother is still in prison. All he has to do is renounce Jesus as Lord, and declare publicly that Chairman Mao is God – and he can come out.

"After the pastor himself had his Bibles taken, he began to pray to the Lord. I will never forget the words he told us, Brother David. He said, 'Lord, You know that the Communists have taken every possible copy of Your Word. You have seen those copies burning. I ask You, would You please speak to someone *outside* of China? Would You cause them to prepare the Scriptures for our people? And Lord, would You bring those Bibles into our land?'

"The tears began to flow from the pastor's eyes when he told us that this day he had seen the answer to his prayer."

It was not only the pastor who wept. When I heard that story, I found it hard to choke back my own emotions. The

142

three of us stopped right there to give thanks to God for the faithfulness of His leading.

* * *

Then Uncle Liu took up the story. "In Canton, we actually came across a Bible School where young Christians are trained to teach others the Word of God."

"But how could they meet for classes?" I interrupted.

"That is just it, they don't," Uncle Liu replied.

I obviously looked puzzled and he continued: "Their system is very simple. Instead of the pupils coming to the teachers, the teachers go to them. One at a time, a lecturer in every subject will visit each one of the students.

"The instructors go from house to house as though they are making social calls. But in fact, each visit is one more opportunity to satisfy the hunger of their twenty full-time students for the knowledge of the Word of God.

"And with each lesson, both teacher and student place their very freedom on the line ..."

* * *

"How bad is their need for Bibles?" I asked.

"Everywhere we went the story was the same," replied Uncle Liu. "In so many towns, the Christian leaders recounted stories of Scriptures being publicly burned in 1966 at the onset of the Cultural Revolution.

"Some of those we visited had no Bibles at all. Others had just one or two which were used for worship meetings, and stored in secret hiding places in between. Many had divided up their Bible into separate parts, so that members of the congregation could each take home a portion to be returned the following meeting – almost like a little library.

"Every group, every individual Christian we met, wanted us to return with Bibles. We have promised them, Brother

143

David, that we will do everything we possibly can to fulfil their requests."

"Amen to that." I told him. "Have they any way of reproducing the Scriptures inside?"

"Only by hand," Joseph explained. "We met one group of young people who would get up two or three hours before work every morning just to copy the Scriptures. But it is slow work, Brother David. And they take a long time to get very far."

We talked late that night, and as it drew to a close, I found myself more heavily burdened than ever to get Scriptures into China – even taking them myself if only I could get into the country.

"Well, Brother David, although you can't get a visa to go yet, we can do the next best thing for you," said Uncle Liu.

"What's that?"

"We have taken many photographs during our weeks away. You set up a time one evening and we'll show you them all."

Next day, I was on the phone to Shan Kumar.

"Shan, you want to see a slide show unavailable anywhere else in the world?" I began.

"Maybe," came that rich Eastern accent down the line. "What is it about?"

"The People's Republic of China."

"Oh. Then I definitely am interested. Where is it to be shown?"

"At your house – tonight I hope."

He chuckled. "Okay, David, what are you up to?"

As I explained, Shan was every bit as enthusiastic as I. And at the first available evening, Joseph, Uncle Liu and I were knocking on his front door.

While the boys were showing us their slides, we saw what they had meant when they spoke of the run-down state of the country. It came alive before our eyes, as we looked at the buildings in need of repair, and the outmoded forms of transport. The propaganda came alive too, as we saw the slogans and posters of the Great Helmsman Mao dominating so many of the scenes.

We were particularly struck by the uniformity of the people. It was hard to tell the women from the men since they wore no make-up and both sported simple, short hair styles. Even more extraordinary were the hosts of people all dressed in the same drab, ill-fitting, blue overalls.

But when the men showed us their close-up shots we saw just how different each person was. An old woman with a well-lined face sat quietly in the bamboo chair outside her tiny home. Children smiled happily as they watched the ducks in a Canton park. An old man with white stubble on his chin stared up at the camera lens, a look of bewilderment in his eyes. Middle-aged parents rode their bicycles home from work, the toll of their daily labour evident in their tired bodies.

Each one was an individual. Each one was living a life of his own. And each one needed the love of Jesus.

*   *   *

Joseph and Uncle Liu completed their showing with slides of our "family" in China. Our necks were craning forward as we saw, on the screen, portraits of our brothers and sisters in Christ; men and women who were risking all to make a stand for Him in that oppressed environment.

As the lights came on Shan turned to the pair. "How strongly are the believers standing under the pressure? Has their witness been extinguished?"

Once again, the answer took us by surprise.

"We had not mentioned this before, but there are many believers in China who told us that they believe a revival is under way in that land."

"You mean to say," Shan protested, "that in a country where it's illegal to propagate one's faith they are seriously contemplating revival? They cannot even afford to open their mouth for the Lord without risking imprisonment."

"I know," replied Joseph. "At first, we could not believe it possible either. But it's already begun."

Joseph went on to explain that twelve months before they had arrived in Foochow, two old ladies had acted on their conviction of revival. They began a prayer meeting, certain that God was going to work in their area.

Their answer came in a visit of a little wide-eyed girl who was demon-possessed. She was also deaf and dumb. As the two women tried to show her affection she retreated and cowered in a corner of the room. The women knelt beside her and surrounded her with their arms as they prayed for her to be healed. Suddenly, the mite let forth an unearthly shriek, despite her inability to speak. Then, she became calm and began to look up with interest as the women spoke to her. From that day on, she could not only hear, but also began learning to speak.

News of her healing spread through the area and soon others came to their home to present their needs for prayer. Each of their requests was met and increasing numbers began to attend.

One night, two hundred people had gathered in their small place for a thanksgiving service. Suddenly, through their singing, came a loud knock at the door. When they opened it, they found an officer of the People's Liberation Army with two of his enlisted men.

"What's going on here!" he demanded.

Their reply was quiet. "We're just holding a prayer meeting."

"And, who are you praying to?" he sneered.

"We are praying to God," they explained.

The soldier's tone was condescending. "Oh, who is your God and what is He doing?"

One of the old ladies spoke out. "Our God is the God who made the heavens and the earth. He is a God who cares for you and cares for us. He became like us to die in our place and He rose again from the grave."

146

He didn't interrupt her so she continued.

"When He was on earth Jesus did many wonderful miracles and He touched people with His compassion and love. We are here, because He has been doing the same wonderful miracles in our midst."

The officer's confidence was a little shaken. "What has He been doing?" he asked.

"You see that one over there?" she replied. "He was sick in his stomach and the Lord touched him. And that one over there? He didn't have enough food. And we prayed to the Lord and the Lord provided food for him. This man here, his leg had a huge sore on it and we prayed for him and the Lord healed him."

Even so the officer was not convinced. "Look at my nose," he mocked. "It's disfigured, isn't it? I've been told I've got cancer. What can your God do about that?" For all his scepticism, the old woman discerned a look of need in his eyes.

They opened the door wider and invited him to sit on a chair in their midst. As they began to pray, he lowered his rifle to the floor and bowed his head. When the prayer was finished, the three men left the house, making no attempt to break up the meeting.

That night, the officer felt a strange sensation in the afflicted area and when he woke in the morning, he found he was completely healed. The man was so excited he returned to the house still in uniform.

"Tell me more about this God. I want to know all about Him." His tone was urgent.

The two explained that Jesus loved him and died in his place so he might be reconciled to God. They pointed out that Jesus was ready to forgive him.

"Do you believe?" they asked. "Will you accept Jesus and start life over?"

He nodded. "I want to give my life to Him – to enlist in His ranks."

News of the officer's conversion spread like wildfire

through the town. The regular meeting grew from two hundred to five hundred members.

The officer was given a copy of the Scriptures and, as he began to share his new-found faith, the meetings increased all the more. By the time Joseph and Uncle Liu had arrived in town, there were twelve hundred people gathered in one meeting in a large house in Foochow.

It was a pattern we were to see repeated over and over again in China: God using signs and wonders, as He had done in biblical days, to draw people to Himself.

The authorities' retaliation, however, was every bit as strong as the movement's growth. They began investigation immediately and, before long, had identified the five leaders of the revival. The day before Joseph and Liu arrived, these men had been arrested and, as an example for the rest of the people, made to look like circus clowns before the whole of the town. Their heads were shaven, their faces painted, and they were forced to wear little dunce hats. After that they were paraded through the streets before being taken off to prison. To our knowledge, two of the five are still incarcerated to this day.

By the time Joseph finished his story, Shan and I were in no doubt about the fact of a revival smouldering in China. This was not the picture of believers in dwindling numbers which we had expected to find under Communism. Here was a church so sold out for Jesus that He was able to work through them in a way far more powerful than through many of us in the outside world.

"How can we help them?" I asked. "What do they want us to do?"

"Well, of course, they constantly requested Scriptures," Liu replied. "But more important than that, they asked us for prayer.

"They long for the knowledge that their brothers and sisters are upholding them daily in the free world. It is no easy thing to take their bold stand for Christ. It costs them everything.

"And the shame of it, Brother David," Joseph paused to emphasise his point, "is that they are already in daily prayer for us in the outside world."

Shan and I looked up in surprise. "What are they praying for, Joseph?" Shan asked.

His reply silenced us.

"They are praying that we might not become too comfortable in our affluence in case our witness becomes weakened.

"They pray that the power of materialism will not extinguish our fire for the Lord."

CHAPTER ELEVEN
The Real China?

A few days later Shan saw us off at Kai Tak International Airport, which juts out into Hong Kong Bay – its green shimmering waters crowded with the traditional junks and fishing trawlers. As Joseph, Uncle Liu and I fastened our seat belts, we savoured the anticipation of soaring over the South China Sea, and the flight back to our families in Manila.

It was not only the flight's take-off that we looked forward to. There was a hope in our hearts that the outside world's concern and interest in China would likewise gain momentum and lift off the ground.

Joseph and Uncle Liu carried their burden for China heavily. Yet they also carried it carefully. On their knees, they would wait on God to find out those friends with whom they could share the vision. Of course, there was so much about their trip that they could not tell. But what they could, they shared with the longing that others might likewise begin to identify with the Suffering Church.

There were some who responded with enthusiasm and encouraged him and Uncle Liu to return to China to learn more about the People's Republic. But far more often, the warnings he knew so well would return. "Can you be sure you can trust an American?" "China is still too dangerous. We must wait until it has opened up again." "It is okay to pray for China, but more than that is impossible." And then would come the most unsettling response of all. "Joseph, you are so young. You have your whole life before you. Why waste it on that country? You could do so much good elsewhere."

Why indeed? Joseph, Uncle Liu and I would meet to compare reactions. It was almost an action-replay of what they had found in Hong Kong before their trip. After all our expectation it seemed we were back to square one.

At the same time, we could see why these reactions continued to come. Mao was still very much at the helm. It did look ridiculous, humanly speaking, to be talking of China at a time when the country was thoroughly sealed behind the Great Wall.

*　　*　　*

Yet hadn't the Lord consistently been teaching us to walk by faith, not sight?

"Father, there has to be a way of bringing East and West together." I had resumed my talks with the Lord around the sloping streets of my home area. Often at midnight I would sit quietly praying in one of its secluded spots, a children's playground in the centre of the subdivision. But I myself was not playing games. I had never been more in earnest with the Lord.

"There just has to be some way for Your people in the outside world to support Your people in China. We are all members of one Body – Yours, Lord. And you call for all parts of the Body to work together."

I recalled a conversation which Brother Andrew and I had shared long before I came to this work full-time – in the hotel at JFK Airport.

"David," Brother Andrew had said earnestly, "What we really need is to bring together every person and every group who has an interest in the Kingdom of God in China.

"We need to encourage one another to get to work behind the Bamboo Curtain. Just think, if every denomination or missionary organisation came together in one conference – how much more we could achieve after pooling our knowledge and insight ..."

He was right. It had been so long since anyone had seriously considered China as a mission field – too long. The church there needed our help; for its spiritual welfare, and for its task in evangelising the People's Republic – in making it God's Republic.

As if reading my thoughts, my Dutch companion continued. "The job is far too big for any of us to work in total isolation. And," he added, "I want our own organisation to be a doormat for others who want to get God's Word into China. It doesn't matter which organisations take the ten million Bibles inside – as long as they walk in response to God's leading."

The title for the conference was to come later. I was discussing our plans in Hong Kong with David Wang of Asian Outreach, when together we both knew we had found the name. The convention would be called "Love China" – for, if we didn't have love for the Chinese, we couldn't begin to serve them.

For Joseph, Uncle Liu and me, that seemed to be the step which the Lord had in store for us next. All of us threw our energies into the mammoth task of mounting the convention.

* * *

Meanwhile, to our joy, letters were starting to trickle out from the precious contacts Joseph and his uncle had made in China. I had never received letters like these before, but they were written in the authentic language of the Suffering Church.

> *I know of your concern for me ... thank you very much for the money you sent ... I will offer your love as a fragrant offering to the Lord, God will surely bless you ...*

Another read:

> *Thank God that under His wonderful leading we now have a regular Christian gathering. Ask God to give opportunity to every family to receive the grace of*

152

God, that their faith my be strengthened ... May you pray that God will manifest His mighty salvation and miracles and that the whole nation may receive religious freedom ...

One came from a widow:

... These few days I recall my husband has been dead for seven years, and I haven't been working for my Lord. I felt so ashamed. Today a sister delivered 100 RMB, a gift from the Philippines ... The faith of my daughter has been shaken. My son and his wife, due to lack of trust in the Lord, don't like to pray, and are attacked by Satan. Suffering drives us closer to the Lord – they, in return, walk away from their faith, and suffer physically and spiritually. Please pray earnestly ...

Finally:

Even though the Christians in mainland could not go into the church to worship God, we can gather about ten persons to worship in the house and have fellowship and prayers. Please pray for us. May God call His own people to work for Him and to proclaim God so loved the world ... Emmanuel.

*   *   *

We were constantly learning of more believers who needed help.

One who required particular support was a woman evangelist from the southern part of China. Miss Woo heard about her first.

"God is performing many, many miracles through this lady, although she has suffered much," she told Joseph on one of his frequent trips to Hong Kong. "Her mother is living here in Hong Kong – out in the New Territories. I think you should take me to see her."

153

She stared hard at Joseph, who looked a little uncomfortable.

"You see," he later explained to me, "it's not that I don't believe in miracles. I have seen God perform them with my own eyes. But sometimes you hear of people who, every time they open their mouths, speak of an exorcism here or a healing there. Yet when you look at their lives, they don't match up with the words they say.

"Sometimes," he added in his own polite way, "I wonder if these people are really quite all right in their minds. And I am not so interested in listening to them any more."

And so he told Miss Woo that he would rather not visit the old lady.

His response had no effect on her at all. "Nonsense, Joseph. We will go tomorrow."

He tried again, "But if she is from the South, I will not be able to understand her dialect."

Miss Woo was not to be deterred. "Then," she beamed, "I will be very happy to interpret for you. We will go, Joseph."

*　　*　　*

An elderly Chinese lady opened the door and welcomed them into the dimly-lit room. Her smiling face contrasted with the shadows of the room and for all his doubts Joseph immediately recognised the glow of one who lived very close to her God.

They sat down to talk and, as the grandmother began telling the story, Miss Woo interrupted every few seconds to translate for Joseph. The old lady's daughter was indeed in southern China, and vast numbers had come to know Jesus through her ministry.

Miss Woo listened attentively with growing enthusiasm as the account continued. But when the grandmother began to tell of the miracles which had occurred, Miss Woo interpreted less and less often. Finally, she sat with a rapt ex-

154

pression on her face, all thoughts of translation completely forgotten.

From the other side of the room Joseph watched the two old saints as they leaned forward in animated conversation. At first he tried to look politely interested, but as the conversation continued, his eyes began to shut.

"Besides," he later admitted to me, "I felt like a post that had been put there for decoration. I knew they were no longer noticing me anyhow."

Slowly his head went down on the sofa and he stretched out to sleep. Two hours later he jerked himself awake ready to apologise for his rudeness. To his amazement, he realised that the pair had not even noticed he had dozed off.

He eased himself back into the sitting position until at last Miss Woo rose to leave. Joseph stood up too and walked across the room to thank the grandmother for her hospitality.

When the door had shut behind them, Miss Woo turned to Joseph and held his arm tight as she looked directly into his face, her eyes bright with enthusiasm.

"You see," she declared in complete confidence. "I was right, wasn't I?

"I told you, you'd be glad you came ..."

*　　*　　*

In the weeks and months that followed, Joseph was to learn that Miss Woo was indeed right. Had anybody less persistent than Miss Woo invited him, Joseph would not have gone to the grandmothers' house. But this one contact was to open up a major new area of our ministry.

Joseph began to learn the story of the grandmother's daughter, Mrs Kwang, and her extraordinary ministry in the southern part of China. It seemed that this lady had begun an evangelistic work which the Lord had multiplied to an unbelievable extent in their region. Hundreds, even thousands of people were accepting Jesus Christ.

The authorities, of course, were outraged. They made many arrests among the Christian workers, persecuting any who were bold in their acknowledgement of the Lord's name. Mrs Kwang herself had been imprisoned three times, and her husband had been in labour camp for many years. Yet, despite all the government's attempts to crush it, the revival continued to expand rapidly. Mrs Kwang and her co-workers remained undeterred in their preaching of the Gospel.

Even while in prison, Mrs Kwang led many to the Lord, both guards and prisoners. Once released, she returned to her ministry immediately. The evangelist toured her "parish" for anything between ten days and three weeks at a time, travelling from town to town, often preaching three times a night. Meetings were held under cover of darkness, often in the early hours of the morning – and were convened in some of China's huge old homes, used in the past by the rich for their extended families. Services were always packed with people, and when the numbers became too great for Mrs Kwang to address alone, the group would divide into smaller units. The sub-groups would go to a different wing of the mansion and there be addressed by the co-workers. She would drop in briefly to see each little gathering during the course of the meeting. It was not uncommon for many to be converted, and likewise many to be healed. The blind, the dumb, the lame were all touched by God. Mrs Kwang used these miracles to point to the living reality of Jesus Christ, and as a result, there were always many won to Christ in each of the towns she visited.

At first, Joseph found it hard to believe these accounts. He was well aware of the vicious and thorough nature of the opposition to Christianity in China, and he wondered how such growth could possibly be taking place. It was not until some years later that he learned how many times God had miraculously been at work protecting His children from detection.

Nevertheless, for all his questionings, Joseph continued

156

to visit Grandmother Kwang. For if these accounts were truly of God, he did not want to miss out. And, as he reported more of the situation to me, I became excited.

Each time I sent funds to Hong Kong for the believers inside, I asked Joseph to nominate some of the Kwang family. Unknown to me, he was still too unsure to do so. The Kwangs' story was so difficult to accept – although he sincerely wanted to believe it. His solution was to send them only a meagre portion of our funds, but subsidise it heavily from his own pocket and Miss Woo's. That way, he reasoned, if the story turned out to be exaggerated or untrue, it would only have been his money that was spent, not ours.

* * *

In addition to the funds going inside, we were continuing to send Bibles to the mainland, largely through the delivery system set up along the various borders. At that time, we had just concluded a delivery of fifty thousand Gospels of John through one of the routes. And five thousand of the New Testaments we had deposited among our contacts in Afghanistan, Burma, Laos and the Himalayas had been carried across into China.

Often these went by donkey; the books were loaded inside potato sacks, a hundred in each sack and two sacks to a donkey. At other times, they were carried by couriers on foot, and transferred from hand to hand until they reached the delivery point inside. For the Bibles that went through the Burma route, we learned that each Scripture had to be handled by thirty-six people from the time it left the Philippines until its final destination inside the People's Republic.

One report of the work came to us from a man who had a regular part in the lonely treks through the Himalayas.

"The Scriptures you gave me have been taken into the Southeast. They have crossed the borders into the mainland. Here my brother gave them to another brother, and he to another. They were passed on and on until all were delivered into the hand's of God's people.

"The travel is very tiring, very difficult. Crossing the mountains does not take a few hours, but rather many days, all walking continuously on foot. We take shelter in the wilderness under the shadow of huge boulders. In the villages we take refuge among the dwellers. These people are very poor."

The verse accompanying this report came from Isaiah 52 : 7. "How beautiful upon the mountains are the feet of him who brings good tidings, who publishes peace . . . who publishes salvation, who says . . . God reigns." (R.S.V.)

*   *   *

At the same time we had also prepared a second courier to travel through China's front door – the Hong Kong border. Ana-Marie Chung was an overseas Chinese girl with a great burden for her own people. Her delivery followed up some of the contacts established by Joseph and Uncle Liu.

One to whom they sent her was the evangelist who had suffered so dearly for his faith. She too was deeply touched that despite persecution he had continued preaching and counselling.

Ana-Marie gave him her expensive personal Bible, having already distributed the few she had brought into China.

The pastor was very moved. In return he offered his own gift; a beautiful rendition of "What a Friend We Have in Jesus," sung in his rich baritone.

But after this came the shock of her trip. News of her activities in other towns had reached the police, chiefly because one person had informed on her. At the next town on her itinerary, the police caught up with her in her hotel.

The secret police were very polite. "We would like to invite you for questioning," they said. She complied. "I knew the Lord was with me," she recalled.

That first afternoon she experienced their idea of questioning. "It was brainwashing. They kept on asking me the same questions even after I had answered them. 'What is your name?' 'What company do you represent?' 'Who is with you?' 'Who did you get in touch with here?'" They questioned her for four hours at a time.

She was told they could not release her that day. She was not to worry, she would be in good hands. Ana-Marie would join the officers for meals, and a nights, a woman officer would keep her company. She decided not to eat until they released her. "I'm just following an old Chinese custom," she explained to them. "I only eat with my friends, not my enemies."

"We're friends," they insisted.

"No. You do not trust me. You treat me like an enemy of your country. I'm a visitor. I have already cooperated, I gave you my answers. Even if you question me for one hundred more days, my answers will not change. No, I cannot eat with you."

They shrugged. The questioning went on for the next three days. Ana-Marie remained steadfast.

At last they gave in. Reading from her passport that her visa was about to expire, they had to release her – none the wiser for all their questioning.

"You know, you should be working for the Communist Party. We need girls like you," she was told. Ana-Marie smiled, a secret prayer in her heart. She knew Who they really needed.

The officers crowded around to see her off. "What will you tell your friends about our country? What do you think of China?"

"What do I think of *my* country? I love it. Jesus loves it too ..." She was on her way.

Her experience brought us in direct contact with the danger of the work. Now we were seeing first-hand the ugly face of the Communist regime, and the machine which controlled it.

The "Spiritual Battle" was no theoretical term; it alone described the confrontation before us as we sought to take the "Sword of the Spirit" into this place, where Satan had unquestionably established control.

* * *

Ana-Marie, Joseph and Uncle Liu had all viewed and reported on China from the perspective of ethnic Chinese visiting relatives. It was not until we heard of a *gwailo*, a "foreign devil", who managed to take a trip that we began to see the other side of the coin; the tourist's China.

Todd Martin from FEBC had managed to take a trip in 1973 as a member of a "special interest group" under official invitation from the Chinese Government. He had been booked onto a highly restricted tour to visit Canton, Peking and Shanghai.

The first thing that struck him was the almost "missionary zeal", as he described it, of the Communist tour guides. Every minute of every day was taken up with a crusade to impress upon the visitors the progress the country had made under Communism. They were shown factories, schools, communes, anything at all which would illustrate the Government's achievements.

Before visiting any of these places the guides gathered the tour group for an "orientation" session. This would entail indoctrination about the subject of the visit: facts and figures for at least half an hour by the Vice-Chairman of the Revolutionary Committee and all of his or her colleagues. To complete the persuasive process, cigarettes would be provided, along with cookies, candies, peanuts, tea, beer or China's famous "Pearl River Orange" soft drink.

Todd found the situation for a tourist uncomfortable. The guides watched them so closely that they were allowed little freedom of movement. One morning in Shanghai he got up at five thirty a.m., well before the set time for breakfast. He wanted to take photos of the people going through their slow-motion shadow boxing exercises on the banks of the Hwang Pu River. He took so many pictures that he ran out of film, and as he bent over to change rolls, an enormous crowd gathered around him peering with interest. At that time of morning, he noticed many people, thousands he estimated, already on their way to work.

When Todd got back for his breakfast at seven thirty, one of his guides greeted him politely. "Good morning, sir. Did you enjoy watching the shadow boxers this morning?"

"Indeed," replied Todd, " but how did you know I was up to see them?" Again the guide smiled. "I saw you there, sir ..."

Todd and a couple of other Christians on the tour were anxious to discover if the church had survived at all under Mao's regime. No photographs of churches had appeared in the Western press. They even questioned whether the church buildings were still standing.

Their background reading had told them of Mao's gradual closure of all churches since he had taken power in 1949. Reports varied but most seemed to agree that before the Revolution there were just under two million baptised members of the Protestant Churches in China. Over six thousand Protestant missionaries were also working in the country.

After setting up the Three Self Movement in 1951, the government had spent the subsequent years consistently closing down more and more churches until only a fraction of the original remained. By the time of the Cultural Revolution in 1966, very few churches were still open for worship. And, under the fanatical fervour of the Red Guards, the handful left were quickly shut down – often accompanied with senseless destruction and violence.

It was not only the Christians that had suffered. The Red Guards attacked with gusto anything and everything they associated with the "bourgeois practices" of imperialism, and all apparent evidence of religion was obliterated in China.

The worst excesses of the Cultural Revolution had come to an end by 1970, so that now, three years later, Todd and the other Christians on the tour wondered if there were any public signs of Christianity re-emerging. They knew of just one officially registered church. It was in Peking and had been opened in 1972 to serve mainly the foreign diplomatic community there.

The other Christian tourists were the first to go hunting for churches in Canton. During the bus tour they had glimpsed a church relatively near the hotel. They chose a moment when the lobby was particularly busy to slip away through a side door. When they reached the church, one stood in front of its bricked-up front door while the other crossed the street to get a photograph. He lifted his camera, focused, and just as he was pressing the button, somebody from the crowd around him jolted his elbow so that the shot would be blurred. The "saboteur" gestured to indicate he should not take any pictures of the church.

A moment later, a big black car pulled up beside his friend standing in front of the church. A window by the back seat was rolled down and a voice spoke to him politely in English. "Would you like to take a ride?" The tourist replied just as courteously: "No, thank you. My friend and I were just out for a stroll." The man in the back seat insisted, but the *gwailo* matched his persistence until eventually the car drove away.

"After all our reading," Todd told me, "this incident really gave us the creeps. The atmosphere was so tense you could have almost cut it with a knife."

Later they tried again to photograph a church in Peking, but once more were without success. Finally in Canton Todd did manage to get the photo he wanted. He had glimpsed the twin spires of the Catholic Cathedral on one of their tours and set out early one morning to find it. On his way he became lost and found himself wandering through the little back streets of the city. He was struck by the cleanliness of the area. Although the homes were very old and often in need of repair, they were nonetheless looked after with scrupulous tidiness, just as those on the prescribed tourist trail. Todd found the extent of their cleanliness remarkable

162

and realised that this was not just a cosmetic clean up for travellers from outside.

By now he was well and truly "off limits" and still no closer to finding the Cathedral. Suddenly he came across a small church right in the middle of the block. On the other side of the street, a man was busy cutting wood. Todd approached him and made a big fuss about taking the labourer's picture as he stacked his pile of timber.

"Of course," Todd explained to me, "I focused on the church behind. To have actually found one I could photograph was like finding gold."

Later, back at the hotel, a fellow tourist approached him. "You were lucky to get your photograph this morning," he began. Todd was a little taken aback. "Why?" he asked. "Well," his friend explained, "I was walking some distance behind you, and when I got there I too tried to take a picture of the old man cutting wood. But just as I was preparing for the shot someone came out of the shop behind me, tapped me on the shoulder, and told me I was not allowed to take the photograph."

It became obvious to Todd and the other Christians that the pressure being exerted in China was coming not merely from the party officials and cadres. The people themselves were so committed to the "cause" that they had become each other's keeper.

"It was not surprising," added Todd, "when you saw the all-embracing nature of the government's propaganda machine."

No matter where they went, the group never escaped some expression or other of the liberation "gospel". Slogans on the streets, posters on the walls, giant pictures of Mao Tse-Tung, all declared basically the same message of belief in the New China. The propaganda was not limited to visual forms, but was also blasted forth from public address systems. It was perhaps to be expected that one should find loudspeakers in Peking's Tien An Men Square proclaiming the virtues of the regime. But Todd also found the same thing repeated along the streets of Peking, Shanghai and Canton – in fact wherever he travelled.

On one occasion the group was visiting a rural commune four hours by train south of Peking. As they toured the agricultural centre they found they could not escape an incessant "voice from on high". The P.A. system was broadcasting a radio programme and in strident tones the commentator was praising "The Great Helmsman" and his achievements. As they went from building to building, watching the varied experimentation with animals, the same voice would persist with its message.

Likewise in the bustling docks of Shanghai, martial music boomed out as the giant ships were loaded and unloaded. The broadcast was peppered with Chinese slogans calling upon the masses to "Serve the country" and "Do your best for the glories of the country".

Nothing escaped the reach of the propagandists. Virtually no artistic performances of any sort were allowed unless they too preached the Communist message loud and clear. Films, stage and variety shows had a religious tone in the way they presented the message.

So persuasive was the message given out that even the tourists found themselves coming away with a feeling that they had visited some sort of land flowing with milk and honey.

"Their response was past the point of reason," said Todd. "I suppose, to start with, we were dealing with mythology's Middle Kingdom, the Great Cathay. That, coupled with the Party's excellent salesmanship, made most of the tourist party quite euphoric about the country."

I recalled what Brother Andrew had said about Communism being a religion. It seemed more evident than ever that Mao had set out to win not only the peoples' minds, but their hearts and souls as well.

* * *

I sat at my desk. The report files of Joseph and Liu, Ana-Marie and Todd were open before me.

I found myself looking at the full force of the Communist juggernaut we faced. Its power was obviously enormous; not only in its blatant, terrifying manifestation, but also in its equally powerful subtlety. The Great Wall was for real – and I wondered how on earth we were ever going to penetrate it. How could we bring any significant aid to our brethren inside?

What chance did we have? A handful of people incapable either of outwitting the Communists in their propaganda efforts or outfighting them in their awesome strength.

The close-up shots from the slides Joseph and Liu had shown us flashed again into my mind. "I love these people, Lord," I whispered, "and if I do, how much more *You* must love them. You died for every one of them."

And they didn't even know it, I thought. They might never have the chance to hear of Jesus as they spent their lives captive to the Communist ideology.

I leaned back in my chair, the impossibility of the task overwhelming me.

"Hey, but wait a minute," I thought, "that's not right. Who has the ultimate control over even the Communist regime?" The words of the Great Commission came rushing back to me. "All authority in heaven and earth has been given to *me*." Final authority had been given to Him, to Jesus, not even to the most powerful of human governments. I sat up straight in my chair with confidence.

The rest of Jesus' words rang with familiarity in my ears. "*Go* therefore and make disciples of all nations ..." That was it. No matter how daunting a government might look we were still to go.

"Yes sir!" I said to the Lord. I pushed back my chair, stood up and called for Beng to put through a call to the local travel service.

165

CHAPTER TWELVE
No Closed Door

"You never give up, do you David?" Beng smiled as she lifted the receiver. We had been through this ritual many times before. For months now I had tried every available avenue to find some way into China, and the travel service was just one of them. As always, Beng came back with the same reply. "They are very sorry, David. There is still no way they can organise a trip for you. Perhaps if you would care to call again in a few weeks ..."

I had received the same response on my numerous "pilgrimages" to the China Travel Service in Hong Kong. Every time I went to the Crown Colony I would try both offices for good measure; the Kowloon office and the main one on the Island.

"We are sorry, but at this time it is impossible for you to visit China," I was always told by a polite but unsmiling counter clerk. "We will take your name and address and contact you if there is any change in the situation."

But the call never came. My brawny frame and pleading look became well known to the staff. Sometimes I would bring Julie and the children too and the whole family would chat with the officials. Always as I entered the office I would pray silently that these people would see past me and my persistence to the very love of Jesus Himself.

On what must have been my thirtieth visit, I felt a slight thaw as the manager called me over to his desk. "Now sir, why do you keep coming back? Why do you want to go to China?" I could imagine what was going through his mind. "Can't I get through to this thick head? If I've told him once I've told him thirty times. Still he keeps coming back."

But the Lord had been teaching me patience, teaching me to love China.

"I am your friend," I replied with a smile. He knew I meant it. What he didn't know about were the hours I had spent walking with the Lord around our home pleading China's case before Him.

While the travel service had consistently refused me, I had tried every other means I could think of. Whenever I went to a country which had diplomatic relations with China, I would try and visit their embassy in an attempt to get my longed-for visa. But to no avail.

* * *

Although I was unable to enter China itself, I nevertheless found myself travelling frequently – too frequently, I thought at times. It was becoming increasingly painful to leave my family so often, with each good-bye more difficult than the one before. Yet they continued to give me such support that it was possible to keep going.

On one occasion I was passing through Hong Kong on my way to our annual conference in Holland with Brother Andrew. I had only been away from home a few days when Julie rang me.

"David? It's Dawn, honey. She had an accident at school today." Julie was obviously biting her lip to hold back tears. "She's broken both her arms."

"She's what?"

Julie went on to describe the full details of the accident. Both Dawn's arms were now in a plaster cast. By the time she had finished, I was ready to catch the next plane home.

"You don't have to do that, honey. That's not why I rang." Julie was emphatic.

"I can't allow you to go through something like this on your own," I protested.

"But we're not on our own. The Lord is beside us.

Honey, I just felt I had to let you know so you could be praying for us."

I thought of the shock Dawn must have undergone and the extra responsibility for Julie, with the other two children to care for as well.

"I've got to come home," I insisted. "It's not fair on you."

"Dave, the kids and I believe the Lord has important work waiting for you at that conference. We all want you to be there."

I had never put the phone down more reluctantly. Long after the call, I sat still, thinking. My family had been contending with so much lately. Just a couple of months before, when I was once again visiting the borders, our family car had broken down while Julie was driving along a busy main road. She had had no option but to leave it there and return home to the family. When she came back for it next morning, she found just an empty shell. Thieves had removed the wheels, the battery, even parts of the engine. The car had been completely cannibalised.

This ministry was taking its toll. Yet Julie's words of commitment to the task echoed in my mind as I set out for Holland.

* * *

The meeting in Holland proved a milestone for Brother Andrew's work. Gathered in his home town were representatives from several different parts of the world; he and his team from Europe, Sven, our U.S. director, and the rest of the team from North America, and others from Africa and Asia.

Although each group was in regular contact with the others, as yet there was no official organisation. Brother Andrew has always been one to keep things small, and he had deliberately shied away from a large-scale body.

That year, however, as we prayed through the vision

God had given him for the Suffering Church, we realised that to fulfil it, the time had come to establish one body which could have branches in each part of the world where the church was facing persecution. With Africa, Asia and Europe represented, it now remained for us to form bases in the Middle East and Latin America.

The name "Open Doors with Brother Andrew" had been established earlier. It was inherent in a statement we had heard him repeat on countless occasions.

"We should never say that any country is closed to the Gospel of Jesus Christ. Jesus told us to go into *all* the world, and if we are obedient to His command, He can open the door of any country for us. In Revelation we are told, 'I have set before you an open door, which no man can shut.' "

* * *

Open Doors. It was true – God promised it in His word. But where was my own open door to China? A few weeks later, back in the Philippines, I had an unexpected visit from a man who seemed positive he had found a way into the People's Republic.

Harold Whitman, a travel agent from Great Britain, had deliberately made a stopover in Manila to make contact with me.

"Brother Andrew suggested you might be interested," he explained, "since I am going to China – without a visa."

"Without a visa? That's impossible."

"All things are possible," was his gentle, but firm reply.

Julie and I seized the first opportunity to invite Harold to supper. We wanted all the details.

"After Manila," he told us, "I fly to Hong Kong. From Hong Kong I go to Seoul, from Seoul to Tokyo, Tokyo to Peking, Peking to Hanoi, then to Bangkok, and finally back to London."

Julie and I looked at each other. Either this guy is a

169

nut, I thought, or else he has plenty to teach me about getting to China by faith. I needed to know more. "How did this start?" I asked.

"Well," he began, "I took my leading from a verse in Matthew, where it says in Chapter 7, 'Ask, and it will be given you; seek and you will find; knock and it shall be opened.'"

"Okay," I said, "Who did you ask?"

"I asked the authorities in China if I could come and visit them. They just telexed me and said, 'We have a room waiting for you in Peking. We shall be pleased to welcome you.'"

I stifled my inner protests and asked him to tell me about the "seek and find" part of the verse.

"I began seeking all possible avenues to China," he told us, "and, since I am a travel agent, I naturally turned to the guide books around me. I've discovered you can fly in from Tokyo to Peking and from Peking to Hanoi. What's more, if you want to get from Peking to Hanoi, you have the 'inconvenience' of staying seven whole days in Peking."

Seven days! How many times had I tried to get into China?

"Tell me," I said at last, "I can see how you 'asked'. I can see how you've been 'seeking'. Now tell me about 'knocking'."

Again it was so straightforward. "When I get to Tokyo I'll just get on that plane and they'll take me through to China. Once we touch down I'll knock on that door and the door will open."

"What about the visa?" I blurted.

There wasn't a trace of doubt in his voice. "Oh, they'll give me a visa when I get there." He obviously read the troubled expression on my face. "Don't you see, David, this is Scriptural," he said. "The trouble is that often we Christians don't practise it. But we can't just sit around waiting for things to fall into our laps. They don't. We have to get on our feet, and take the Lord at His Word."

I shook his hand as we rose to leave. "Man, if it works

for you, send me a postcard from Peking because I want to know." Could the answer really be so easy?

Three weeks later, as I sat working at my desk, Beng knocked at the door with the day's mail. "David, there's a postcard here for you. It's from China."

* * *

I lost no time after that. Shan Kumar and I, together with another friend, Derek, followed Harold's example, and like him received an official invitation to Peking.

The three of us travelled to Tokyo to await our flight to Peking, China's "forbidden city".

On the day of our departure, all seemed to go just as smoothly as we could have wanted. Our passports were examined and passed at the counter of China's own airline – CAAC. The Chinese clerk checked with his computer and confirmed that our names were on the flight. He tore the coupons off our tickets, handed us our boarding passes and took our luggage. As I stood watching our three bags on the conveyor belt I thought my heart was going to burst. "Lord, we're finally on our way."

We watched our bags pass through the black rubber flaps and disappear from view.

Almost involuntarily, Derek found himself voicing his inner thoughts. "It's too easy," he murmured, shaking his head. The fellow behind the counter looked up. "What's too easy?" he asked.

Derek did his best to appear nonchalant. "It's just that we don't have our visas for China."

Suddenly we were involved in a complicated conversation. Finally the counter clerk ordered, "Please give me back your boarding passes. Come upstairs, I want to talk with you." We could see from his expression that, for some reason, he thought he had lost face through the incident. He didn't want it to be "easy" to get into his country.

In his office, we tried to explain. "Look, we've got a

171

telex here. Our hotel rooms have been booked and our visas will be given to us on arrival." The airline official just looked at us. "But you don't have a visa in your passports. You cannot go." He added a parting shot as he raised one eyebrow. "As you said, it was too easy."

While we waited for our bags to return, I stood on the ramp gazing dumbstruck at the plane we should have been sitting in, a CAAC Boeing 707. It was painted white, and bore a bright red Chinese flag on its tail, complete with five golden stars.

I watched the jet taxi down the runway and take off – and some part of me went with it. Had that counter clerk not taken offence, we would have been on that plane. He had taken a simple comment and thrown it right back in our faces.

I learned a lesson that day. When God is putting something together it always fits – in that sense it is "easy". We just had to be able to trust Him and go forward in confident faith. Even a moment's hesitation could be used by Satan to thwart us. We couldn't afford to entertain any doubts. We were simply to follow – and allow God to make it as easy as He wanted to.

* * *

Meanwhile the date for the "Love China" conference was steadily approaching. Shan was programme director. Between us we had to come up with publicity material for the conference and a theme on which the week was to be based. With the publicity deadline imminent we met for a final evening of planning.

"The theme needs to be a prayer," I said to Shan. "I agree, but what should the prayer say?" he asked. Together we knelt beside the bed in my hotel room. For several hours, we prayed and talked and prayed some more, until we were of one mind.

Several weeks later, as delegates filed into the huge conference room at one of Manila's big hotels, two sights met their eyes. The first was a wall-length blown up photograph of Communist soldiers on the march, and the second, above it, was the prayer we had chosen. *"Lord Jesus, through us let the people feel your love."*

*   *   *

More than 430 delegates from twenty-three countries gathered with us to consider how to give the Chinese people the best opportunity to hear the Gospel of Jesus Christ. "Love China '75" was the first full-scale gathering since 1949 of evangelicals concerned about Christian witness in China.

After the conference, one of the main speakers flew on to Hong Kong with Julie and me. I had first met white-haired William Willis and his wife, Fanny, during the evangelistic campaign we had held while on furlough in the States. I told the Welshman of my vision for China and he had committed himself to pray daily for me. When William Willis said that it really counted for something, as I knew that saintly old man gave seven hours of every day to prayer. His fervour for the Lord, coupled with his white hair and authoritative manner, reminded me of an Old Testament prophet. Mr Willis had followed God faithfully ever since he had become a Christian during the great Welsh revival in 1904.

When we reached Hong Kong, he spent the whole of our first day in prayer, and the next, until at last, when lunch was served, he joined the rest of us. After the meal, he took me on one side. "Young man," he said in a soft Welsh accent, "the Lord has given me a message for you. But I am not to tell you what it is until I've looked into China." I was impatient. "Couldn't you tell me now?" I asked. But the diminutive clergyman was insistent, and I didn't argue.

The following day Shan and his wife, Neta, took the four of us to the Lok Ma Chao look-out; the famous tourist spot

173

in the New Territories from which one can see right into China itself. The pastor's spectacles glinted in the bright sun as he peered down on the patchwork fields below and watched Chinese labourers at work. From our vantage point, it seemed we simply had to reach out to touch the people of China, separated from us only by the narrow winding Shun Chun River.

At last, Mr Willis took my arm and drew me aside from the little crowd of "China watchers". "David, you remember yesterday I told you that I had a message from the Lord for you?" I nodded. All day I had been trying to curb my impatience.

"The Lord has told me that the door into China will open for you. And the door will never be closed for you and your friends. You will be able to go in and out as you please." He paused to allow his words to sink in. "Can you believe that, young man?"

"I believe it," I said. I meant it.

Yet as I gazed into the distant blue-green hills of China I thought, "Lord, you know I'm prepared to believe it. But how is it going to be possible?"

*   *   *

A few weeks later I applied yet again to visit the People's Republic, this time with my whole family. At last the staff at Hong Kong's China Travel Service told us it might be possible to get a visa.

Then we were shocked to hear that the Russian Embassy in Peking had been bombed. The China Travel Service confirmed our fears: "We are sorry, sir. No more visas can be issued until the trouble is dealt with."

The family coped well with the news. "Guess the Lord had other plans for us, Daddy," said Dawn. The three D's (Dawn, Deanne, David) had grown to trust God more and more in recent months, particularly as we as a family had seen Him continuing to meet our personal needs.

Deanne and David had been with me one Saturday morning when I had decided to look for a new car. Earlier that day, while in prayer, I had asked the Lord why we did not have a car for me to use for the work. The constant use of public transport was eating up funds, and I felt certain a car would be more economical.

"Why don't we have one, Lord?" I had asked.

In the quiet of the moment, His voice seemed to answer me. "Because you never asked me. I would have given you a car by now if you had turned to me."

I told the children of my prayer while I took them to the barber that morning. Deanne always accompanied me for hair-cuts, insisting that the barber could not do it correctly without her. David had come to make his contribution too.

"Do you think you could trust the Lord for a car?" I asked them.

"You bet, Dad," said Deanne confidently, as she took a critical look at the barber's scissors.

After the hair-cut, we went over to a car dealer's and began looking around. One vehicle that caught my eye was a brand new green Toyota.

"That's a knock-out, Dad." David grinned with enthusiasm.

"Yeah, it is, isn't it?" I agreed. "Tell you what – why don't the three of us pray over this car and ask Jesus if He would find a way to let us own it for the work?"

The two nodded and together we walked across to the Toyota. Under the hot sun, we placed our hands on the little car. "Lord, we are asking You if You would allow us to have this car. And Lord, we are thanking you in advance for it," I said.

"Amen," chimed the other two.

Next day, I went back to the yard and discussed the price of the car with a salesman.

"Sir," he said cheerfully, "if you pay in cash we can take three thousand pesos off the price."

"I'd be happy to pay you in cash," I replied. "But could you give me a credit line on it till the end of the month? I don't have any money for it right now."

"Certainly, we can do that. In fact, why don't you fill out an order form right away?"

"But I don't have any money."

"That's okay. Sign here." As I filled out the order form, he asked me what kind of work I did. We chatted for a few minutes, and then he excused himself while he went to consult with the manager.

Shortly afterwards, the manager came out of his office. "You want to buy that green Toyota?" he began.

"Very much. I don't have the money yet," I responded. "But I'm believing I will have it within thirty days."

"Then you may take it right away," the manager said.

My eyes popped in disbelief. "But I don't have ..."

He smiled. "Take it, sir. We know we will get our money back. And we believe in the work you're doing."

So, with an empty bank account, but a very grateful heart, I was able to drive that brand new car all the way home to my amazed family.

It took only twenty days before, unaware of our need, friends in Rolling Hills, California, once again sent funds for our family's expenses.

* * *

Once again we had all seen how trustworthy our Lord was. We had now to trust Him with our visit to China.

"Well, Daddy?" the kids declared after our plans for the trip were cancelled. "Where do you think Jesus means us to go?"

We spent some hours discussing the decision. As a family, we had been staying in Hong Kong, at our friend Derek's home, waiting for the visa. Now we sat in his living room with maps and tourist books in front of us, while he and his wife sympathetically offered us encouragement.

Finally we reached a decision. Since the China trip was to have been followed by a trip to Holland anyway, we decided to take a holiday re-tracing the footsteps of Paul on his journey around the Seven Churches. This was our first furlough in six years and it was my way of saying "thank you" to my family for their patience and support.

We flew to Istanbul and began our trek through the beautiful terrain of this Muslim land. We enjoyed Ephesus particularly. We saw the dungeons where Paul had been in prison, we stood in the Coliseum where he had ministered. To this day, the book of Ephesians is one that truly "comes alive" for us.

We left the ruined city to drive through Turkey's beautiful countryside. Quite unexpectedly, as the picturesque scenery slipped by, I had an inexplicable conviction that God was speaking to me. It was the same inner voice that had spoken to me about the green car. This time, it seemed, God was telling me that I should go to Romania. "Why, Lord?" I wanted to know. Came the answer: "When you get to Holland, tell Andrew what I have said. He'll tell you why."

We continued our "apostolic journey" through Greece and Italy, then took a flight over the Alps to Holland. As the plane touched down at Schipol Airport in Amsterdam I looked forward to seeing my "brother in the battle" again. At last, too, our families would meet. I was also eager to find out about Romania.

"Of course, David." Brother Andrew's face lit up with enthusiasm. "Of all the countries in Eastern Europe, only Romania and Albania are allies of China. The rest are linked with the Soviet Union. If you go to Romania, you'll have no problem getting into China. Do you know you can even fly from Bucharest to Peking?"

I hadn't known. At last it seemed that door was opening up before me.

"The Spirit of the Lord is talking to you. I say go, David. Take your family to the United States and then come back here from California. We'll arrange for your trip to Bucharest."

"And," he added with a cheeky grin, "why not take some Bibles for the Romanian Christians along with you?"

Although the two of us met for several days of conference, our time was not all hard work. Our wives and children immediately felt the same bond that we had experienced. We took outings together, drinking in the charm of Holland; its canals, windmills, bicycles, and the cool air that was so different from the constant humidity of Manila. The final touch came when Brother Andrew and his wife Corrie presented each of our kids with a pair of genuine Dutch wooden clogs. With typical thoughtfulness, they had chosen those with an American colour scheme — red, white and blue.

* * *

I followed Brother Andrew's counsel. We spent three weeks in California for the final leg of our furlough; visiting our family there, calling on friends, and joining in the bi-centenary celebrations. Then I put Julie and the children on a plane for Manila, and returned to Holland. Awaiting my arrival was a ticket to Bucharest and large bundles of Bibles.

The morning of my flight, Hans, Brother Andrew's assistant, took me to the airport. We were driving past endless fields of colourful tulips, still damp from the night's rain, when suddenly we saw two magnificent rainbows arched across the sky.

"Why look!" Hans declared. "Today you'll enter two Communist countries. The rainbows are your confirmation of peace that you won't meet any storms in Czechoslovakia and in Romania."

"But there should be three rainbows. I'm going to Peking too," I bantered.

"Well, two out of three isn't bad."

Then about half an hour later, I saw it ... the third rainbow in the sky. "That means I am going to get into China," I exclaimed delightedly, and settled back in my seat to enjoy the trip.

*   *   *

In Romania, the Lord indeed opened doors for His Word as ninety Scriptures found their way unhindered into the hands of the believers. Now it only remained for the door to open into the People's Republic.

But when our plane touched down in Karachi, Pakistan, en route for China, it seemed that the door was going to shut right in my face. It was a body blow, quite literally, that floored me. For two and a half days I lay writhing in agony with one of Karachi's notorious viruses. My stomach was in knots. I had a fever and I reached complete exhaustion from the toll it took on my system.

As I lay on the bed, doubts started to crowd my mind. "David, forget the Peking deal. They won't give you the promised visa. Besides, you're sick. Man, you've been mistaking your own will for His. See, He's sent this illness to show you that you're wrong. Wrong!"

The questions came thick and fast as the room seemed to spin around. I felt there was a furnace in my head and even the free-flowing perspiration could not put out the fire. Suddenly I realised that God *did* want me to go to China – how else could I explain that unexpected leading to come via Romania? This then had to be the work of the Enemy. I knew I was in a spiritual battle and I should be fighting, not surrendering to the enemy's plans.

I got to my knees at the side of the bed and asked the Lord to take control of the situation. "Lord, you've already defeated Satan on the Cross. Not in my own strength, but in Yours I claim the victory." Within a couple of hours my fever had left me, the cramps had completely stopped, and I felt as if I'd never been ill at all.

That evening my step was light as I walked on to the tarmac and out to the waiting jet. The midnight flight over the Himalayas was unforgettable. Looking down I could see the spectacular mountains, their jagged snow-capped peaks fluorescent in the moonlight. They seemed to be never-ending, peak after peak, as our Boeing 707 winged its bumpy way eastward.

At six o'clock next morning the first rays of the new day's sun began to reach through the darkness. As I surveyed the scene below, I realised that for the first time I was looking down upon the People's Republic of China. My face pressed against the window, I gazed on the towns and little villages and the long stretches of cultivated land. Down in those green and brown patches lived the people for whom I had prayed, worked and lived since 1972.

It was as though I was coming home.

All of a sudden the pilot's voice came through the plane's P.A. system. "Ladies and gentlemen, in just a few minutes we will be landing in Peking." At last we touched down. As the plane taxied towards the terminal I looked out of my window to see in full colour a giant picture of Mao Tse-Tung. I knew I was in the People's Republic of China.

When we came to a stop, the aircraft was immediately surrounded by soldiers in green trousers, matching tunic, red collar and Mao cap. As they began to filter onto the plane, a customs officer stood at the front to address us. "Ladies and gentlemen," he said in perfect English. "Please present your passports." "Oh Lord," I thought, "they want my passport and it doesn't even have a visa in it." Sweat trickled down inside my shirt.

The officer began to move through the plane collecting passports. When he reached me he said politely, "We've been waiting for you, sir. Please follow me."

He took me to the immigration department and began to process my application for a visa. After the paper work was finished, he disappeared without explanation. For ten minutes I sat there, wondering what would happen. He finally returned, and handed me my papers.

"Welcome to the People's Republic of China." I looked down at my passport, and there was the visa stamp.

I thought back to the advice that Brother Andrew had frequently given me – that since Jesus has already given us instruction "to go" on His authority, we didn't need to wait for any further permission. Once we stepped out, God would do the rest.

The man was still talking. "Sir, you are welcome in our country. But on this occasion you can only stay a few hours. We cannot accommodate any visitors in Peking because all buildings in the city have been evacuated after a major earthquake. Everyone has been moved out onto the streets."

The famous earthquake of 1976 left massive damage in its wake, causing death and destruction almost without precedent. I later learned that as many as 750,000 were estimated to have died in the catastrophe. The full brunt of the earthquake had been borne by the city of Tangshan, but the shock waves had reached Peking. Even in the capital it was to prove months before the people could move from their temporary shelters on the streets, back to their homes.

I was shocked at the tragedy, and disappointed. Yet I soon understood why the Lord had brought me at this time. Within the confines of the terminal itself were hundreds from Tangshan, Tientsin and Peking. They were being evacuated to safer parts of the country.

The people and their tragedy stared starkly at me. I saw the privileged ones, men in their grey uniforms, members of the Communist Party. I saw peasants – obvious by their faded, threadbare clothes and lined, sallow, faces etched with hopelessness. Others were from the cities since their faces were smoother, better filled out. Yet their expressions too reflected the strain and shock of their ordeal.

Many of the people cried openly, others were silent with the depth of their suffering. Ideological difference or not, they were behaving as any other people would after a tragedy of this magnitude.

"Now you've seen them, David," the Lord seemed to tell

me. "The people I've laid on your heart. I wanted you to see them in a moment of great tragedy when they were most human, most vulnerable, most lovable; when no Communist ideology, nothing on earth except My comforting can ease their pain."

Four and a half hours later, as I walked across to report for the return flight, the counter clerk smiled. "Please know you will be welcome back any time to the People's Republic of China."

* * *

The plane touched down at Manila Airport, and waiting to meet me was Julie. I put my suitcase in our car, and the motor revved as we set off for home. "Honey," she said, "You remember the letter you sent to Peking?" I nodded as I drove. It had been a formal request for an invitation to visit the People's Republic, which I had sent some time before.

"Well," she continued "you have an answer here." Her eyes twinkled as she spoke.

"Have you opened it?" I asked, trying to concentrate on my driving. She was openly smiling now. "As a matter of fact, I have. It just happens to be ..." she paused, enjoying the opportunity to keep me on the edge of my seat, "an official invitation from the government asking that you visit them as soon as convenient."

I felt like bouncing through the ceiling of the car. I had hardly left China, when I was on my way back. The Communist immigration official had told me I would be welcome any time. William Willis had said the same. The Lord had opened the door and it was not going to shut again.

CHAPTER THIRTEEN
One Step Ahead

Just ninety days after I received it, I "accepted with pleasure" the Chinese government's invitation. This time I was not going on my own, but with James Wee, the younger brother of Billy – my old friend from the "Love Song" days at FEBC.

The slow train to China departed from Kowloon station, winding its way for an hour and a half through the New Territories to the border town of Lo Wu. James and I rose from our seats with a silent prayer on our lips. Here our bags would be searched.

We had decided that James would bring only his personal copy of the Scriptures. I was to carry the twenty Bibles we hoped to give to Tan Hoc Tue, a contact of Joseph's in Kwantung province.

We quickly passed through Hong Kong immigration, and as we walked towards the Lo Wu Bridge I saw a sign with the simple words: "To China". I shook my head, hardly daring to believe that within minutes I would be standing on Chinese soil.

We picked up our bags, heavy with their precious cargo, and walked over the border bridge – the famous "Bridge of Weeping". It had earned its name through the sorrow of the many unsuccessful escapes from China. These desperate men and women, unable to bow to the Communist regime any longer, would plunge into shark-infested waters for the long swim between the mainland and Hong Kong. Half never made it to the Crown Colony. If they managed to evade the sharks, they still faced the risk of being spotted by Communist patrol boats. For those who managed to emerge triumphant on Hong Kong's shores, another fate often awaited – that of being handed over by Hong Kong police to Communist authorities and dragged mercilessly back to the People's Republic of China, over this very bridge, the "Bridge of Weeping".

As I walked across, I noticed a huge red and white slogan of welcome: "Long live the Great Unity of the Peoples of the World".

Thinking that the customs men might tire a little if they checked the many other visitors before us, James and I held back until most had gone through. When our turn came we silently told the Lord yet again that we were counting on Him now.

The official motioned us into the search cubicle and asked James to open his bags. "What have you to declare?" James showed him his camera, wristwatch, currency, jewellery, and cassette recorder. He seemed happy enough with these, but then his eyes fell on the large black Bible. "What's this?" he said, thumbing through it with interest. "I'm a Christian," James said with a smile at the impassive officer. "That is my personal Bible."

Thinking of the twenty I had stored away in my suitcase, I watched as the customs man examined it closely.

"Since it is in English, you may take it through." I was next. I moved my case and shoulder bag along the bench towards the officer and waited for the confrontation. "That's okay sir," he said, and waved me on. "You can move through. No need to check ..." I was not about to hang around for him to change his mind. With a thankful heart, I picked up my luggage and followed James.

After a sumptuous lunch provided by the Chinese government, we boarded the train at Shun Chun station for the two hour trip to Canton. I savoured the landscape and peasant life of South China as we meandered through the red soil and curved hills of Kwantung province. Peasants were hard at work in the fields, wearing woven broad-brimmed hats. A few little children ran about, pointing to the train. Water buffaloes splashed around in the rice paddies, their black skins shining like wet umbrellas.

Canton is a city of three million souls and almost as many bicycles. The railway station, a cavernous building, was festively decked with thick strings of firecrackers and red banners. It was 23 October, 1976. The place was crowded and the excitement in the air was almost electric. A powerful sound system filled the building with "The East is Red" – a booming martial hymn sounding as though a million Chinese were all singing and marching onward to Mao's Kingdom come. This time it was not Mao they were hailing, but Hua Guo-feng, who had just been proclaimed Chairman.

One fourth of the world had a new leader. What a time to be in China. As we drove from the station, I couldn't help recalling the night at FEBC, so long ago, when I had read Psalm 37 and been told of the fall of China's leaders. Now it was happening. Did this mean, as I had understood that evening, that after their fall the country would open up?

The cacophony of the firecrackers surrounded us all the way to our hotel and, after we had checked in our bags, we returned to the street to take in the scene. By that time an impressive procession was underway.

At first I thought the soldiers had been called out to pay homage to the new Chairman as they marched proudly down the main avenue in green uniforms decorated with the red star. But as the sea of marchers seemed to bear down upon us, I realised there were just as many in blue as green. Blue was the colour of China's civilians. The people themselves had spontaneously joined the joyful throng to express their hope for a wonderful new future under Chairman Hua. Their faces were alight with expectation. They seemed to be looking heavenward as they lifted their heads in an almost religious display of nationalistic fervour.

But what of their ultimate future? I asked myself. "Lord, how many of these people will have a chance to hear of you before they have burned out their lives working for Mao,

Hua, whoever? Each will spend his life giving his all for the State. But upon his death what will the State have to offer him in return?"

* * *

That evening, as we took a walk through Canton, we glimpsed the double-edged significance of Hua's accession to power.

When we stepped from our hotel we felt the hot air clutch at us as in a sauna. I had donned a blue denim outfit; shirt, trousers and matching cap in a bid to identify with the people.

At the end of our street we came across a crowd gathered round an enormous Chinese billboard. As the only Westerners in that group, we received many long, hard looks. We tried to smile at those around us, but most immediately glanced away, embarrassed to have made eye-contact.

While we watched, a poster of the newly denounced "Gang of Four" was being pasted into position. Madam Chiang, Mao's widow, and the three radicals formerly from the Politburo, Yao Wen-Yuan, Chang Chun-Chiao and Wang Hung-Wen, were depicted in ridiculous poses. They were skewered like pigs on a barbeque. Mao's discredited wife, Chiang Ching, was wearing a black ball-gown with rings on her fingers and bells on her toes; the very essence of decadence itself. Through her nose was a ring, and tusks were growing from her nostrils. The idea was to convey her as having a "ferocious" appetite for power. Within the week, the whole world would learn about the "Gang of Four".

I thought back to Brother Andrew's words at our first meeting. "If they do not have an enemy on the outside they create an enemy on the inside."

Suddenly three soldiers with rifles bore down on the multitude. As James and I were the only foreigners, they stared at us with particular interest. Then, since the group's gathering was peaceful, they strolled on.

We made our way back to the hotel as quickly as our aching feet would carry us. Our hearts were beating faster than usual after our encounter at the billboard. As we wound through the alleyways, we passed narrow-fronted, crumbling brick houses, leaning against each other unevenly. Clothes hung drying on wires across the alleys, as though flags signalling to the outside world that there was life inside. The muted light coming from low-watt bulbs, the old banyan trees lining the road, even the yellow moon hanging low across the trees, gave the whole scene a feeling of timelessness, an air of long ago.

But for James it was very much the present that was on his mind. Back in the hotel he was strangely subdued. "What's got to you, James?" I asked, though it wasn't hard for me to guess. Poor James had to face the prospect of a Bible delivery when together we had spent the day witnessing the strident militancy of the country's regime. The penalty for any mistake could be arrest and even detention. It could mean he might never see his family again.

"Let's pray, Brother David," he said at last.

Later that night James was restless, his mind still churning over the danger of his position. Next morning over breakfast I could read the tiredness in his face. The following night was no better; nor the next.

On the fourth day we set out for the town where we would meet Mr Tan. When we arrived, I stayed alone to pray while James went to the house. It would have drawn too much attention if I had gone too. James had to climb three floors before he reached the believer's tiny two-roomed apartment. He took no Bibles but brought personal gifts of food and clothing. That night he planned to organise a rendezvous for the Bible delivery the following day.

Brother Tan was all smiles as he graciously welcomed James into his tiny home. He was alone with his wife, but he explained to James that believers' meetings were held frequently in his flat.

"How many come, Brother Tan?" James asked.

"We have a fellowship of ten people in this part of the city," he replied. "But they only ever come here two at a time. When the first two have finished their time of worship with us they leave and later on another pair will come."

James promised to meet Brother Tan again with the Bibles at a large restaurant the following day. But that night, as the two of us laid our plans before the Lord, James' sense of uneasiness grew stronger. The two of us fasted and prayed until 11.30 next morning. Yet James' conviction remained the same.

"David, I just don't feel comfortable about today. I don't believe I have the Lord's peace about it."

I agreed. Something did not feel quite right about making the delivery – it seemed as if God was cautioning us. "Don't take the Bibles. You go ahead and meet Brother Tan anyway. I'll stay behind to pray some more."

James took a cab to the restaurant. When he came back, a few hours later, his lips were pale. "Praise the Lord I did not take the Bibles," he commented quietly.

When he had arrived at the meeting place he asked the taxi driver to wait outside until the meal was over. Inside the restaurant he nervously looked around for Brother Tan, but there was no trace of him.

"Would you like to sit down and order, sir?" the head waiter approached him. "Perhaps in a few minutes," James replied absently. He strolled around the large eating house trying to look as casual as possible. After ten minutes he stepped outside and began to walk back towards his taxi.

When it came into view, he stopped dead in his tracks. The cab was being searched inch by inch by police. One was looking in the front seat, bent over to examine every nook and cranny, a second was searching the trunk, and a third had even removed the back seat to make a thorough check. James did the most natural thing he could. He strolled quietly back to the restaurant and ordered himself a meal. "But my chopsticks were shaking, Brother David,"

188

he said with a weak smile. After the meal he again approached the car, and found the police gone.

"Did the driver say anything?" I asked James.

He shook his head. "Not a word. I guess this kind of thing is pretty common."

How thankful we both were that he had not taken any Bibles with him. We were doubly thankful when we later learned that Brother Tan had, in fact, been waiting in the restaurant. But God had not allowed them to meet. He had been one step ahead of them both all the way.

Although, when we left the next day, the Bibles were still safely in my suitcase, we were not downhearted. We had seen God at work in the eight days we were there. He had given us the chance to look into the very face of Communism. He had enabled us to make contact with believers. And He had protected us at every turn; for if the Bibles had been found even at customs, all our future deliveries would have been jeopardised. Above all, the Lord had taught us the essential lesson of walking in response to His leading only. That lesson would prove fundamental to all future courier work.

We felt disappointed, of course, that we had been unable to deliver the Scriptures, but God in His perfect timing had other plans.

We were there, after all, to do His will, not ours.

*   *   *

After our time behind the Bamboo Curtain I was more determined than ever to support the believers inside. By now my old friend Robert Foster had joined us full-time, and all of us in Manila concentrated our energies on the provision of Bibles and financial aid for the contacts Joseph had established.

Miss Woo also continued to work very closely with us. At long last, Julie and I had come to meet this gentle Chinese sister, who had welcomed us with open arms.

Our difference in nationality had, by this time, become secondary to our one-ness in Christ – and it was His love which she reflected in the support Miss Woo tirelessly gave Open Doors.

She had become our link between the believers in South China and the outside world. It was through her that we channelled our funds to support the believers there. She also brought us regular news of the ever-growing revival taking place under Mrs Kwang's ministry.

Through Miss Woo we met Grandmother Kwang, who wrote to the family inside about us.

A few weeks later I received a letter which I will treasure all my life. It was from Mrs Kwang herself.

> From my mother's letter I have learned of your love for me, which touched me deeply and made my tears flow. Although this world is slowly changing, the love of my God does not change. Your love really comes from the Lord, which is forever, and the longer it gets, the deeper it becomes. This love makes me feel refreshed.
>
> My beloved! "They which run in a race run all, but one receives the prize ... We are going to obtain an incorruptible crown." So, let us run together!
>
> My soul is knitted together with yours. God has made my heart to be united deeply with yours. I love you very much. I always pray for you at night.
>
> Our family here loves you very much and greets you in peace.
>
> Your cousin who always remembers you.

*　*　*

Early in 1977 James and I planned to make another trip into China, this time with our wives, and Brother Andrew. We were to deliver Scriptures to another of Joseph's contacts in Kwantung and while there James was also planning to meet his friend, Tan Hoc Tue, to deliver the promised Bibles.

Previously James had experienced no difficulty in obtaining his visa. But this time he simply could not get his papers through. As he prayed about the situation, he felt the same restraint which he had experienced in Canton. The Lord was telling him not to go on this trip. Finally, therefore, on the day of our departure, we waved good-bye to a rather thoughtful James – all of us wondering why he was not to come with us.

For Brother Andrew, the China of 1977 was vastly different from the China we had visited in 1965. Gone were the averted eyes, to be replaced instead with a shy openness, even a welcoming smile. The people seemed to have a hunger for something, a vulnerability, a need.

Our Chinese hosts were very keen for us to attend one of their famous operas. The performance we watched was typical of the government's propaganda machine. Twirling figures, clad brightly in red, extolled the virtues of Chairman Hua and the State, at the same time denouncing the Gang of Four.

As operas are difficult for Westerners to understand, English captions from the libretto were projected on to a screen at the side of the stage.

– "Wise Chairman Hua smashed the Gang of Four and shook Heaven and Earth."

"Heaven?" Julie leaned across to whisper in my ear. I didn't know heaven fitted into Communist philosophy?"

– "Chairman Mao delivers us from suffering." Mao was dead, yet lived on as the people's "saviour".

– "On what basis should our policy rest? It should rest on our own strength and that means regeneration through our own efforts." I looked at Brother Andrew after that one. Communism was truly a religion.

– "May the good news wing to all corners of the land."

"Amen," Brother Andrew let out a deep sigh beside me.

191

"Please, Lord," he pleaded in a whisper, "May indeed the *Good News* wing to all corners of this land."

The performance continued, as the colourful figures gestured towards the audience. Their voices rose in ever-increasing crescendo, as evangelistic fervour filled the hall.

Again, I turned to Brother Andrew. But he was no longer looking at the stage. His gaze was concentrated on the rapt expressions of the faces around him.

"Just look at these people," he said at last. "Whatever the State tells them to think and do, they comply with. This week, they are to hate the Gang of Four and smile at the *gwailos* (foreigners). Last week, the *gwailos* were their enemies and the Gang of Four their heroes. They don't have a mind of their own any more. They can't afford to – it is too dangerous!"

He lowered his eyes, burdened with the sight before him. "All they have ever known is lies and hatred. They are not their own any more – they belong to the State. And yet every one of them has been bought with a price – bought by Jesus."

The three of us, right there in the middle of the opera, bowed in silent, longing prayer. It was some minutes before the show could take our attention again.

During the tour, we were taken to a school in Canton where children were being taught to read an English primer. "The sun is bright. The sun is high up in the sky and springs from the east. The sun is red. Chairman Mao is the sun."

Brother Andrew was as irrepressible as ever. "David," he confided as we stood in a classroom. "I feel like shouting, 'Yes, but Chairman Mao is dead now, yet the sun still rises and sets. So who is the sun?'"

As the little children gathered around us afterwards, he picked them up one by one to give them a hug and a kiss. But I knew the prayer in his heart.

We could not deliver the Bibles for another three days,

so we spent the time drinking in all we could of this changing China.

One morning Brother Andrew and I sat on a bench in a square in Canton watching the mass of humanity before us. A number of friendly passers-by addressed us from the crowd.

"Hello!" they shouted cheerfully.

"Hi!" we replied.

Their smiles became broader. "Hi!" they repeated, copying the intonation in our voices.

"You have a lovely country," I called.

They nodded some more. "Lovey countee ...". Still smiling, they did their best to imitate the sentence though its meaning was lost on them.

The game continued for some minutes, the two of us calling various phrases, and the little group struggling to master the new words.

Before they left, we gave them the best phrase of all. "God loves you! God loves you!" we called. "He died for you."

By now they were grinning from ear to ear. "Goh ruv ... Goh ruv ..." If only they had known what they were saying.

We waved good-bye, and as they left, Andrew's voice became serious.

"David, the need here is great, and the people are so ripe for the Gospel. Now I can see more clearly than ever why the Lord has given us a vision for ten million Scriptures." He went quiet for a moment, deep in thought. "You know," he said, "you are never going to make that target without more people to help you. You must find others willing to bring Bibles too."

"But that's no easy job," I replied. "Most people think it is crazy to talk about a ministry to China. Even more are frightened about what might happen if they get involved."

Andrew looked at me with understanding, yet his conviction remained undaunted. "But Jesus told us to 'go into *all* the world'; not just those parts where Christians get the red carpet treatment."

"Still," I persisted, "many people fear that even if they manage to get into China, they don't know what repercussions they might face inside."

"Then let me remind you that Jesus told us to *go* into all the world. But where does he say we have to come back again?"

For a moment, I sat nonplussed, taking in his reply. Then, breaking into a hearty chuckle, I clapped him on the back.

"You're right, Andrew. Man, you're absolutely right."

I grinned at him, expecting him to smile in return. Yet for once Andrew, who always laughed at a good joke, was deadly serious. "Then why do you laugh, brother? This is not a laughing matter."

"I – I just hadn't thought of it that way before."

"Ah. But you see this is our problem. We think we should only go into a country if we can be sure of our return. Jesus never promised that."

He wagged his finger at me.

"Just think, David, when you were trained as a Marine, did they guarantee you a return if they sent you to war? No! Well we are at war too, spiritual war. If we spend our time worrying about what might happen to our safety, we will never get into the battle."

"But," I intervened, "how can I ask that commitment of people?"

"Jesus asked for it, you just have to repeat His words. All around the world people are singing about the fact that they are going to heaven. If they believe that, what is their objection to getting there a little earlier? Those who want to go into China for the Lord can and will do so. You just have to find them."

My laughter had long since disappeared. I got up with my goal clearly before me. There were people who cared

enough, and trusted the Lord enough, to go to China. We
had to find them, and bring them to help those dear
believers inside, while there was still time.

*   *   *

Brother Andrew could not afford the time to stay with
us. But as we saw him off at Canton Station, his con-
tagious enthusiasm for the task remained with us.

A key verse from Psalms is one we claim in any delivery
of Bibles, and never did it apply more aptly than on this
occasion. "I cry out to God Most High, to God who fulfills his purpose for me." (Ps. 57:2).

As soon as we set out to make the transfer we knew we
had trouble on our hands. A number of men happened to
fall in with the crowd behind our tour group.

We had agreed to meet our special "friend" in the park.
As soon as I spotted the woman I went across to speak to
her – only to find myself followed by one of the six men.
After a brief conversation, I wandered casually away, realising there was no way we could hand over the Bibles
under these conditions. Julie and I began to admire the
picturesque park, wandering aimlessly around it with our
"friend" observing from afar. Nevertheless, we could not
shake the men off, and we knew we were in for a very
long afternoon.

Dusk was approaching and still we had no idea how the
Lord was going to "fulfill His purpose ..." We knew only
that we had to be very sensitive to His prompting when
the time came.

Then a commotion broke out a hundred yards away
between two very angry men. Our followers, who were
obviously secret police, rushed to the scene of the fisticuffs,
leaving us alone for the first time since we had arrived at
the park.

"David, your shoulder bag ... hurry!" Julie did not
waste any time. "I'm going to the 'comfort room' and I'll

be needing the tissues in this bag," she said, eyes twinkling. I understood.

When our friend saw Julie walking towards the ladies' toilet, she understood too, and quickly stepped inside. It was all unrehearsed, yet the Holy Spirit had shown them what to do.

Before Julie reached the toilet, the policemen were back with us. They followed Julie to its entrance. From their vantage point they could see us sitting on a park bench forty yards away.

Fifteen minutes ticked by. There was still no sign of the girls. The policemen were getting restless, and so were we. Did the girls intend to remain inside until the men left? How long would it be before they entered the public toilet and caught Julie and the girl with the packages? We prayed and prayed, helpless to do anything else. "Lord, bring them out in five minutes before the men get any bright ideas," I begged.

A minute after that prayer, Julie re-appeared – not from the "comfort room" as I had expected, but down a little hill to one side of me. There was a big smile on her face, and as she waved her hand in greeting I could just make out a brief "one-way" sign.

The policemen, not having seen the other woman enter the rest room, followed us out of the park and to our hotel, before calling it a day.

What had happened inside the comfort room?

"There was a rear exit," Julie explained.

"We slipped out the back way, walked a few yards down a beautiful pathway there – and, since the Lord had already seen to it that no one else was in sight, we made the exchange."

"Why did it take you so long?" I asked.

"Well, it was very pleasant there," she replied. "And the work was hot after all. We decided we had at least earned ourselves a cup of Chinese tea ..."

* * *

On our return to Manila, we found James Wee anxiously awaiting news of the trip. As I told him the story, the two of us could not help wondering once again why he had not been permitted to come with us.

Five months later we had our answer. James and I were once again on our way to Kwantung, loaded with Scriptures. This time, James felt certain the Lord was giving him a green light for his trip.

Once inside, James lost no time looking up his friend, Tan Hoc Tue. "Brother Tan, I wanted so much to visit you earlier this year but the Lord seemed to prevent my coming. Here though, at last I have brought your Bibles."

Brother Tan fought back tears as he picked up each one and lovingly examined it. Then he gave thanks to James, but above all, to the Lord for the protection of His Word.

Afterwards he looked at James, bright-eyed. "My brother, this was the Lord's own timing. It would have been wrong if He had allowed you to visit me on your last trip.

"You see, I have been under close scrutiny by the authorities in recent months. One of my children," he paused as his face clouded with sorrow, "had tried to escape just before that visit but was caught and brought back here. Our family was immediately subjected to continuous observation."

"Were you harmed in any way?"

"No. But they knew about my being a Christian. And during Brother David's last trip, they took me to a nearby church to warn me off."

"Why did they take you there?" James asked.

Brother Tan gave a little shrug. "They have photographs there of believers; those who have been persecuted or imprisoned for their faith. They showed me these pictures and asked me whether I knew any of the people. Then they threatened me with a similar fate.

"And so, my brother," he concluded, "you can imagine what might have happened if you had visited me then. It

197

was definitely the Lord who prevented your visit."

After recounting this conversation to me, James came to a pause, knowing that his question had been answered. "It's like last time, Brother David," he said softly. "The Lord is one step ahead of us all the way ..."

CHAPTER FOURTEEN

The Year of the Tourist

I jumped as the telephone rang. I had been reading a report from one of our couriers.

"Hello?" Without thinking, I picked up the receiver before Beng could intercept the call. "Who is that?"

"Hong Kong calling," came the operator's stilted accent. A moment later an enthusiastic voice was chatting excitedly down the line.

"Brother David, Brother David, I have important news for you."

It was Miss Woo.

"You won't believe what has happened. Praise the Lord with me ..."

"What is it, Sister Woo?"

"Oh, Brother David, I don't know where to start. It's – it's – the Grandmother. She has just called me."

"You mean Mrs Kwang's mother?"

"Yes." She sounded breathless. "One of her grandsons has managed to leave China. He's here in her house!"

Young Daniel Kwang, just nineteen years old, had somehow or other managed to get out of China.

*   *   *

The next day, Miss Woo and I were knocking at the door of Grandmother Kwang's house in Hong Kong. As it opened, I found myself greeted by a slim, rather shy-looking Chinese youth.

"Brother David?" he questioned a little tentatively

"Yes," I nodded and next moment I was giving him a giant bear hug. That was as much as we could communicate directly with each other – Daniel spoke almost no English.

As we sat in his grandmother's living room, Miss Woo interpreted Daniel's conversation for me. "How are your parents?" I asked, pausing for Miss Woo to translate. Back came the message. "They are well. They are praising the Lord for His goodness. They send you their love. They want me to tell you they pray for you every day."

His reply touched me. I still could not get over the fact that these people, with all their difficulties, could bring themselves to care for us as well.

"We are praying for them, too." I said. "You bet we are."

As Miss Woo translated, a smile spread over his porcelain-like features.

"How are you, Daniel?" I continued. "Are you all right after your trip out from China?"

"I am fine," I was told. "The Lord is very wonderful in bringing me here. You want to hear how He brought me?"

I nodded and he plunged into his story. On Christmas Day, 1975, the Lord had told him in prayer that he was going to leave China. He was even given the precise date on which he should apply for his exit visa. Daniel had shared this with his mother and some of the other believers. They had all kept it to themselves but had prayed regularly about it.

When the date actually came, over twelve months later, he went to the immigration office and placed his application. The official behind the desk knew all about Mrs Kwang and the thousands she had brought to the Lord.

"Are you crazy? Who do you think you are? Of course you cannot go, your mother is a criminal, an enemy of the State. Get out of here!"

In blind anger the official began to beat Daniel about the face and body with his fists – until, with a final outburst of disgust, he abandoned him and strode back to his office.

As the man walked away, Daniel laid his case again before the Lord. "Last year, you told me this was the date for me to come. I don't understand what is happening. Please show me your power."

At that moment, the man inexplicably came to a halt. He turned around to face Daniel, and asked in a new tone of voice: "Is your name Daniel Kwang?" As the young boy nodded, he added, "And do you live at ——?", giving the Kwangs' address. Once again Daniel confirmed it, amazed at his change in attitude. Without offering any explanation the official had done a complete about-face. "Then," the man concluded, "come with me."

"Why?" I asked Daniel. "What made him do that?"

At that precise time, Daniel explained, in Mrs Kwang's home, about three hundred believers had been gathered for fellowship and instruction. The meeting over, they had all set out on their walk home when the Holy Spirit suddenly stopped every one of them, telling them to return to the meeting and pray for Daniel. The Lord impressed upon them that the boy needed their intercession immediately. Mrs Kwang was most surprised to see them all returning, but when she asked them why, everyone gave the same explanation.

"The Lord spoke to me saying that your son is to get his visa for Hong Kong. I have come to pray for him and give thanks."

Later that night, Daniel received his papers.

* * *

Daniel knew that now he was outside China, one of his responsibilities would be to present the needs of the Suffering Church to the free world. But to do this, he had to master the English language, in as short time as possible. We talked and prayed together that night until we came up with a solution. If he lived with a family who spoke only English, he would have to learn the language quickly.

Although our Hong Kong workers, Pastor Ward and his

201

wife, Anne, were elsewhere at that time, I quickly offered their services, assuring Daniel they would be delighted to have him come and live with them.

It was only a matter of time, once they had returned, before the two were happily welcoming their new teenage "son". "He has become a 'Timothy' to us," they were to tell me after a few weeks had passed.

As the months went by, we began to get more information from Daniel about the extent of the revival the Lord was bringing about through his mother's ministry. At the same time, accounts were coming in to us of similar revivals, on a lesser scale, in central and northern China as well. We saw the truth of the believers' forecast during Joseph's earlier visit, and Brother Andrew's prediction back at our first meeting. God was indeed bringing about revival in the People's Republic. With each report, we understood better why the Lord had given us the vision of ten million Scriptures for this immense nation.

To date, however, we were so far from that target that our efforts looked almost laughable. A few overseas Chinese and a handful of Westerners had been involved in courier trips, delivering Bibles in their twenties, thirties or at the most, forties. At the same time our couriers in bordering countries were continuing their deliveries through the unfriendly mountain passes into China. But all of this was hardly a beginning.

We now had contacts set up throughout the country just waiting to receive Scriptures. But where were we to find the couriers to take them in? And even if we could find them, how were we to get enough teams through that Bamboo Curtain to satisfy the church's needs?

* * *

Unexpectedly, the answer came early in 1978 over a Hong Kong breakfast of cinnamon rolls, orange juice and coffee. I was reading the *South China Morning Post* when

I suddenly came across a tiny advertisement entitled. "Tours to China". I looked more closely and found they were offering four day tours to Canton and eight day tours to Peking. The paper gave the name of the travel agency concerned – just a commercial travel organisation, not even the China Travel Service.

I rubbed the sleep from my eyes. When I thought back to the number of times I had tried every available means of getting into China over the past few years, it seemed almost impossible to be reading an advertisement like this.

Yet was it so impossible? We had been watching for change in China since 1976, when Chou and Mao had both died. According to what Psalm 37 had said, several years before when I was back at FEBC, China would open up once the two had fallen.

My mind went back to a strange tale Daniel had told me about the day that Mao died. "During that afternoon, the sky became very dark in our area, and lightning and thunder came. It was so strong that the old people, even those in their eighties, said that they had not seen anything like it in fifty years. They came out of their houses to look at it, and then turned to each other and said: 'The old man is dead. Chairman Mao has gone.' And they rejoiced." A little later, news reached them from Peking that the Helmsman had indeed died at that time.

Daniel had gone on to explain that these people believed, as happens so often in the Bible, that earthquakes signal a change of some kind. When China's devastating earthquake occurred in 1976, therefore, they were expecting to find something different happening in the country. Their chairman's death, just one month later, only confirmed their expectation.

Now the extent of that change was becoming apparent for all to see. I took the advertisement excitedly to Pastor Ward and Anne, asking them to check it out. Within weeks staff workers from Asia and the United States were booked on tours not only to Canton and Peking but Shanghai and

203

Nanking as well. It seemed that 1978, to continue Chinese tradition, was indeed "The Year of the Tourist".

* * *

It was not long before James Wee and I were treading again the by now well-beaten path to the home of his ancestors – this time making our second trip to Peking.

The Sunday after our arrival we took some Bibles to the home of a Christian friend, and after just a few minutes with him, our host went to his front door to welcome a young European Christian – John. He was living temporarily in Peking and spoke almost perfect Mandarin.

John sat down to join us and our natural topic for conversation was the church in China. As time slipped by I began to feel this meeting had not been a coincidence. John was obviously burdened for the needs of his brothers and sisters.

I prayed silently that if the Lord would have us establish some sort of link-up with John, He would make it clear. Instinctively, my eyes sought James', and I knew he was praying the same way. Finally I took a deep breath and broached the subject.

After explaining about the kind of work we were doing, I opened up my briefcase and took out a number of Bibles. "We believe these came through Peking Airport customs control undetected, as a miracle," I said.

John said nothing but I noticed him swallow hard. I went on. "Are you willing to trust God with us? Would you take these Bibles from us now, believing that God will provide you with a Chinese Christian to whom you can pass them on?"

There were a few minutes' silence while John digested all that had been said. Again I looked to James, and knew he was praying about the outcome. Later, John was to tell us that although he was a little taken aback with the way the conversation had gone, we had nonetheless been expressing many of the things which had been heavy on his own heart during his time in China.

"I'm willing to take them," he said at last. "But please understand there is no way I can pass them on now. You'll have to provide the contacts for me."

By now, having seen the Lord's confirmation of this meeting, I could smile confidently. "Let's trust the Lord together, brother," I said.

"Our method is not to simply leave Bibles lying around in public places. We firmly believe we should place them in the hands of known Christians who need and long for them. I believe God is in our meeting and He will lead us to the right believer!"

The four of us knelt on our host's floor, the Peking sun warm on our backs as we prayed together.

"Dear Lord," John prayed, "I believe these Scriptures came in as part of an on-going miracle and I am willing to become a part of it too, open to what you will do with them and with me in the days to come."

His words were to prove prophetic. In the weeks and months ahead, John was to become our principal connection with the Suffering Church in Peking.

* * *

No visit to Peking is complete without a walk through its famous Tien An Men Square, and for me it held special memories of the last occasion I was there.

Just twelve months earlier I had decided to take an early morning stroll before James had woken. I put on my Levi outfit and Mao cap, slung my camera over one shoulder, and stepped out into the vast square to take some photos. The first thing that met my eyes were the people, thousands of them in uniform – lined up in three solid sections. The People's Army were in green. The policemen were in blue and white. The sailors, also in blue and white, looked spruce in their caps and sailors collars. All stood in line on the south west of the square before the Chairman Mao Memorial Hall and Mausoleum. They waited patiently to pay their respects to the entombed Mao.

As soon as I appeared a thousand eyes focused on me. I was the only foreigner in the entire square at that time of the morning. I smiled at them. Nobody smiled back.

I decided to join the long line of mourners and pay my own respects to their leader. It was an endless wait as the line slowly inched its way towards the crystal coffin, surrounded by its many offerings of brightly coloured flowers.

I could not help wondering yet again at the amazing hold that even in death Mao had over his people. Here they were queued in their thousands paying tribute to a man who, according to the Guinness Book of World Records, was responsible for the deaths of more people than any other person who ever lived. More than Hitler ... Stalin ... Amin. A man whose pictures had adorned almost every home, shop window, public building and billboard, the object of adulation, even worship, by the people in their millions.

When my turn came to stand before this giant of twentieth century history, I looked down to see a small, sallow, shrivelled body. The formerly red, full cheeks were now sunken and yellow. The dark eyes, once bright with ambition and power, were now shut. Modern China's self-made god was patently mortal.

I took off my cap and bowed my head in silent prayer. "If only Mao knew You ... but You have Your plans and he was part of them." I said. "Lord, use this moment in China's history to lift the minds of Your people here beyond their 'political father' to their one true Father. Bring them back to Yourself."

I replaced my cap and turned to walk past the long line filling the length of the square. As curious faces turned to stare I smiled at each one, inwardly repeating my prayer as I went.

* * *

The moment I enjoyed most in all my frequent trips was my return home. Julie had made it a tradition to bring the children to meet me unless they had school the following day. When I stepped out into the heat from the airport's immigration section, there would be an enthusiastic chorus of voices calling my name.

My welcome at home would be just as warm. Deanne never failed to organise a large greeting sign to hang outside the house. If I had been to a country in the free world, the poster would be covered with appropriate symbols. If not, she and the others would be careful not to give away a hint of where I had been.

There was no end to their ideas. As well as the posters, the three D's would sometimes greet me with helium-filled balloons bearing the words: "We love you Daddy", and accompanied by smiles bigger than their faces.

On those nights when school prevented the kids from coming to the airport, I always knew I'd find three sets of eyes wide open when I tiptoed into their rooms. In the dark, they would give whispers of welcome and news which simply couldn't wait till morning. "I'm on the school basketball team, Daddy." "I can do a new turn on my skateboard now! I'll show you tomorrow!" "Sleep good, Dad. We missed you!"

When the house was settled. Julie and I had an opportunity to share the happenings of the days or weeks we had spent apart. Then we would spend time together with the One who had faithfully cared for us in each of our separate situations.

During one of my evenings home, as the two of us were reading our Bibles, Julie unexpectedly laid hers to one side and looked at me intently.

"David," she began. "You know something?"

"What's that?"

"You've been reading quite a large hunk of your Bible tonight."

"Uh huh."

"Do you realise, honey," she continued, "that ten years ago you wouldn't have been able to do that?"

I put the Bible down slowly.

"I mean when we were first married you could not read the way you can now. I think the Lord's been working a slow but steady miracle right under our noses."

I stopped to think about it in those terms. When, I wondered, had the changes begun? At college, reading had still been a struggle, and it was only a little better after we were first married. "Maybe it really started to change after I met Jesus," I said. Goodness knows I had asked Him about it often enough.

"And all those hours you spent reading the Bible under Mr Roy's direction," Julie mused. "Perhaps the Lord used those, honey ..."

The two of us talked at length about it, trying to isolate the time when some sort of major breakthrough had come. We couldn't. It had just been a slow, quiet improvement that the Lord had given over the years since I handed my life – and that problem along with it – to Him.

Even now, I was no speed reader. And I was not comfortable reading in the public eye. But, as Julie and I talked that night, I realised that the crisis of reading was now a thing of the past. God had brought me to the point where reading, instead of something to be feared, was a pleasure.

That evening I recognised the full extent of His working. And gratefully acknowledged that here in my own personal life, just as when crossing the borders, I was seeing the God of the impossible at work.

* * *

On my next trip to Hong Kong, I found that Pastor Ward had already begun organising the tourist trips that could be used for courier deliveries.

On each of the available tours visitors were being booked

from the United States – and, as fruits from an earlier trip "down under", from Australia and New Zealand. Each of them was tightly screened and carefully prepared for the trip. The utmost caution needed to be taken for the protection of the believers inside. The teams were also counselled for their border crossings.

"There is no way that in our own strength we can out-smart Communist officials," they were told. "They are trained to perfection. The only way to get God's Word into China is to allow Him to do it for you. Your part will be to make sure you are walking close to Him so that you can sense His leading as He does so."

Their suitcases had no false compartments, the Bibles were simply placed inside. Then, after committing their way to the Lord, the tourists would be on their way, Brother Andrew's well-known prayer in their hearts: "Lord, in my luggage I have Scriptures that I want to take to Your children across the border. When You were on earth, You made blind eyes see. Now, I pray, make seeing eyes blind. Do not let the guards see those things You do not want them to see."

Time after time they would return from their tours with faces shining, having witnessed God indeed make seeing eyes blind. Something always "happened" to distract the customs guards just at the needed moment. It was never the same thing twice – the distraction each time was different, and always outside of the courier's control. Only the principle remained the same – that God would clear the way for His Word to go through.

One of the first tourist couriers, Jim Cooper, had to face the rugged Shun Chun customs hall. It is a wide room divided into narrow compartments, with several customs men in each. The ratio of customs officials to visitors was strictly one to one. As Jim entered the room, he was instructed to take his suitcase to one of those on duty, towards the end of the room.

He walked towards the man, only to find, at that

moment, that another guard had unexpectedly become free. The official at the end then gestured for Jim to return to the other one. Jim obediently did so, only to be told smilingly by this guard to go back to the original one. Again Jim did as he was instructed, but by now the customs officer at the end was laughing – and proceeded to send Jim yet again to his colleague. The two continued their game of Chinese "ping-pong" with Jim, who by now was laughing along with them. Eventually Jim placed himself equidistant between the two, put his bags on the floor and his hands on his hips, saying: "Come on fellers. We have to come to a decision about this. Others are waiting." At this the guards chuckled heartily and with a wave of their hands gestured for him to pass on, bags unopened. Jim happily complied, inwardly marvelling at his Lord who not only cleared the way for the Bibles to come through, but obviously had a sense of humour as well.

Accompanying Jim on his delivery were four other couriers. They too passed through Shun Chun without one Bible being detected. All of them met outside the hall in grateful spirits, silently praising the Lord in between smiles at local officials.

On their tour inside the People's Republic, Jim and his friends were suitably exposed to all evidences of progress under the new regime. They were taken through a porcelain factory. They visited schools, hospitals, communes, parks, each representing the smiling face of the China of the late seventies.

Posters through the streets left them in no doubt that the Gang of Four were still very much to blame for every ill in current Chinese society. Although the policy of the Gang was no different from that of Mao himself, the current government could hardly blame their national god for the excesses of his regime. Far better to find another scapegoat to bear the brunt of the criticism, without toppling Mao from his pedestal. The people still needed their former object of worship. Yet their new leader also required his own recognition. And where once it was only Mao that presided over factories, streets, homes, shops and all other venues, now Hua's picture hung alongside – just as large and dominant. Indeed in some places, Mao was not even to be seen – only his successor.

Not unless they were asked, would the guides refer to one other aspect of life in China at that time – religion. Everywhere Jim went he kept his eyes peeled for church buildings. Ofter he found them standing closed like silent monuments to a bygone "superstition", nailed and boarded firmly shut. At the front of one of these, some enterprising locals had erected a bamboo frame on the dusty, dilapidated church steps, and were busily drying fish there.

More frequently, he discovered, they had been reallocated for other functions in the community. Some had become administration buildings, others used for industry. Frequently, the crosses on the top of church steeples had been torn down to leave only the stump. On one church, the cross had been broken but not removed – it had been left welded into its bent position as a symbol of the East 'breaking' all imperialist influence from the West.

Perhaps the church that moved them the most was a building now used as a munitions factory. The Sword of the Spirit was being replaced by the weaponry of militant Communism.

The doors of the churches in China were closed as tightly as they had ever been.

* * *

But thankful as we were for these Westerners who responded to the needs of the believers, we still needed more overseas Chinese burdened enough for the church of their motherland to get involved as well. How much more they could do, speaking the language, looking much the same as their fellow countrymen, and how much better we could understand the Suffering Church through their face-to-face communication.

211

Peter Wong, one of the first, was a doctor with a practice in a Western country. However, he had relatives in China whom he had never met, and he knew that some of them had been Christians before "liberation". He longed to visit them to discover whether they still believed. He also wanted to use the opportunity to deliver Scriptures.

When the doctor arrived at customs, a young woman official came to check his bags. Before leaving, he had carefully placed his Bibles in the middle of his clothing. He had then stuffed his belongings at the side of the bag, above and below the books. He had even put some New Testaments in the pockets of the trousers he had packed. As the girl began to search his luggage, it was as though her hands were guided. She placed them at the sides of the suitcase, on top of it, and then, as if still not sure, she pulled out one pair of trousers as far as the top of the leg. Before she got to the pocket however, she seemed satisfied and pushed the clothes back in again. Dr Wong let out a long inaudible sigh. Just one or two more inches, and she would have found the Scriptures.

"Welcome to the People's Republic, sir," she said as she closed it with a snap.

Once inside the country, Dr Wong lost no time in finding his family. He visited the uncle who he knew had formerly been a dedicated Christian, and chose a quiet moment to broach the delicate subject.

During the Cultural Revolution this man, a top professional in his field, had been reduced to the role of janitor for his faith. Recently he had been restored to the position his ability merited.

"Do you still believe?" Dr Wong had whispered.

"In my heart, yes," came the reply. "But I never speak to anybody about it."

"You mean you have no fellowship?"

The doctor's relative was adamant. "None."

Dr Wong also talked this time at length with another cousin. After a family banquet, most of the relatives remained in their living room, watched a colour television.

212

Only the cousin retired with Peter to talk in a separate room.

"I shared my testimony with him," he told me. "And to my surprise my cousin revealed he too had been a Christian for three years before 'liberation'.

" 'Well, of course, our beliefs are all different now. I hold a responsible position here.' " Peter grimaced as he repeated the reply.

"My cousin then tried to keep the conversation on political lines and gave me a well rehearsed list of the evils of the Gang of Four. But I felt I needed to know where he stood. 'Are your beliefs really changed? Has your faith really gone?' I asked him. 'Do you truly no longer believe?'

"My cousin would not give any answer to that. He seemed embarrassed. I think I knew what was really still in his heart but he could not show it to me."

* * *

As China's door opened ever wider many more Westerners like Jim Cooper, and overseas Chinese like Dr Wong began to pour through it. Together with the Bibles still coming over the mountains from the bordering countries, the "sustenance" for the Suffering Church was gaining in substance week by week, month by month. The scope of the work increased correspondingly, and so it was with grateful relief that we welcomed Todd Martin on to our team in the Philippines. He had been teaching for some years in the States, but moved back to Manila to develop the communication arm of our ministry.

On the borders, one of our largest deliveries ever had just taken place. Three thousand men had found a way to cross into China from Burma, at one time. They went on official business – in order to do a favour for the government. All, however, were carrying Scriptures, and once across the border, every man was caught.

"If we cannot bring in these Scriptures," the leader told

their captors, "we will not eat or drink. We choose to fast and pray until you release us and the Bibles."

"Then you will starve," said the Chinese officials.

The leader's tone was quiet as he tried to convey the love of God to his interrogators. "I do not think we will starve. Our God will take care of us."

"Chairman Mao and Chairman Hua have taken care of us," the Communist replied stonily.

The Bible couriers would not give in. They made it plain that, unless they were allowed to take in the Scriptures, they would not continue with their official business either.

After forty-eight hours, they were released, and every copy of God's Word went with them into the People's Republic.

The size of the border work was increasing all the time. In India we had just ordered twenty thousand Scriptures to be printed, and these had already begun to trickle into China via different routes in several border countries.

As the Bibles found their way into China, more and more joyful letters continued to make their secret way out. More than anything, we were touched by the sense of one-ness these letters expressed. Despite barriers of geography and ideology, the unity of the Body could not be broken.

> *Cousin, your love for us is like the Lebanon Water from the mountain stream flowing from a far, far place to our place – touching every one of us. Although we are far apart, the love of our Lord is like the golden chain of life that ties us, binds us strongly together.*

This writer was obviously a pastor.

> *I am the shepherd in the field, and have felt the reflection of the warm sunlight from above. The sheep in the flock jump for joy and are also comforted because of your care and concern.*

214

Another "cousin" wrote:

> *You have given a great contribution to our Father God's House, and the help always comes on time – every time. Your burden for the relatives in the mainland is His mission for you. We are happy and rejoice because of you and would like to give our big thanks. Hallelujah! Praise the Lord! You have a share in our work...*

And of course, our mail frequently included letters from Mrs Kwang.

> *The wonderful grace of Jesus is poured out unceasingly upon me. His mercy is my psalm, the song in my mouth and the joy in my heart.*
>
> *How wonderful is the work of the Holy Spirit! We are separated in two different countries, yet He has nevertheless matched us together in one Body. This is Life within life that causes us to be of one mind, one spirit and one heart.*

The growth in the number of believers was obviously continuing.

> *Thank God for His exceptional grace. He has blessed His family here, so that more sheep are being born and nourished. They go in and out safely. We are walking under His grace and loving kindness. These are all the works of the Lord.*
>
> *"May the Lord who walks among the seven candlesticks walk with you. May His right hand firmly hold you. May the heavenly peace, comfort and power of the Holy Spirit fill your heart.*
>
> *Your sister who remembers you in the utmost.*

215

CHAPTER FIFTEEN
Sweeter than Honey

The little blue taxi drew to a halt outside the university in Canton. Beside the entrance, stood what seemed at first to be a "welcoming committee" – a jeep manned by two green-clad soldiers with loaded rifles.

Joseph was making his first trip to China in four years. After a period of full-time study, he had returned to our team and was visiting one Chinese family that every one of us longed to meet. Joseph was on his way to meet Mrs Kwang.

He glanced out of the window and took in the menacing scene. Beads of perspiration formed on his forehead and a jumble of thoughts crowded his mind. Did they know all about him? Had they been expecting his visit? Did they know Mrs Kwang was inside? She had been secretly staying with a doctor's family in this university to escape the eyes of the authorities.

He fumbled in his pocket for the driver's money, silently praying at the same time.

"Lord, I don't know what to do now. I just trust you to work it out." He reached over to open the door. "And one more thing, Lord," he added as he gathered his bag, "please don't let them see how nervous I feel."

His youthful features made it possible for him to look like an overseas student. Taking a deep breath, he smiled at the expressionless soldiers and walked by. They made no move. Once past them, he let out a sigh of relief. Had they been placed there for his sake, they would have acted by now. Even so, he could feel their eyes boring holes into his back as he walked into the university grounds.

Joseph had no idea where to find the doctor's rooms in the large university. Daniel had told him only that the medical man lived on this campus, and that he simply had to ask around for him by name. "But don't mention my mother, of course," Daniel had warned.

For the soldiers' sakes, Joseph was doing his best to look nonchalant. But with no idea in which direction to turn, he was quaking inwardly.

"Yes, can I help you?" asked the girl receptionist.

"Please, I am looking for Dr Chang. Can you tell me where to find him?" Dr Chang was the son of one of Mrs Kwang's friends. At his mother's request he had offered Mrs Kwang lodgings, since university residents did not have to register their address with the local authorities.

"I'm sorry, I have never heard of Dr Chang," said the girl behind the desk, and Joseph's heart dropped for the second time that day. "What now, Lord?" he groaned inwardly. Could Daniel have given him the wrong information?

Nevertheless, he took the form the girl offered to fill out the reason for his visit. In one section he had to state his relationship to the person he had come to see. "Well," he smiled to himself, "I am her brother in the Lord." Picking up the pen he wrote confidently: "Relative".

The girl spoke again. "Every doctor here has a clinic. Why don't you go to each one until you find the one you want," she suggested helpfully.

He turned around, stealing a quick glance at the gate. The soldiers' eyes were still following him. He had no option but to continue. With a prayer that God would guide his steps, he began walking towards a cluster of medical rooms.

In the first one he chose, Joseph asked a nearby doctor if he happened to know where Dr Chang practised.

"I am Dr Chang. Can I help you?"

"You are?" Remembering the presence of others in the room, Joseph had to restrain his exuberance.

"Doctor, I'm very pleased to meet you." He leaned closer, and said quietly, "I'm here to see Mrs Kwang."

"Is she expecting you?"

"Yes, it has all been arranged."

The doctor led him to his quarters and, though Mrs Kwang was out at that moment, invited him to wait. He ushered Joseph into the second of the two rooms in his apartment before excusing himself to return to his patients. In that inner room, Joseph would be safe from the risk of observation from passers-by.

An hour later Mrs Kwang appeared at the door, returning after a secret preaching engagement. The glow in her expression struck him immediately. Somehow he had expected to see a gaunt, even scarred face. Instead he was looking at one that radiated nothing but tranquillity and love. He stood up, poised to offer his hand, a "hello" on the tip of his tongue. Before he could say a word, she took the wind out of his sails.

"Brother Joseph? Praise the Lord! Let's pray."

Next moment they were kneeling side-by-side on the floor, worshipping the Lord together. Some minutes after, they rose, tears of joy brimming for both of them. Then came the formalities.

"How do you do, Brother Joseph. I have prayed for many months for this meeting."

The pair sat down on the sofa for the start of many long hours together as she shared with him the story of the church in her province.

Normally, for security reasons, Joseph would not visit a contact in China more than twice. But this time both of them felt it safe to make an exception. At the end of every day, Joseph knew there was more that needed to be said. "We can continue tomorrow?" he would half-question as the afternoon drew to an end.

After five days, they finally brought their talks to a close. Joseph had brought her fifty-six Bibles to distribute among her co-workers. Delightedly she had taken them. But when he had asked her how many more she needed, her reply set him back on his heels.

218

"Dear Brother Joseph, we could use, at the very least, one thousand Scriptures."

* * *

Now that we knew Joseph had actually met the evangelist, Julie and I could barely suppress our enthusiasm as we awaited his return from the trip.

When, at last, he reached our home and we had sat him down in our living room, a host of questions tumbled out one on top of another.

"How is she?" "What does she look like?" "Where is Mr Kwang?" "Did you meet any of the other believers?"

Joseph lifted his arms as if to block the oncoming tide of queries. "I will answer all your questions," he laughed. "But if it's okay with you, just one at a time."

Remembering our manners, we got up to offer him a cup of coffee and a snack.

"Yes, they are all very well. Yes, I did meet some of the believers. Some of her co-workers visited her while I was there. Mr Kwang is in their home town.

"Have I answered all your questions so far?" he smiled.

"All but one. You haven't told us what Mrs Kwang looks like."

"Ah. She has black wavy hair, brown eyes, and a round smiling face," his voice became wistful, "in which you can almost see the presence of Christ Himself."

Joseph went on to tell as much as he could that night of the stories and teaching Mrs Kwang had given him.

"She would stop her story every few minutes, Brother David, just to speak of the goodness of the Lord, and His care of her family and of the believers. Really her eyes were just alight for Him. She constantly exhorted me to trust in Him alone and stand on His Word. Oh – her knowledge of the Scriptures ..." he broke off, shaking his head, "just fantastic!"

"So you no longer have any doubts about her and her work?"

219

Joseph didn't say anything. He did not need to. His expression spoke for him. "Do you know, the first thing I saw when I arrived at her place was an enormous pile of mail – all of it from Christian leaders throughout the country. It was huge. I tell you – God is doing a mighty thing through that woman. It's not because she in herself is extraordinary. She is just a beautiful, motherly, loving lady. No – it is because she walks *so* closely to Him that He can do a great work through her."

Since her latest imprisonment, the evangelist had been relentlessly sought by the secret police. They wanted to get her back into prison and keep her there for life. But, amazingly, every attempt they made to find her was unsuccessful. She told Joseph that, since her last imprisonment, the Lord had promised her she would never have to face another arrest.

Subsequent events had proved Him faithful to that promise. Frequently when she was holding a meeting, the Lord would warn her of danger and tell her when she should bring it to a halt.

On one occasion, she held a series of gatherings lasting several days, instructing her co-workers. Their pattern was to spend the morning in teaching, break for lunch, and then resume for the afternoon. On the final day, when Mrs Kwang had finished preaching, she was on the point of telling the co-workers to go out for lunch before resuming for their final session in the afternoon. But at that moment, she felt the restraint of the Lord. She was certain He was warning them of danger and urging her to complete her teaching then, instead of breaking for a meal.

Mrs Kwang asked the co-workers to stay while she concluded her instructions to them. Then the entire group left, without further delay, to catch the ferry home. Just after the last believers had gone, the secret police arrived in force. They stood guard at every door of the house, planning to pounce at the first sound of hymns being sung. Their vigil of waiting, however, was rewarded only by silence.

Nevertheless, tense with expectation, they hung on. Nothing happened. Eventually one could wait no longer.

"I'm going in there," he told his colleagues. He entered the house like a lion going in for the kill – only to return through the front door minutes later, a sheepish look on his face.

"They're not here! Where on earth ...?" His commander cut across him. "The pier, they must be at the pier."

Together the police ran towards the river as fast as they could, but arrived just in time to see the stern of a ferry disappearing downstream.

"Stop!" shouted the irate Communist leader through cupped hands. "I order you to turn back."

The ferry captain was a Christian. He smiled quietly to himself as he kept the boat on course. His wife sat behind Mrs Kwang, giving her words of encouragement until they were out of view.

* * *

I shook my head in amazement. "That's got to be the Lord," I said to Joseph. "There just isn't any other explanation. How did the Kwangs get to hear the rest of the story?"

Joseph smiled. "One of the workers at the pier was a Christian and he heard all about it from the soldiers. You know, Brother David, that is just the thing! In their area the revival has spread so far that there are believers in all walks of life."

He continued to speak of the many other miracles which Mrs Kwang had told him. One that touched me particularly was the account of a co-worker whom the Kwangs affectionately termed "the Old Man". He had come from a very poor family, and much of his early life had been a daily struggle. This preacher, whose life had been one of great fruitfulness for his Lord, had been forced as a child to leave school, because he had never been able to master reading.

"In fact, his family was the poorest in the whole village,"

Joseph explained. Because of his poverty, when the Communists came to power, they made him chairman of their area – to prove a point. They gave him a big house to live in and double rations of rice. But he loved the Lord so much that he just used his home for worship meetings and distributed all his rice among the hungry believers – until he ran out himself.

"Eventually the government became aware of his activities and ordered him to choose between his new-found position and his faith. Knowing that he was going back to life-long poverty, he nonetheless told them, 'I will not disobey my Lord.'

"He once again became the poorest man in the area, without house or accommodation. This happened during the early days after Mao took power, and the Christians he knew were either too poor to help him, or were themselves in prison. One person did manage to provide him with a small room to use, but he had no way at all of obtaining food. For some days he lived there, with water as his only sustenance until he grew weak with hunger.

"One morning, when he awoke, he noticed a big hole in the wall, and did his best to repair it. He brought a number of stones to block it in. But within a few hours, there was another large hole, and he decided that for some reason, this was from the Lord. Later he saw a large rat come through the hole. The rodent made several visits and brought him sweet potatoes, nuts and vegetables."

I interrupted him. "For the old man to eat?" I asked.

"Yes," he repeated. "The rat brought him food. Otherwise he would have starved to death.

"Every morning the rat kept coming to him, bringing him enough food for that day. Sometimes, when he was expecting someone else to visit him for the day, the creature would bring him a double portion of food."

"How long did this go on – a few days?" I was still incredulous.

"Several months."

222

I shook my head and Julie turned to me. "But honey, we have accepted all that for Elijah, when he was fed by the ravens at the brook. Why couldn't it happen in twentieth-century China?"

I guessed it could, but it was still quite incredible.

Julie squeezed my hand. "How big is your God?" she smiled.

*　　*　　*

Far into the night, Joseph recounted more about the time he had spent with Mrs Kwang. But the final surprise was yet to come.

"Brother David, she would like more Bibles."

"Fine," I said, "I was thinking of sending in another team soon."

"Well, actually," he paused as if taking a deep breath, "she has told us how many she needs."

"Even better then. How many?"

"They need a thousand."

For a moment I didn't say a word. His news had precisely the effect on me that he had anticipated.

"But," I said at last, "the most we've ever taken through Hong Kong is fifty!"

"I know, Brother David, I know," Joseph shook his head.

My thoughts turned inwards. One thousand seemed impossible. Surely a delivery that size meant biting off more than we could chew. What if it failed? For a moment it was easier to play safe rather than stick my neck out yet again and risk making myself and the organisation a laughing stock. How in the world could we do it?

And in that question, I had the key to my answer. *We* couldn't. That was the beauty of it. It would be the Lord Himself who would make the way . . .

"I cry out to God Most High, to God who fulfils His purpose for me," I said aloud.

The other two looked up at me, their heads nodding

with understanding. The verse had become a favourite with us in this work.

"Well," I concluded, "if the Lord is ever going to have us bring ten million Bibles to China, it's no doubt time we started taking in more than fifty a time."

I winked at Julie. "He's the same God today that could feed Elijah by the brook – I guess we can trust Him for a thousand Bibles!"

* * *

Much of the planning for the delivery took place with Daniel in Pastor Ward's tiny Hong Kong apartment. For forty-eight hours we crowded around a table along with the other team members, preparing our strategy. Joseph, whom we considered our key team member, had suddenly become very ill, and with dismay we realised there was no way he could come with us.

Yet still the Lord was saying, "Go". On the second night we all packed our suitcases, praying over every Bible that we placed inside. Despite myself, and the direction I believed God was giving us, I was still unable to suppress doubts about the mission. Was I sure it was right to endanger all these people, to try to deliver by far the largest number of Bibles we had ever attempted? What if I had made a mistake, read God wrongly? The whole thing could fall down around our ears, and worse, place the believers inside at risk. Once again I called upon Him to lead us and fell into a fitful sleep.

The following morning, the team assembled for final worship and prayer; James and Lyn Wee, another overseas Chinese, Beng, Julie and myself. We linked hands around the table as a sign of the bond that joined us together and bowed our heads for prayer. American voices mixed with Filipino and Chinese as we sang together, "He is Lord". We followed it with a song of commitment, "Father I adore You, lay my life before You . . ."

When we arrived at customs at Shun Chun, we were

carrying between us nine hundred Bibles. The other hundred were to follow in a later delivery. Each of us passed through without incident until it was James' turn to be checked.

The border guard opened James' suitcase and began to search inside. He took some minutes over it, delving deep with his fingers. At last his hands came to rest on the thin layer of clothing covering the Bibles. James broke into a cold sweat, convinced the man must have felt the books. There were so many of them.

"Dear Lord, protect Your Word. Stop him, Lord." All of a sudden, the guard straightened and pulled the lid of the suitcase shut.

"Please pass on, sir. Everything is in order."

James joined us and together we boarded the train for Canton. In the carriage he quietly recounted the Lord's protection at the border, and all of us gave silent thanks. I looked out of the window at the by now familiar sight of South China's fields, trees and rounded hills delineated against a cloudless blue sky. The whole scenario reminded me of words from Jeremiah 32:17: "Ah Lord GOD! It is thou who hast made the heavens and the earth by thy great power and by thy outstretched arm! Nothing is too hard for thee."

"Not even nine hundred Bibles, Lord?" I whispered.

As soon as we were settled in Canton, we took to the streets with relish. I loved being back in China. Somehow, though, there seemed to be a subtle change between this visit and our last. Julie noticed it first. "The hoardings, David. The posters, they've changed."

She was right. The attacks on the Gang of Four no longer dominated the scene. Instead, a new kind of emphasis was being presented to the people; its colourful campaign designed to reach into their drab lives from every street corner and building face, lifting their aspirations to a higher plane.

The Party Central Committee had launched its crusade

225

for the "Four Modernisations".

The government's aim was to bring China up to par with the Western world by the year 2000 in four different areas – agriculture, defence, technology, and industry.

Mammoth posters dwarfed the inhabitants of Canton, depicting the coming utopia and urging them to work towards it. I was reminded of Hollywood as I glanced at them. In the Ben Hur tradition of lettering, a seemingly three dimensional golden message almost lifted off the wall with the proclamation: "1985 to 2000". Apparently by that time grain and steel production were to reach their target. The gold lettering was built up like a tower, complete with red star on top, and stood against a backdrop of cascading fireworks.

Others depicted the goals for technology and defence. They displayed rockets after lift-off, nuclear submarines, supersonic jets, lofty antennae transmitting to satellites. The whole picture was like the setting for a "sci-fi" movie.

The people themselves were represented by a selection of workers from different sections of society – all gazing to a bright sky filled with technological wizardry. Underneath were Chinese characters which read, in translation, "Ardently struggle to make our country a modern great power within this century".

Most disturbing of all was an enormous poster dominated by the two giants of recent Chinese history. The solid, practical Chou en-Lai was set against a dream-like portrayal of twentieth-century life; replete with skyscrapers, jets zooming upwards, oil rigs, radio and television towers and the ubiquitous red flag. Chou was holding a scroll which apparently laid out the plan for the "Four Modernisations". Behind him stood an even larger figure, dressed entirely in white. It was an ethereal Mao, his face lit up by a shaft of light that seemed to be coming from heaven itself. In front of the two marched thousands of minescule Chinese figures, no bigger than Chou's fingernail. The tiny marchers were wearing brightly coloured clothes – in stark contrast to the dull blue "uniform" of the real live Chinese in the streets beneath. Letters on the poster described the "Four Modernisations" as the "grand behest" of the two leaders, who for the moment seemed established in their god-like status.

The opening of China became all the clearer to me. Obviously, to achieve these goals, the country would have to invite the Western nations to share their expertise and knowledge. No longer could the Great Wall shut the People's Republic off from the rest of the world. China would have to woo the West and win it – to reach its target.

But, I wondered, once its needs had been met, what then? Would the honeymoon be over, and the nation once again turn its back on the free world? Or worse, would it use that newfound progress against the other powers?

All at once it came home to me that we had not much time in which to work. The Lord had, in His wisdom, allowed China to embark upon its current programme, and the openness this brought was our ideal opportunity to bring spiritual food to the believers. We had to act, while we had time.

"Brother David, we don't have long now. It's time to get back," James' voice cut through my reflections and brought me down to earth with a jolt. "We must be on time to deliver our gifts."

He was right. We hurried off to organise the Bibles and, despite my high-flown contemplations, I broke out in a cold sweat of nervous anticipation.

Julie and I stayed behind when the others boarded their taxis to deliver their cargo to Mrs Kwang's contact.

Our part in the afternoon's work was to stay on our knees from the beginning to the end of the operation. In one sense, we longed to have gone out with the team, but we all knew that would have been folly. Even before setting out on the trip, we had accepted it would be impossible for Julie and me to assist physically at this point in the delivery.

227

The others would melt into their surroundings so easily, while we could jeopardise the whole venture with our unmistakable Western looks.

A few hours later, the team was back, beaming with delight as we gathered for thanksgiving prayer in our room. All seemed to speak at once in their eagerness to tell how well the afternoon had gone.

"Not a single hitch, Brother David," James concluded after the excitement had settled a little. "We set off for our destinations, and in no time at all had delivered all of the Bibles."

Apparently when they had greeted one old believer it had been impossible to converse because he spoke a different dialect. James had simply handed him his "consignment" – and then, in an effort to communicate, had reached out to give him a warm hug, "God loves you, my brother," James whispered in his dialect.

That night we went out for a Chinese banquet to celebrate. Spirits were high as we seized our chopsticks and tucked into fish, chicken, pork and rice, cooked a dozen different mouth-watering ways. Over lychees and Chinese tea we fell again into conversation, against the clatter of dishes and lively chatter.

"You know, David," James became serious for a moment. "This afternoon was so easy, almost too easy. I can hardly believe it." He raised his delicately patterned cup to take another sip of jasmine tea.

I smiled happily at his comment. But deep inside his observation recalled another occasion when those words had been spoken. Tokyo Airport. The time when we had missed out on our trip to China because of doubt. The incident was like a mirror to me now as I realised I too had been carrying doubts about the success of this venture until this moment. It was as though the Lord Himself had rebuked me. When He was putting something together he made it not only possible, but in a real sense so "easy".

If He had dealt with nine hundred Bibles this way, He

could have guided through twice that number – even triple. Why, oh why, hadn't I been able to trust Him with more?

* * *

Before the year was out, Joseph had one more trip to take to China – one which was to bring him unexpected answers to some of the questions from his trip four years earlier.

His first surprise came when he returned to see his relatives in Canton. On his last visit, when Joseph had spoken to them of the Lord, their reaction had been one of polite indifference. This time, they were far more interested, each set of parents gathering around to accept a Bible when he had finished his "sermon" of greeting.

One of the uncles even followed Joseph when he later left the room.

"Nephew," he said quietly, "I believe in God now. Listen: 'For God so loved the world that He gave His only begotten Son, that whosoever believes in Him should not perish but have everlasting life.'" He beamed proudly as he finished.

"How do you know that verse?" asked Joseph in surprise.

"Don't you remember?" replied his uncle. "When you left us after your last visit you wrote that down on a piece of paper for each of us."

Until that moment Joseph had forgotten the incident.

"You see Joseph, ever since that time, I have put it in my heart and prayed every day according to what you told me. And now, I have great joy in my soul. I am so grateful you told me about Jesus."

There was more to come. "Do you remember, how my two children were chronically ill when you were here before?"

Joseph did remember that. He had advised his uncle to pray for them.

"You told me, 'Jesus is alive and He can heal the child-

ren,' and so I tried it. One of my children had been sick
with asthma but the doctors could find no cure. The other
was also very ill and no medicine could help him either.
Even myself, Joseph, I had migraine which would never go
away. But after we'd prayed the Lord healed all three of
us."

His conclusion was joyfully simple. "I believe in Jesus.
Jesus is alive."

That incident, and many like it, left Joseph with a deep
conviction that overseas Chinese Christians proved ideal
evangelists in China. From that time on, Joseph was irrepressible. Whenever he met with Chinese believers in the
West, his challenge was always the same.

"Even if you cannot bring Bibles to China, you should
still go there. Why not? You'll be able to witness to your
relatives."

"But," he would add with his warm smile, "how much
better if you take in the Word of God too."

* * *

One man whom Joseph particularly wanted to see in
Fukien was Pastor Chai, the pastor who had so wanted help
in getting his daughter out of the country.

Joseph was very apologetic on their arrival. "I am sorry,
pastor," he began quickly. "We have tried to help with
your daughter, but have not had any success."

"Oh Joseph, you can stop trying," Pastor Chai assured
him, to his astonishment.

"Why?" Joseph remembered all too clearly how much
the father had longed to see his daughter outside China.

"She has decided to stay, Brother Joseph. You know we
have a great revival taking place in our town right now,
in fact in many towns in China. One day, after we had
seen many people converted, I took my daughter aside
privately to talk to her. By this time, we both had the
opportunity to leave the country.

"And so, I put the question to her: 'Daughter, you have

seen the revival which is going on in China, the many new believers that need pastoring. You know both of us have the chance to leave the country. My dear, if we go out it will be for your sake, I want you to have a good future and to know your father loves you. We can go for your sake. If we stay, this is for God's sake and for China's sake. Which do you like?'

"My daughter looked at me a moment and then said: 'Papa, we stay. I'll help you. We stay in China for the Church.'"

A lump came to Joseph's throat. He knew the struggle this must have meant for the father. But as the daughter entered the room, he saw such radiance on both their faces that it was obvious they had no regrets.

That night, the extent of the revival became very obvious. The pastor had immediately scheduled a meeting of the same congregation with whom Joseph had secretly worshipped before.

Or was it? Instead of the fifteen people he had met last time, there must now have been sixty or seventy present. The room was crammed to capacity.

Even so, the pastor later explained, this was a comparatively small meeting. "There have been so many conversions, specially among young people, but here in the city we have to keep the numbers small. Out in the rural areas where the Communist authorities do not have such tight control, hundreds attend meetings at a time."

Joseph found the same pattern throughout his trip. Christian leaders in each town recounted extraordinary growth in the numbers of believers during the recent four years.

It was estimated that the church had increased by an unbelievable four hundred per cent since 1949. And eighty per cent of the new believers were young people, below the age of thirty.

But with the enormous growth had come an equally great hunger for the Scriptures. "We must have Bibles, Joseph.

231

These new believers desperately need the Word of God to grow," he was told in each town.

The same words were expressed to him again and again – the only difference being the kind of Scriptures they preferred.

Many requested the Union version of the Bible; the traditional translation, akin to the Authorised Version of the West. Others preferred more modern translations for the needs of their region. The range available was increasing all the time. Their requests included, 'The Living Bible' in Chinese, the 'New China Bible' published by Asian Outreach, the Bible Society's 'Today's Chinese Version', and the New Chinese Bible Commission edition. It was the Union version, however, which we were asked for the vast majority of the time.

There was a difference, too, in the choice of script. The age-old written language of the country has consisted of thousands of complicated characters. Chairman Mao, however, instigated the establishment of a new script, with fewer and simpler characters for the people to learn. Since the new script is the one being taught in schools, many of the young people have difficulty reading Bibles printed in the old script.

Joseph took careful and detailed notes in each town. He recorded the number of Scriptures wanted, the version, the choice of script, and whether the whole Bible or just a portion was required. It had become a policy for Open Doors always to take to churches specifically what the church itself requested.

The believers' profound and consistent hunger for the Word of God stirred Joseph deeply. One believer he met, who was living in retirement and a poor man, even pushed money into Joseph's palm, insisting: "This is so that you can buy more Bibles for my people when you leave here."

"No," Joseph exclaimed. "There are people in the free world who can afford to give offerings. You keep this money."

His protests fell on deaf ears. Finally he reluctantly accepted the money, pocketed it, and then brought it out again with a gentle smile.

"Brother," he said, "I have recently been given some money. I would like to donate it to you to pass on to your brothers and sisters in prison. Will you take it?"

Joseph also told me of another Christian he had met with a strong burden to get Scriptures to his people.

"He was an old man," he explained, "who had just been released from prison when I arrived. His hand still bore a jagged scar from a shrapnel wound he received from the soldiers.

"But when he heard about the Bibles, he immediately wished to help. 'I want to distribute Scriptures for you,' he told me. 'I have many contacts in other provinces.'

"I could hardly believe him. Only days before he had been in jail for his faith. And yet he was prepared to risk another prison term. And for a second offence, his treatment would be worse than the first.

"But the old man would not give in. 'The price is not as high as the one my Lord paid for me,' he said.

"'Besides,' he added, 'my brethren are so hungry for the Word. I will take it to them, Joseph. The Lord will guide my steps.'"

The day after they met, Joseph collected two hundred Bibles which had previously been delivered to the city, and left them for the old man to deliver if he still wanted to go ahead with his plans.

Later we learned that every single copy had been transported hundreds of miles – each one placed by that scarred hand into the eager hands of believers in the north.

*   *   *

In keeping with the believers' hunger for Bibles, Joseph found their gratitude overwhelming. Often, to his embarrassment, they would insist on giving him something in return.

"But they could not afford it," he explained later. "Many

of them were on wages as low as forty RMB per month –
£13.00. I did my best to dissuade them." But he was always
unsuccessful.

One old lady of seventy-eight touched him particularly.
She brought him a large jar of the best honey in the area,
"as my offering to the Lord".

When I heard of that lady, I was reminded of the first
trip I had taken to China, via Romania. After I had delivered the Bibles to a pastor in Bucharest, he had also
brought me a gift of honey to convey his thanks.

The two incidents gave me new meaning for a verse
from Psalms which I had previously thought little about.
It was Psalm 19:10 – David's description of God's Words:

> *More to be desired are they than gold, even much
> fine gold; sweeter also than honey and drippings of
> the honeycomb.*

CHAPTER SIXTEEN
The Body Broken

The law of the People's Republic states unequivocally that
any person who has been imprisoned is forbidden to leave
the country – ever. Thus, when Miss Woo told us that the
Kwang family might be coming out of China, we were
amazed. We knew that only a miracle could bring them out.

Daniel showed us how to trust. "A long time ago, when
my mother was in prison, the Lord told her that the whole
family would one day leave China. They will come out. We
just have to pray and pray."

That was precisely what he did. Every morning when the
Wards awoke, it was to find that Daniel had already been
on his knees since at least four a.m. After some hours, the
slim quiet lad would emerge for breakfast and then excuse
himself and retire again to his room. There he would bow
before his Lord – not only for his family, but also for all the
believers in China, and the church in the West as well.
Visitors to Pastor Ward's home often noticed that, even
during the day and evening, Daniel would frequently leave
the room.

"What is he doing?" they would ask their host.

Pastor Ward's smiling reply was always the same. "Oh,
he's just gone off to pray."

I had spoken often with Brother Andrew about the need
for intercessory prayer in this ministry. "David," he had told
me, "we need to find people around the world who will become intercessors for the Suffering Church.'

In Daniel, I had seen what he meant. Just as I had seen
in Mrs Olsen in New York City long ago, and in Welshman
William Willis. In fact, before I had ever set out for Asia, old
Mr Willis had spoken to me about this kind of prayer in his
Southern Californian home.

"Son," he had said, "do you know what an intercessor is?"

I had to admit that I didn't.

He sat me down on the floral sofa. "In Ezekiel 22, where the Lord had decided to destroy the land, it says in verse thirty, 'And I sought for a man among them that should ... stand in the gap before me for the land, that I should not destroy it, but I found none.'

"That is what God is seeking for now – men to stand in the gap. Men who will intercede for others.

"Now David, I have a question for you."

"Yes, Mr Willis," I had felt like a young boy at the feet of his grandfather.

"Tell me lad, what does your prayer cost you?

"The Bible says that when Jesus was in Jerusalem, he wept over it. It also says in Hebrews that Jesus offered up his prayers 'with strong crying and tears'. Is that the way you are going to pray over your mission field?"

I looked away, feeling a flush rise to my cheeks. But Mr Willis fixed me with his eyes, and then spoke again, a resonant tone in his voice.

"I'm not going to let you go without one more verse, David." It came from Jeremiah 13 – "My soul shall weep in secret places."

Mr Willis concluded: "You mark my words, lad, an intercessor is a man who prays and weeps in the secret place of prayer until God stoops down and dries his tears."

The last ten years had taken me to that place many times on behalf of China – for the millions who needed to know Jesus. Now it was time to be there again, to join Daniel Kwang in intercessory prayer for the exit of his whole family from that country.

* * *

Before long, we saw God's answer to those prayers – as He showed once more how much greater He is than any

236

man-made system. When we later heard how He had prepared the way for the family to leave, we knew it was unquestionably a miracle.

Four weeks before they left the country the family had heard nothing about their visa applications, which had been filed some years earlier. However, one morning in prayer, Mrs Kwang sensed the Lord's voice telling her that they would leave the country in one month's time. She was to leave China in order to tell the world of the needs of the Chinese believers, and to tell the world to prepare for Jesus' return.

In the meantime, she was told to instruct her co-workers for the month remaining, so that they would be equipped to carry on after she had left.

She informed the other believers and they were astonished. "That's impossible!" they protested, "no one can leave the country after being imprisoned – and you have been inside three times."

But the evangelist was sure this had come from God. She spent the whole month in instruction, and on the final day commissioned each co-worker to continue the work.

The following day, a government official came to their home. "Come with me," he told the family. "You are to go to the police station. Your papers are waiting for your exit from the country."

While the Kwangs were filling out their forms, the local authorities suddenly realised that one parent had been in labour camp and the other in prison.

"Wait a minute! Stop right there. *You* have no right to leave the country," shouted a clerk behind the desk. "Those papers will be ripped up immediately."

Commotion broke out and, in the confusion that followed, the Kwangs were asked to withdraw. A Christian, who worked in the office, later told them that while they waited angry officials suggested they call the soldiers in immediately.

But God's hand was to be made unmistakably plain that

day. The senior officer on duty unexpectedly announced that he had been one of Mr Kwang's interrogators in labour camp. To the group's astonishment, he spoke up on his behalf.

"I called upon this man, time and again, to deny his faith," he told the men before him. "But he would not do so. Even in the face of death itself he still would not deny his God." He gazed across at the calm figure of Mr Kwang. "I have respect for this man," he concluded quietly.

Then, dispensing with the law of the land, he walked across to sign the family's papers.

On their way out of the country, the Kwangs had to face one more obstacle. They were travelling by bus towards the border, but the route required them to make a ferry crossing. On the particular day of their trip, as they came towards the water, they saw an impenetrable fog – so dense that the ferries could no longer pass through it. The family prayed that the atmosphere would clear to enable them to cross.

As the bus reached the pier, the fog indeed began to lift. The ferry started its engine and the bus drove on board. After they had reached the other side, the passengers looked back. The fog had returned. They later learned that no more buses passed that day.

*   *   *

An urgent phone call at the office was my first indication that the family were on their way to Hong Kong. I had in fact just returned from the colony, having ordered thirty thousand New Testaments from Hong Kong's Bible Society that weekend. Eugene, an executive from our Californian base, was in town and the two of us quickly packed our bags to catch the next flight to Kai Tak Airport.

When the plane landed we took the first taxi we could find to the home of Grandmother Kwang, where by now the family would have arrived. As we stepped inside, I recognised all the family immediately because I had been carrying a picture of them in my Bible for eighteen months. It is not normal for Chinese people to reach out to Westerners, especially a Chinese woman to a man. But at that moment tradition was put aside as they offered us their open arms, and tears of joy and gratitude to the Lord were on every face.

When at last I was able to speak, my first question concerned the "family" who had been left behind in China. As they began their reply the Kwangs motioned us to take a seat. We crowded around them in the little room, with Eugene sitting on the edge of a bunk bed and me precariously balanced on a small wooden stool.

Our interpreter that night was Ruth, a gentle European friend of the family who spoke fluent Mandarin. As the tale unfolded she translated stories about the Lord's family inside – particularly about the Old Man. "He sends you his greetings in our one Lord, Brother David," the mother said.

"As do all the 'family' there," the father added with a beam.

It was not long before all of us had bowed our heads in exuberant prayer. When we came to a close, we were treated to a beautiful Chinese meal cooked on a tiny stove in the corner of the room. I had eaten sumptuous Chinese food in many different places, but none could compare with the beef, vegetables, noodles and rice that we shared that night. As we ate, Mrs Kwang spoke of the nine hundred Scriptures that had been delivered earlier, and the other hundred that had followed.

"When we heard that the nine hundred had come through, we held a meeting of praise and thanksgiving to the Lord. The tears were running down our cheeks," she said through Ruth.

"To us it was like the time when the children of Israel crossed the Jordan. The Lord miraculously opened the way for His purpose to be fulfilled."

A look of shared joy spread from face to face throughout the family as they realised what she was talking about. In the flow of Chinese voices that followed, I recognised just one phrase which I had heard Daniel use before: "Tsan mei Chu" – "Praise the Lord".

"And what are their current needs?" I asked. "How many Bibles do the believers require now?"

As Ruth quietly translated their reply, she had no idea of the effect it would have on me.

"She says they need thirty thousand Scriptures – immediately, Brother David ..."

It took me a minute to catch my breath. I had just ordered that precise number of Scriptures, three days before, without an inkling even that the Kwangs would be coming out, let alone requesting such a delivery.

Thirty thousand was an enormous load to consider taking to China at one time – even one thousand had been overwhelming. But with such evidence of the Lord's authorisation, there could be no doubt that this was the next step for Open Door Asia.

"This has to be of the Lord," I said, when I finally found my tongue and explained what had been happening.

Mrs Kwang lit up with delight as Ruth interpreted. "Now," I added, "all we have to work out is His way of getting them there."

We talked for some time about plans and strategy for "Project Jordan" as it later came to be called among the staff – based on the family's comments about the children of Israel crossing the Jordan. For security's sake, we also gave it a public name for Christians in the Western world. That name was Project Rainbow.

Later in the evening, we again discussed numbers with both father and mother. "Tell me, honestly," I said, "will thirty thousand be enough?"

"No," Mrs Kwang replied, "not really."

Mr Kwang spoke up. "To be frank, Brother David, the thirty thousand would satisfy our immediate needs, but in fact, our overall need is for one million."

Eugene looked at me, startled, and I knew what he was thinking. If one family could ask for a delivery of this size to meet the needs they knew of, how many more Bibles must be required by the many other groups throughout the country?

It was becoming ever clearer to us why the Lord had given the vision for ten million Scriptures for China.

* * *

In response to the Kwang's request we began to set up research probes. We also continued to send teams to other parts of the country where deliveries were needed. Eugene and I set off on the first of several trips together.

One visit required us to touch down at an airport in the southern part of China, and there we were immediately assigned an official guide. His name was Chang Lo, and he was instructed to accompany us for the few hours of our stopover.

All our luggage was left at the airport except for the briefcases and cameras, and we set off for a mountain park in a car booked in advance by Chang Lo.

The park gives a magnificent view of the surrounding area, and as soon as the car came to a halt, I strode off to snap some photographs.

While I was gone, Eugene and the guide sat on a bench to admire the scene. Eugene later told me he felt the Lord prodding him to witness to the young man as they sat together. Yet he wanted to resist the urge because he knew this was not our priority. If the Communist reported such a conversation, it would endanger our real mission. It is our policy that evangelism is the responsibility of the Chinese themselves, and our role is to support them through prayer and the supply of God's Word. Rules however can be overruled by the Lord Himself. Eugene could not get away from the prompting of the Lord that morning.

241

"Father, help me to do the right thing," he silently prayed. "I'm not going to speak unless you make it plain to me that this is Your will."

They talked in English, and Eugene soon discovered his companion was a university student. Chang Lo's parents were cadres, both holding official positions within the community. As he described his family's work, entertainment, and school activities, Eugene came to sense the colourlessness of their lifestyle. In turn, Eugene told his friend about his family in America.

After several minutes of small talk, he asked Chang Lo about churches in China. The question seemed strange to his guide. He knew of no church in his area that was open. The Cultural Revolution had closed all churches and, he reasoned, there could be no need for them now, since there were now no more Christians.

"Have you ever heard of a book called the Bible?" Eugene asked cautiously.

"Yes, but I have never read one," Chang Lo replied. He was twenty-one years old.

"What would you do if you saw one?" Eugene continued.

There was no hesitation in his companion's reply. "Oh, I would buy it," he said.

"Why?"

"Because I like to read many books."

Chang Lo began to inquire about young people in the United States, even asking whether young Americans attended church. Then he recounted an incident concerning his English teacher from Great Britain. This man had told the class about a day when he had lost his house key, and how after he had prayed, God had helped him find it. Eugene smiled, knowing how closely this paralleled the story in my own life.

"Do you believe my teacher's story?" Chang Lo asked.

That was the opening Eugene had been praying for. He thought about the biblical principle of sowing, watering and reaping.

242

"Yes, I do believe the story. That is just the way God works. Would you like to hear more about God?" With a wide smile, Chang Lo nodded his head affirmatively. But where could one start with someone who knew nothing about the Bible, God, Jesus, or salvation?

Eugene began at the beginning. He talked about creation, God's love, His Son Jesus, and the plan of salvation. These were all new words to Chang and he was asking for definitions. Suddenly, Eugene remembered that when they first sat down together, he had given his guide an English/Chinese dictionary as a souvenir.

For two hours they looked up relevant words in the dictionary together. As they discussed their meaning, Eugene used them to explain the Gospel. The guide listened with rapt attention, eagerly hanging on every word. He fired many questions in his obvious hunger to know the truth.

Finally, Eugene asked quietly: "Chang Lo, can *you* believe?"

The young man's eyes were steady as they held Eugene's. "Yes." he said with conviction. "I can believe – just the way you told me."

Eugene longed to give him a Bible, but all our Scriptures were packed in the luggage at the airport. Looking up, he saw me walking back in their direction.

"David," he called, "do you have any 'apples' with you?"

"Just one," I replied. "My own."

"Would you like to give it to a new brother in Christ? He's very hungry," Eugene grinned.

"Sure, I'd love to."

When we said good-bye at the airport, we told Chang Lo of the many brothers and sisters in Christ who would be praying for him. With a firm handshake and a smile, he walked away. But suddenly he turned and, half-running, came back. Placing his hands on Eugene's shoulders he added: "God bless you."

On the plane, Eugene sat beside me, wistful. "I may

never see that lad again," he began. He turned his head to take in the sight as the aircraft broke through the clouds into glorious sunshine. "Correction," he added with a smile, "one day we will meet in heaven."

*   *   *

A few months later, another journey took Eugene and me straight to Peking. We had already supplied believers there with three hundred cassette tapes of the spoken New Testament, and Gospel music.

On this trip too we brought tapes, four tape recorders they had requested, along with one hundred New Testaments. In addition, we brought several transformers so that the tape recorders could be worked on the local voltage. That trip ran particularly smoothly. Everything went straight through customs. Nothing was touched. No questions asked. We were through with a greeting of welcome.

It was Holy Week when we arrived in the city, still carrying our "gifts". Before they could be delivered, we had arranged to meet with John, our new Peking contact. He had sent us a number of reports since we had met him the year before.

After our first meeting, we had delivered to him a continuing stream of Bibles. His accommodation was a far from private dormitory shared with others, and his only place for storage was the floor under his bed.

"But I have had no fear of being found out," he told us. "I know the prayer Brother Andrew uses as he takes Bibles into Communist countries. 'Lord, make seeing eyes blind ...'

"I have asked the Lord to do the same for the books under my bed," he explained. "And a real peace has grown upon me as the weeks and months have passed. I have had absolute confidence that the Lord would keep my hidden material secure."

"And has anything been found?"
John smiled. "No. Nothing."

*　　*　　*

After some months, John had met his first contact from the secret church. For him that meeting ushered in months of blessing and caring fellowship. Like the Old Testament account of the widow with the cruse of oil, the Lord never allowed him to run out of Bibles. Whenever they were needed, John had sufficient to supply.

John had also learnt more about the Suffering Church in Peking, and in other parts of China – since many had come from all over the country to work in its capital, bringing with them news of Christians in their respective home towns.

His report revealed another aspect of the broken Body of Christ in China. As he talked, we began to understand the full extent of the hurts which had been inflicted on that Body, and the traumatic effect these wounds had left on many of the believers.

"Many have now reached the point where they no longer feel able to attend worship meetings," he told us. "They know that if they congregate in groups larger than two or three people they run the risk of being charged as 'subversives'.

"Some are frightened even to visit other Christians – if those believers have been bold in expressing their faith. They are worried that the black mark placed against their brethren will brand them as well."

John had spoken to one believer who lived down the hall from an old Christian lady well known for her courageous stand for Christ.

"Do you have fellowship with her?" John asked.

"Oh no, we don't dare," replied the Christian. "She is very carefully watched. Her husband has been in jail for many years, and although he came out for a short time, he would not stop witnessing. Now he's gone back in again."

"How does she live?" John asked.

"Actually, her health is not too good. We think her life is probably very hard."

"Nobody looks after her?"

The believer shrugged his shoulders with embarrassment. "She seems to manage on her own. She's very strong and she trusts the Lord."

There was an awkward silence. "Sometimes if no one's looking, we try to say a word of encouragement."

John persisted. "Will you try to have more fellowship with her? I would particularly like you to pass on this small New Testament."

The Christian looked at the floor. "Well, perhaps ... now that things are a little easier ..."

His eyes sought John's. "But please pray for us. Oh, please pray."

*   *   *

"During times of extreme persecution," John explained, "some believers reneged on their faith and were coerced into exposing their fellow believers.

"The betrayal might take the form of participation in 'struggle and criticism' meetings, or of giving assistance to the government in drawing up charges of 'counter-revolutionary' political crimes against the Christians. Other believers cooperated with the government without meaning to. They were just too naive to realise the implications of their actions."

His expression hardened a little. "Of course there were also those who had been impostors all along. These people just pretended to be Christians from the start and were planted in the churches by the Communists. They have caused great damage. Their method is to draw unsuspecting believers into positions where charges of illegal activity can be laid against them.

246

"I'll never forget the words of one believer who shared his pain with me. 'Persecution and physical suffering are terrible,' he told me 'but to be betrayed by other members of the Body of Christ is the most bitter blow of all.'"

Of course, this pattern was repeated throughout the country, but the wounds were taking longer to heal in Peking, where the intensity of government restriction had eased only slightly during the post-Mao era.

* * *

Some of John's accounts of suffering etched a permanent impression on our minds. One woman had already lost half of her family to prison and to death when she was assigned to a labour gang. Her duties were to break up rocks and build roads. Day after day, the toil drained her strength until eventually there was nothing left for her but bitterness and pain.

Finally there came a morning when she believed she had reached the end. The pressures were crushing her and the believer felt she could not go another step. She wondered if the Lord would require her life of her. At that moment, she turned her head wearily and standing beside her saw an old woman she had never met before. The woman asked a simple question, "Do you still believe?"

The believer nodded, almost unable to form the words. "I – I still believe."

"A bruised reed he shall not break and a smoking flax he shall not quench," the old woman quoted from Isaiah 42. Then she turned away and walked out of sight.

With these words, the believer's heart began to lighten. She felt the strength of the Lord flowing into her being. It was as if the Lord had given her a sign that He would not allow her to be broken completely through her persecution.

That night, she made diligent inquiries as to who the old woman was, but no one seemed to know. She had come and

247

as mysteriously disappeared ... But the believer had received a touch from the Lord.

* * *

Another believer suffered unforgettable humiliation at the hands of the Red Guards during the Cultural Revolution. The man had been dragged from his house and the guards had hung a placard around his neck which read: "—— is a bastard". The Red Guards incited others to gather round and taunt him. The man was agonised and shamed beyond bearing. He pleaded with the Lord to deliver him. "Why am I suffering like this, Lord? Please release me from it. I cannot bear much more."

At that moment, one of the guards began to jeer at him, shouting: "Hey! This man is not suffering nearly enough. I have a better idea. Why don't we take that card off and replace it with another one that says: 'Jesus Christ is a bastard?'"

The Red Guards laughed as they carried out his plan, and the believer felt his heart would break. "To suffer for you Lord, is terrible, but this, this ..." As he wept for the humiliation cast on the Lord's name, and as the hatred around him grew, unaccountably he sensed his spirit begin to lift. He felt the presence of the Lord in his heart and it was as if Christ, indeed, had come to bear the mockery and pain in his place. And then he understood: Christ *has* borne our sin and shame on the cross, Christ has taken away our pain and death.

* * *

John concluded his report with a picture of the "aboveground" Christians meeting in China. The registered church in Peking had just started to undergo major changes. The Three-Self Patriotic Movement, which had been obscured during the stormy years of 1966–76, had been revived

early in 1979. And the Peking Three-Self Church on Dong
Dan Street had begun to show evidence of the change in
atmosphere.

Numbers had started to increase from that February
when about forty people were attending the service regularly. Sermons had been introduced along with more fervent
prayer. Foreigners still made up a significant proportion of
the congregation, but now more Chinese were beginning to
attend.

The world was witnessing the advent of China's new
"openness" on religious matters.

After our meeting, John and a Chinese Filipino who had
come with us transferred the "gifts" we had brought to their
destination. When the delivery was completed, they were
given a dozen hot freshly-boiled eggs still in their shells.
Knowing what this gift must have cost, the pair protested
that they could not accept it, but the believers insisted.

"Please tell our two brothers that we are praying for them
and are so grateful for the love they have extended to us.
We, the church in Peking, cannot allow our brethren from
the West to go empty-handed."

The following morning was Easter Sunday. Eugene, our
Chinese friend, and I met John soon after sunrise. Together
we travelled the thirty miles north to visit the Ming Tombs
– where thirteen majestic "shrines" stand, their curved roofs
golden in the sun, and their walls a deep red. The cloudless
sky was rich azure, with just a whisper of wind through the
pines and juniper trees around us.

The four of us gathered in a secluded spot to spend time
in remembrance of the "broken Body of Christ" in China.
The Lord's presence was very real to us as we worshipped
together during that communion service.

We sat among the ancient tombs, housing history's dead
emperors, and my thoughts turned to a similar setting
among the pyramids of ancient Egypt. Each one was a
monumental demonstration of its ruler's quest – man's quest
for eternity. Beside the shrines we bowed our heads to the

249

Living Christ whose resurrection from the dead was being celebrated all over the world that morning. The One who said: "He that believeth in *Me* shall live for ever."

We took the eggs as the bread, and "broke and ate them". For the wine, we took the people's drink in China, their Pearl River Orange. And together, the four of us remembered the words of the Lord when He commanded, "As often as you do this, do it in remembrance of Me."

CHAPTER SEVENTEEN
The Lion and the Lamb

"Brother David, Project Rainbow is in danger!" Joseph was talking breathlessly on the line from Hong Kong. "There's no way we can get thirty thousand 'apples' delivered under current 'weather conditions'. There's been an unexpected change in the winds."

"What did you say?" I sank into the chair at my desk as I tried to take in his message.

"We can't go ahead as planned, Brother David. It's too difficult. Perhaps we could take on a smaller project instead – one which we carry out slowly, in small deliveries ..."

I knew there was no way Joseph could describe the "change in the weather" over the phone. "Hold everything," I told him. "I'll be over to see you on the first available plane."

Project Rainbow was already well underway at the time of his call. Throughout the world we had alerted our supporters to pray for "Rainbow". We didn't tell them what the project was, we just asked them to bring it daily before the Lord.

In the United States alone, we had sent out ninety thousand prayer letters and we knew that in Australia and New Zealand ten thousand people were interceding for us.

In Japan too we had many people praying since the church there had recently become deeply committed to the needs of the Suffering Body. I was touched by the extent of their commitment; remembering too vividly the beach games I had played as a boy – childish in every sense of the word. These dedicated Christians in Japan were unconsciously a rebuke to me – in the love and care they displayed towards not only the Suffering Church of China, but to me

251

as well. They were standing with us in Project Rainbow.

Even beyond our immediate region, there were thousands more prayer partners in Great Britain, the Netherlands, Africa and Latin America.

We had received one particularly moving letter from a lady in America who had been awoken in the middle of the night and told by the Lord to pray for something called "Rainbow". She had been obedient though at that time she did not have any idea what it was.

In addition to those outside China, there were many on the inside who had also been praying and working towards Project Rainbow. They had prepared a comprehensive line of delivery to transport the Scriptures once they arrived in the country. They had also planned where the deliveries would go, and many of those awaiting them were pastors or lay-preachers with a "flock" to feed.

Everything, it seemed, had come together so clearly. How could the Lord be stopping us now?

When I arrived in Hong Kong, Joseph and his assistant, Mark Tao, poured out the reason for their worry. A courier recently travelling with a load of Bibles into China had found it impossible to deliver his cargo to its destination. He had been painfully conscious of the ever watchful eye of Communism, always on the alert in that country. In the end, still oppressed by the tension of the regime, he had returned across the border with his Bibles intact.

"They have tightened the security inside," Mark declared. "We cannot possibly take in thirty thousand."

"Perhaps we could think again, Brother David," said Joseph. "If we take in a proportion, maybe half of that number, we can do it in smaller amounts – it will be less noticeable. Then gradually, in time to come, we can send in more."

"But thirty thousand is the number God gave us," I replied. We had felt positive that this was to be our next delivery ever since the Kwangs' exit from China. It was the express request of the family to meet an urgent need. And it matched precisely the number I had ordered immediately prior to their arrival.

In my heart I felt certain we should go ahead. If Satan wanted to try and bluff us, we had to stand against him.

"I believe we should proceed as we intended," I said at last. "But why don't we put a fleece before the Lord? I will ask Julie and the children if they would be prepared to go on a delivery mission."

The pair looked up with interest as I went on.

"If they will go, and the Lord allows *them* to have a safe delivery even at this time, we will take that as His authorisation for Rainbow to go ahead."

"Won't they need a Chinese team-member?" Joseph asked. "Where will they find one?"

"We'll let that be the final confirmation from the Lord," I said. "We will trust Him to provide one for us." I grinned. "I believe He will."

One week later Julie arrived in Hong Kong accompanied by Dawn and David. Although their tickets to China were booked, they as yet had no Chinese team-mate – and it was only twenty-four hours till their departure. They knew that if the Lord did not provide one their trip would be off. And likewise, according to our fleece, Project Rainbow would have to be abandoned, and a much smaller delivery undertaken.

Late that afternoon, Mark was walking down Kowloon's Nathan Road, when suddenly an old friend called to him. "Mark, I was going to call you today. How are you?" Mark chatted with his Chinese friend for several minutes until, finally, the man mentioned the reason for his planned call.

"I have to go into Canton tomorrow. I thought I'd let you know in case there is anything you needed to be done in there ..."

The following morning the team, complete with its Chinese member, entered the People's Republic for the delivery. As if to prove to us that He was in control, the

Lord did not even use Julie for the Bible "drops". Although she was the experienced senior member of the team, at the moment it happened she had been called upon by another Westerner for help with an urgent personal problem. So it was the kids who carried out the transfer with their new Chinese friend.

Afterwards young David was asked how he had felt about the delivery. Would he do it again? "Of course," David said confidently, "the Lord made it real *easy*."

There was that word again, "easy". And it was related, as in all the previous instances, to ventures where God had shown Himself so fully in control that everything had fitted together perfectly.

Satan had been bluffing once again. Project Rainbow *was* to go ahead as planned.

* * *

The funds had all come in, the Bibles were paid for, and the couriers who were to take them were undergoing preparation. It only remained for the last-minute arrangements inside China to be finalised. This task fell to Joseph and Mark who set off for a month's journey to complete the master plan for Rainbow. Concurrently they took the opportunity to check out the needs of the believers in other parts of China. It was a two-fold expedition.

As the pair travelled in the southern and coastal regions of the country, the first thing which struck them was the overwhelming evidence of China's ever-widening revival. In the cities, where the control of the authorities is greater, they found meetings of anything up to a hundred people. Out in the countryside, however, the meetings were often attended by several hundred, a thousand, or even two thousand at a time.

"These areas are much harder for the authorities to police," Joseph told me later. "Besides, since South China and the coastline are so much in the eye of the tourist, the authorities cannot afford to take such a hard line with the Christians, or the West will hear about it."

Elsewhere, however, it was a different story, despite China's overall softening on religious affairs. In northern and inland China, the authorities could take whatever measures they liked, with little chance that news of it would travel to the West. We knew of Christians in several provinces who were still in labour camps, and of tight restrictions placed upon any Christian activity in the cities.

Joseph and Mark were not surprised, therefore, to find small meetings in the urban north. In Peking itself, it seemed impossible for groups to meet in numbers larger than six at a time. On average the numbers were somewhere between three and ten in the towns on the boys' itinerary.

It was in the rural areas that they met their surprise.

"Can you believe it, Brother David," Joseph continued, "they also have meetings of up to a thousand people! In fact, in one province we know of, there are one million Christians."

"Are you serious?" After all I had heard about these regions, it seemed impossible.

"Absolutely," he replied. "And these Christians, Brother David, have made a profound impact on their province. Do you know that they are so conscientious in their daily work that their output has exceeded the quotas – and many Communist officials have become Christians through their witness."

Joseph broke into a chuckle. "So now, if they want to, they can sing in their home services at the top of their voices. All one thousand of them if they like. No one minds a bit."

"And," he finished, "one time when they held an evangelistic meeting, they borrowed the P.A. system from the Communist officials!" He laughed as he saw the astonishment on my face.

"Praise the Lord, Brother David. This revival is His doing."

255

It was just as the believers had predicted and prayed about for so many years. Thousands, even millions in all parts of the country were becoming dissatisfied with the emptiness in the "religion" of the State, and turning to Jesus. Brother Andrew had anticipated it too, and Joseph's extraordinary news recalled for me an allegory the Dutchman had once recounted about a lion and a lamb.

"Tell me, David," he had asked, "if I let a lion loose in my back garden with a lamb, what will happen?"

"I'd give the lamb five seconds," I had replied.

"Ahah. But suppose I separate them first. Then starve the lion while I feed up the little lamb and wait until the lion is too weak to raise his head. If at that time I let them loose again in the garden, what would happen?"

"Not much, I guess."

"You're wrong, brother. The lamb would be the victor. If he wanted to, he could even step on the lion and proudly proclaim himself the conqueror.

"You see, David, the lion is the State, and the lamb is the Suffering Church of Jesus Christ. If we feed it, it will become strong. And the emptiness of atheism will, in due course, come to an end – as the people discover the vacuum of moral virtue and spiritual value in the system of the State. And so the lamb will conquer."

I turned to Andrew with a smile. "Now I understand," I said. "So *that's* why Jesus said, 'Feed my lambs ...'"

* * *

Throughout their trip, Joseph and Mark had been carrying a number of New Testaments which they had progressively given away until, by the time they reached Nanking, only a few remained. They had also been carrying a very large Bible complete with concordance and references, suitable for a pastor. In all their travelling, Joseph had not yet felt led of God to give this one away.

The address of a Christian woman in the city had been

given to them earlier, and the two decided they would call on her. To their surprise, she was not there when they came. Instead, they were greeted by two young men whose poverty was evident by the worn condition of their clothes. Yet in their faces, Mark and Joseph could see a radiance and love which struck them immediately. One in particular whenever he spoke seemed to have an aura of gentle authority.

The four talked about their reasons for being there, and the young men explained the Lord had brought them five hundred kilometres to the city.

"We believe the Lord has a Bible waiting for us somewhere here," one of them said. "We know that the lady of this house sometimes has a supply of them. She's in Shanghai trying to get some now. We are waiting for her return."

"How did you get here?" Mark asked.

"We came by two trains – it's been several days since we set out."

"Where did you sleep along the way?" Joseph by now felt fairly sure these men were genuine Christians, but he wanted to keep the conversation going a little longer until he was positive.

The younger of the two replied: "We come from a very poor province. After our travelling expenses, it was not possible for us to stay in hotels. We just slept on public benches or on open ground."

Joseph and Mark looked at the pair with deep concern, and a conviction that they were telling the truth.

"Brothers," Joseph began, "we have two New Testaments, we could give you." He moved towards his briefcase and the two men followed him immediately. He gingerly opened it to extract the Scriptures. He didn't want to lift the lid very high in case the men saw the large Bible – which, in his mind, was still reserved for a pastor.

But as he tried to shut the case, the believers in their enthusiasm grabbed the lid – wanting to see inside for themselves. Joseph tried again to close it without success.

The men opened it fully and caught a glimpse of the large Bible before Joseph could hastily get the lid down.

"Please may we have that one," they begged. "Please ..."

Joseph slowly withdrew the large Bible and looked up at them. "I will be frank with you. All along I had planned that this book should go to a pastor. It is a preacher's Bible."

The two men nodded with understanding.

Joseph continued: "Will you make me a promise? When you return will you hand this to your pastor so that it can be used most fully."

They smiled in agreement.

During the hours of discussion that followed, however, it slowly became evident that one of these two himself held meetings in his home town. His aura of spiritual authority continued to command respect from Joseph and Mark, yet with it came a humility which had made the man hold back from revealing the fact of his house meetings earlier in their discussions.

Nor would he willingly have parted with the next piece of information had Joseph not quizzed him thoroughly.

"How many come to your worship meetings?"

The believer's reply was quiet.

"Usually there are eight hundred."

"And who leads them?"

"I do."

Joseph looked at his brother in Christ with new understanding. "Then you are the one! It is you for whom this Bible has been intended all along. Keep it, brother, and may the Lord magnify your ministry as you preach from His Word."

The group bowed for a time of thanksgiving and praise; each one feeling overawed with the way God had been so obviously authorising the events of that day.

When they resumed their discussion, Mark asked the young pastor how he had been managing to preach to his congregation without using a Bible.

258

"Once a week, I have been cycling to the home of a preacher in a nearby village. His was the closest Bible to our area. I have been borrowing it for the time of our meeting, so I could use it for preaching. Then after the meeting, I cycle back to return it."

Deeply challenged by the young pair's commitment, Mark and Joseph spent the remaining hour discussing their needs for Scriptures among the fellowship group. They parted with the agreement that we would get several hundred Bibles to them as soon as we could set up a delivery system.

When Mark and Joseph got back to report to me, they were more convinced than ever that we were walking in God's will and that the thirty thousand had to go ahead. The necessary delivery lines had been confirmed during their trip, and the enormous needs of the country had been reinforced for them a hundred-fold.

The stage was set, all was ready. We had only to wait for the countdown to Project Rainbow.

CHAPTER EIGHTEEN
The Smile on the Face of the Tiger

Several thousand Scriptures went through. Then two of the delivery loads were discovered at customs.

The officials who found them were not at first able to identify the Bibles, never having seen one before. It was with great pride therefore that a more senior one pronounced his recognition of the Scriptures. "These are Bibles," he said importantly. "Bibles! You spell that B-Y-B-L-E-S."

The men were told to leave their Scriptures at the customs hall for collection on their departure from China. A few days later they brought their cargo back to Hong Kong where it was re-packed into other suitcases and taken straight back into the country.

However the discovery at customs brought immediate repercussions for those inside. Joseph had been awaiting the team's delivery and, as soon as he learned that some Scriptures had been found, he informed his link-man among the believers. The mutual decision was to pray. No one knew what to do next.

That night as he lay sleeping, Joseph had a dream in which he saw our Bible storeroom in Hong Kong. The place was completely empty. Every Scripture had been removed from the shelves.

Next morning, he met again with one of the believers. "Joseph – what do you think?" the man said nervously. "Does the Lord mean us to stop? We feel very scared ..."

"Me too," said Joseph. "And we can certainly shut the delivery down, if you believe we should." The Christians in China knew that they only had to give the word, and the flow of Bibles would cease.

Both became silent, wondering what was the right course

of action. Then Joseph remembered his dream.

"Brother, let me share something with you." He told the believer what he had seen the night before, and as he did, his friend's face relaxed visibly.

"To me, Joseph, I would say God is encouraging us. If that warehouse were empty, there is only one place the Bibles could have gone – here.

"I believe that is the answer to our prayer."

Ever cautious, Joseph urged him not to make any quick decisions. But by the close of their time together, both were sure. The Lord was saying, "Go".

The rest of the delivery continued unimpeded. After several days, two and a half tons of Scriptures had been carried by hand through the Chinese border, including those discovered and halted on their first attempt.

The final crossing, the one which emptied Joseph's "room", involved Eugene, Shan, Mason, an American, two overseas Chinese and myself. It was no easy task carrying the load of Scriptures across the border – particularly as some of our team members were women. The task was not made any lighter by the fact that Shan had broken his arm a few days earlier. It had been set in plaster and was supported by a sling.

Yet I came to give thanks for both, for during the customs check we nearly found ourselves in trouble. Eugene was the one an official chose for close questioning, holding his visa in one hand, while asking him to open his bags.

"Excuse me, I wonder if you could help me?" Shan asked the official. "I hurt my arm just recently and it is still giving me a lot of pain. I will need to sit down very soon. Can you show me where to find a seat?"

With that the customs man lost interest in Eugene. He handed back his papers and waved him on his way.

The rest of the Bibles went straight through without a hitch. Mason and I assisted the women with their bags and, in each instance, the guards chatted only briefly with us before sending us past. Their attention, once again, "happened" to be diverted elsewhere.

We knew that the ease with which this was happening had nothing to do with us, or our own cleverness. We were seeing God at work, once again making seeing eyes "blind". There was almost a timelessness about that moment, as though we were all part of something much bigger and greater than ourselves. Again the Psalmist's words echoed in my ears: "I cry to God ... who fulfills his purpose for me."

Nonetheless, as the suitcases were being loaded onto the trolley at the other end of customs, ready for delivery to our hotel, all at once my heart quailed within me. The enormity of the operation, from a human viewpoint, suddenly came home; that so many Scriptures should pass through at one time, without a single detection. We had never attempted anything this size before.

Almost without realising it, I found myself confessing: "Lord, I never want to go through this again. Never!"

Next minute I realised what I had said, and shamefacedly asked His forgiveness. "I'm sorry, Father. If You really want me to, I will do it, Lord. But it will have to be in Your strength alone ..."

* * *

By the time we got to the hotel, I was slapping Shan on the back. "Do you realise," I said delightedly, "the Lord even had a purpose in your broken arm? He brings every little detail together to achieve his purposes. Praise God!"

"Amen to that," Shan responded. "All things *do* work together for good ..."

By now he was sitting down and nursing his painful arm. He glanced up at me with a look of mischief on his face.

"But next time, David, if we need a limb broken – we'll make it yours, all right?"

* * *

Now that we had brought the Bibles into the country, we were to wait while they were distributed to the Chinese Christians themselves. The seriousness of the situation threatened, at times, to overwhelm us all as the thousands of Bibles continued to find their way into the hands of those who had requested them.

The believers involved in the line of delivery needed great sensitivity to the Spirit's leading every time they ventured from one home to another with a Bible. Our role was to support them on our knees, praying that no mistake would happen with any one copy of the Scriptures.

At last we received the message we had been waiting for. All the "apples" had been taken safely to their destination without a single loss.

The delivery of that news came in a form which took us completely by surprise. We received a knock on our hotel door, and opened it to find a delegation of Chinese standing outside.

It took only a moment to realise who these simply-dressed people were. Although we had never been introduced, one look at their shining faces and broad grins told me they had to be believers. One of them carried some dried figs, another held hand-embroidered table cloths, and a third had brought a sheaf of Christmas cards.

I welcomed them into our room pinching myself at the same time to make sure this was really happening. With security risks so great, none of the Christians had ever dared visit a team of Westerners before. The government authorities had eyes and ears in every hotel. Their people were posted on each floor. If they had realised who our visitors were, and why they had come, their situation could have been very serious indeed.

The little group sat down to share with us their joy at the arrival of the Bibles, and insisted we accept their gifts. "The church wants to thank you. We are here to let you know what you and your team mean to us." They passed around the dried figs and we ate them together as we sipped traditional green tea.

The believers remained with us two hours, telling of the situation for their brethren. Despite the pressures and difficulties they face, these believers, like the Kwang family, could only speak of the goodness of their Lord. Finally we linked hands in a circle and bowed to worship Him together. I wanted to weep as we prayed, East and West joined as one.

At last we rose and the believers came to each one in the team, hugging all of us in turn.

As I said good-bye, I couldn't help adding: "I'm still amazed that you've come out so boldly to see us."

The leader of the group replied with a shake of his head. "It was nothing. Our mighty God walked before us, as we came here." He chuckled for a moment. "It's not only the customs officials whose eyes He can 'blind'. We were not followed. Praise the Lord, Brother David."

* * *

Knowing that the Bibles were now safely at their destinations, we spent our remaining time in China fulfilling the role expected of a tourist. As we did so, we saw yet another in the series of ever-changing faces of the country.

The posters, as usual, heralded the change. Although we saw occasional signs urging the people towards the Four Modernisations, we saw many more promoting local products. Watches, colour televisions, sewing machines, and fans were advertised in place of the political posters. One advertisement even promised its readers "Recovery of youth" if they would only buy the tablets on display. And it was with an oddly familiar feeling that we looked up to see Western cigarettes being promoted in the centre of the city.

One evening I took the opportunity to walk down the same streets I had trodden so long before with James Wee. The ageless quality could still be felt as I wandered through back alleys. There was, however, an all-important newcomer – the television. Every second or third house had a set, displayed in place of honour in the living room. Close by, it was common to find a modern electric fan whirring proudly. And, in the second room of the little homes, I heard distinctly Western music coming from many brand new cassette recorders. These three items were obviously the longed-for possessions of every householder.

How could the people afford such purchases? I wondered. Some would have been brought in from outside the country by relatives, but others would also have been bought by the Chinese themselves. What with?

I received my answer during tours which we took in our remaining days in the country. The government had introduced a system of monetary incentives in order to get maximum work efficiency from the people. Communes competed with each other for the greatest productivity. Within each commune, the workers who laboured the longest hours and achieved the most, earned more points than the others. And more points meant more pay. Each was granted a private plot of land to grow crops that could be sold at the market. Factory workers were divided into teams, and urged to compete against one another. Again, the best team received the best pay.

"Not that our people lack anything," our guide hastily explained, "but if they know they can earn a little extra money this way, it helps them work harder. Then our country can progress further along the road to modernisation, like your countries in the West."

During our visit to the city, we went shopping in one of China's famous Friendship stores. Entry was only given to Westerners or overseas Chinese. Outside the store many local Chinese were waiting as overseas relatives purchased items on their behalf. After we had shopped, I stood watching the eager crowd for a few minutes. Their faces were alight with expectation, watching for their promised goods with all the excitement of kids under a Christmas tree. As shiny new bicycles, colour televisions, fans or other treasures were brought from the store, the new owner would beam happily, and walk tall as he took it proudly to his home.

At that moment I came to sense a fundamental change underway in China. In order to achieve its Modernisation programme, the country had needed to give its people new motivation. Had it given them a new god at the same time? One which was every bit as powerful and influential as their recently deceased deity? Was the new god of China to be Mammon?

Some months later, we were to see further changes in the country which confirmed my thoughts. Chairman Hua, the hand-picked successor to Mao, stepped down from his position as premier of the country.

At the same time, Mao, the old god, was being progressively dethroned through a series of moves by the party. Pictures of Mao began to come off walls, statues were removed from their pedestals.

This replacement therefore was to be more than just a change in personnel. Mao was slowly but surely to be toppled from his pedestal and "Mammon" called upon to unite the country for its "golden" future.

* * *

On the final day of our time in the country for Project Rainbow, Eugene was to receive a surprise farewell visit. His siesta was disturbed when one of our team took him a message that he was needed in another room for a meeting. He came quickly. But when the door was opened to him, he found the room so dimly lit that he could not recognise the figure inside.

A soft voice speaking broken English greeted him. "Hullo. I was hoping I would see you again."

As Eugene's eyes adjusted to the gloom, he saw a familiar face. It was Chang Lo, the guide he had led to the Lord earlier that year. He was astonished – how had the man found him? Who had told him he would be in China again? The two clasped hands and began laughing with joy and excitement.

At that moment, the other five of us on the team emerged into the light from the shadows of the room, and shouted as one, "Surprise!"

Chang Lo had brought gifts for us – bags of dried sugared dates. We in turn gave presents to him. For three hours, the seven of us talked and laughed and took pictures. A polaroid camera allowed us to give Chang Lo photos of the gathering.

Finally he explained how he found us. One of his co-workers, another guide whom we had met previously with Chang Lo, had seen us at the hotel and phoned his friend to let him know. During our conversation, we discovered it was the last day in that city for all of us. Chang Lo's assignment terminated that night. The following day, he would return to his home, and we would be leaving the People's Republic.

Eugene took time to give him suggestions and encouragement in his Bible Study – wishing they could both stay much longer in the city to give the young man time to become grounded in the Word. Chang Lo was also having difficulty in his prayer life, and Eugene helped him with that too. All too soon, it was time to leave and the rest had to remain unsaid.

Early next morning we were to board our bus for the train station. We were walking through the hotel lobby carrying our luggage, when unexpectedly someone took one of Eugene's bags – a smiling Chang Lo. He helped Eugene onto the bus and sat down beside him. "Did you not realise that I have the authority to accompany you?" he said with delight.

Once more, the two talked about the Lord and Chang Lo promised again to read his Bible and pray regularly. His official status made it easy to get Eugene past the checkpoints. Chang Lo walked him through, beaming proudly, as though accompanying a great dignitary.

But at customs it was time to say a final good-bye. Knowing Chang Lo's assignments were never to be in that city again, Eugene found it hard to leave him. He asked if the young man had any needs, money perhaps for university or clothing. "No," came the reply, "money would only create a problem for me."

Chang Lo's smiling face became serious as he finished. "You have given me the Lord. That is enough. God bless you, you are my spiritual father."

* * *

As tourists, many of the team members involved in Project Rainbow had opportunity to visit the increasing numbers of Three-Self churches opening up in the major cities of China. This was the time when reports of China's new policy of religious freedom were reaching the international press.

All around the world people were asking why the People's Republic had suddenly reversed its position on religion. Its reasons were gradually becoming clear.

The new government with its single-minded concentration on achieving the Four Modernisations had adopted a far more pragmatic stand than its predecessors. The current leaders wished to harness all energies towards the fulfillment of their new goals. Therefore to a certain extent differences of philosophical opinion could be overlooked in an effort to bring together all groups in the country into a "united front".

Not only was the Three-Self Patriotic Movement re-established, but also the Catholic Patriotic Association, the Chinese Islamic Association, and the Buddhist Association.

For the moment at least, the country's basis for unity was not to be so much agreement on ideology, as mutual commitment to the economic progress of the nation.

Far more important even than this, was China's new

need for the West. Its goals of modernisation would never be achieved without Western technology and know-how and the Communists knew this would not be forthcoming unless they demonstrated respect for the individual's right to belief.

Renovations began to appear in the churches of Canton, Shanghai, Peking. The choice concentrated on the tourist belt where travellers could observe the government's demonstration of its new freedom, and carry impressive reports back to their various homelands.

Whatever the government's reasons, and however long this new relaxation was to last, grateful believers turned out in their thousands to worship in the new-found freedom of the officially-sanctioned Three-Self churches.

While in Shanghai, I attended a service at the Moore Memorial Church. On the Sunday it opened people in their enthusiasm had lined up to the door hours before the service. Everything had been emotionally under control until the pastoral prayer, when many of the congregation sobbed openly at this opportunity to worship in public after years of subjugation.

Another of our couriers attended a service in the south. The church seated about one thousand four hundred people and that day it was estimated there were one thousand five hundred people present. Later, on Christmas Sunday, there were two thousand eight hundred – double its capacity. They were jammed against the walls; it was impossible for all of them to get inside.

During the service our friend attended the sermon preached was based on the text through which I'd been led to the Lord. "God is a Spirit: and they that worship Him must worship Him in spirit and in truth." (John 4:24).

The preacher at the service was undoubtably a born-again Christian and proclaimed as strong an evangelical message as possible in the official church. He was one of five or six pastors allotted to that place consistent with the pattern throughout all Three-Self churches. Among them, there is always at least one official Three-Self man along with a number of other pastors. Many of these have been brought back into the ministry from the places of secular employment where they were forced during or before the Cultural Revolution. Some have served terms in prison.

That year had brought my old friend Pablo to work full-time with us at Open Doors. He and Todd Martin played strategic roles in Project Rainbow, and seized their opportunity to visit an official church together.

They noticed, as did all our team members elsewhere, that there were very few Bibles in that church. Afterwards, Pablo approached one of the pastors to discuss the matter. During the service he had watched this man closely, and felt a spiritual one-ness with him – he seemed definitely a born-again Christian.

As they talked alone, Pablo asked him if he would like a copy of *Decision* magazine in Chinese. The pastor gratefully accepted it, and then Pablo carefully broached the subject of Scriptures.

"How is the situation here? Do you have enough Bibles or do you need more?"

The pastor lowered his tone. "We need them very desperately. Anything we are brought, I would be glad to accept."

Pablo's question had been basically one of research for the future. Much as he longed to help meet that need, he knew that at this stage, it would be foolish to deliver any Scripture loads directly to the Three-Self church.

After they had talked for some minutes a number of other pastors and interested tourists joined in too, including Todd. One of the pastors was a man with whom Pablo and Todd had felt no sense of unity at all; they strongly suspected him to be the official Three-Self "eye" in that church.

During their discussion, Todd, in his own diplomatic way said: "You know, we have a lot of Christian Chinese friends in Hong Kong. And they're always wondering what they can do in a practical way for their brothers and sisters. What can we tell them? They were wondering, for example, if you would need Bibles."

Without hesitation, the man our team suspected replied with a resounding "No."

His vehement comments were interpreted by the same pastor who had previously spoken to Pablo in private. The man's expression was completely impassive as he translated the message: "He says to tell you 'we have no need of Bibles in China.'"

The pastor continued: "He also says to tell you we are printing our own Bibles next Spring and we will have adequate supply. Therefore, we don't need any."

The believers had, however, already expressed to us their doubts about the government's plans. To date it had *promised* to publish some 130,000 copies of the Bible. How far would these go in replacing the hundreds of thousands burned during the Cultural Revolution? And, if they were to be replaced, how many more would be needed to keep up with the four hundred per cent increase in the Chinese church?

Pablo and Todd knew, moreover, than when Christians in the Suffering Church received a Bible officially, they placed themselves at great risk because their names were registered with the authorities. They became easy targets if ever the government decided to clamp down on religion.

Later we were to learn of an even more disturbing condition for the purchase of a Bible. Believers told us that they would be instructed to register not only their own names, but also that of the person who had led them to Jesus Christ.

The Three-Self Movement claimed to be the tool through which the government was offering Protestants freedom of religion in China. The statement was published and welcomed in the outside world, but how close was it to the truth? Although many believers had ventured out to worship openly in the new churches, many many more showed tremendous wariness, if not outright suspicion, over the revival of the Movement.[1]

One fact could not afford to be forgotten. An intrinsic part of all Communist ideology is atheism. Therefore, when such a government speaks of religious freedom, their claim needs to be examined closely.

Certainly the worst excesses of the Cultural Revolution stopped with the death of Mao. According to the Three-Self leaders, the Gang of Four alone had been responsible for persecution of Christians. Now that the villains had been exposed, the country could be rehabilitated to the freedom of the period prior to the Cultural Revolution.

But what freedom was that?

Our research showed us that in the late fifties, well before the Cultural Revolution, the number of open churches in China had reduced drastically. On average, only about 10 percent of churches were still in use, even at that time.

Most of the pastors had been taken away from their home towns and, at best, given jobs as rural labourers. I thought of some of China's giants of faith; Wang Ming-dao, Watchman Nee, the daughters of John Sung. All had been imprisoned, brain-washed, tortured for their faith. Many who had been imprisoned back in the fifties are still incarcerated today for the "crime" of preaching and simple obedience to their Lord.

Believers throughout the country had told our team of the horrors of the labour camps, house raids, imprisonments, or, for the "lucky" ones, job demotion – all of which dated back well before 1966.[2]

Even the Three-Self Movement's newly established policy of freedom in preaching had its own restrictions. During his travels Joseph was told of a number of topics which Three-Self pastors are required to avoid in their sermons. The list has not been proclaimed publicly – but is given behind the scenes to pastors to ensure they do not infringe party policy.

The topics included:

- Tithing. (This would affect the economy.)
- Day of rest: Sunday. (This would affect production.)
- Healing and exorcism.
- Marriage between believers and unbelievers.
- Second coming of Christ. (This might undermine the people's single-mindedness towards the Four Modernisations.)

Limitations on preaching extend not only to sermon topics, but also to permitted audiences. Preachers are not allowed to address Communist officials, nor are they supposed to evangelise young people under the age of eighteen.

One young girl, the daughter of a Three-Self pastor, summed it up succinctly. "My father really loves the Lord," she explained, "but he feels as though he is preaching with his hands tied behind his back."

There is considerable discrepancy between the government's claims of religious freedom, and the reality of the situation. Indeed, one of the senior administrators of the Three-Self Movement, working under its Bishop Ting, recently expressed his frustration to one of our workers.

"I am sick of being a puppet for the government – having to repeat the same lies," he said wearily. "And I'm just about ready to tell the Bishop so."

Although the Three-Self church is a government institution, there are many different kinds of people within it.

"You cannot know for sure," John, our Peking contact, told me. "There are those who are certainly fakes, planted by the government to spy on others. There are some who have succumbed to the pressure of the government, knowingly or unknowingly, and have allowed their faith to be compromised as they act in the Party's interests. Others are genuinely doing their best, in a situation of compromise, to worship their Lord and serve His flock."

Compromise. That was the key. Even at best, the believers who were prepared to go along with the government church knew that they had to compromise to do so. That hurt. That caused them to suffer too – to be just as much in need of our intercession in the Free World, as their brethren who risked all to worship in the secret churches of the country.

Who could criticise the majority of Chinese believers who choose to stay outside the officially sanctioned body of religion?

One of our Chinese staff workers, Mee Lei, spent an afternoon in Shanghai listening to a middle-aged Christian woman who had refused to attend Shanghai's open church.

"All those who go to the church regularly have to place their name and address on the register. That is what happened before the Cultural Revolution too. And then when the authorities wanted to persecute us, they knew exactly who we were and how to find us. Most of us are not prepared to take that risk again."

Mee Lei asked her whether she knew for certain if there was any danger associated with joining the Shanghai church.

The lady's face clouded. "I do know there is a group there who pretend to be Christians, but who are really placed in the church by the Communists themselves."

'How can you be sure?" asked the young courier.

"Because when I was younger and attended university, this same group pretended to become my friends. I believed them to be Christians and shared openly with them. When they had finished learning of my activities, they reported me to the authorities and I was expelled."

Mee Lei did not know what to say next. "It must have made you very sad," she faltered.

"Oh, not really. It doesn't matter now. As long as I am faithful to the Lord, that's all that matters."

"Why then do you think the church was opened?" Mee Lei asked at last.

Her friend smiled. "To impress the tourists," she said. "It's really a government-run thing, you know. The Three-Self pastor is hired by the government and they pay him a good wage for being there."

Her face became very serious as she gave Mee Lei a warning. "You know, it is no longer wise to offer Bibles to the officials in that church. They have a new policy now. Before, they used to say they did not need any. But now they are cleverer. Now they will say yes, and when you bring them Bibles, they will accept them, and either destroy them, or put them in some place where it is difficult for Christians to get access to them."

Mee Lei gratefully listened to the believer's counsel and was touched by her faithfulness despite her suffering. It was obvious that the lady lived alone. Mee Lei asked if she were a widow.

The woman shook her head. "I have a husband – he is a pastor. Many years ago, the government forced him to work as a rural labourer in order to stop his preaching to our flock here."

Mee Lei's heart went out to her. "Do you ever see him?"

"Yes, once a year he is allowed to spend one week with us."

Mee Lei was silent, expecting that the lady might break into tears as she told her story, but she remained dry eyed. "The Lord is good to us," she smiled. "He gives us all we need."

"Does that mean you never wish you could leave your country?" said Mee Lei.

"Oh, I could leave if I wanted to," her companion replied. "I have a brother who could organise my papers. But I don't want to. The Lord wants me here in China where I can be a support to my husband and where I can serve the believers."

275

The government may have been proclaiming its new religious policy to the West, with a smile on its face. But that grin is much like the satisfied smile on the face of the proverbial tiger. Behind it, the teeth are still as sharp as ever.

1. Believers expressed similar reservations over the later institution of the Christian Council of China. The C.C.C. is a sister organisation to the Three-Self Movement, and has been allocated a range of responsibilities in the area of pastoral work. With its inception came an announcement understood to imply the legalisation of China's home churches. This news has been welcomed in some circles, but has also caused many believers to request renewed prayer. They fear that the apparent ratification may be used to bring house church members into the open, where the authorities can clearly identify them.

2. Prior to publication, a new wave of short-term imprisonments and interrogation of house-church leaders began. Believers inside are deeply concerned that more will follow.

CHAPTER NINETEEN
China's "Number One Enemy"

The officer's voice rang out across the square, over the heads of the huge crowd. "These people have sinned against the State." His words trembled with anger. "Now they will pay the price."

A small group stood apart. Among them was Mrs Kwang. She watched as the guards released the safety catches on their rifles. "Father, forgive them," she prayed, echoing the words of Jesus as He faced His death on the cross.

"Take aim ... fire!"

The crack of rifle shots echoed through the square as the soldiers fired into the men and women before them. Many slumped to the ground while others remained standing. Mrs Kwang was unhurt.

The Communist leader turned to address the survivors and the huge audience. "If you engage in counter-revolutionary activity, you will face the same death," he warned. He turned on his heel and marched from the square, his men following.

Mrs Kwang and the other survivors walked slowly back to join the hushed crowd.

"Many believers were filled with fear after these warnings," her son Daniel explained. "Many fell from faith."

The church in China was beginning to discover who the *real* believers were.

*　　*　　*

Despite the apparent "thaw" of the late nineteen-seventies, the Chinese Christians had many painful memories of the "tiger's teeth". The experiences of Mrs Kwang, which we had finally pieced together from Daniel's accounts, illustrated how shallowly these memories were buried. The planning of Project Rainbow had required many long days and nights of preparation, often in conjunction with the Kwangs. Our discussions had brought to light an astonishing story.

"My mother was eighteen years old when she began to preach in our little church," Daniel told us. "She was especially gifted in evangelism, and the church started to grow very fast. But the government had been closing down churches all through China, and after she had preached for just one year, they came to our area.

"My mother did not know it then, but the authorities planned to arrest her on a certain night and her co-workers along with her. When she was praying that morning the Lord warned her that she should leave our town and visit a friend in another part of the country.

"The officers arrived that night and immediately nailed shut the doors of our church. Then they went to the homes of many of the believers and co-workers and herded them into trucks to take them to prison."

"How did they know where to find these people?" I asked.

He gave a helpless shrug. "Oh they got their names from the church register that had been introduced under the Three-Self Movement.

"Anyway, once they were in prison, the guards treated them very badly. Many were killed – thousands. Others were tortured and offered freedom if they would deny Christ and inform on the other Christians. There are many still in prison, even today," he added, his eyes holding mine steadily.

"When my mother returned, she only had to look at the church door to find out why the Lord had taken her away. When she saw it, she broke down and cried. She wanted to be with the believers, even if it meant imprisonment. But straightaway the Lord warned again that she had to leave the area."

278

The family's own grandfather was among those taken to gaol. The prison guards had been instructed to make a point of using violence on the prisoners and one particularly sadistic guard entered the old man's cell armed with a bottle.

"Here, 'Grandfather', I have a present for you," he said, bringing it down on the old man's head with a crash.

The blow was so savage that a blood vessel was broken in the skull and he began to haemorrhage internally. The bleeding did not stop for days and eventually the authorities had to admit him to a nearby hospital. But after a few short weeks, his pain-wracked body could fight no longer. Their grandfather went to be with his Lord.

*　　*　　*

"My mother knew," Daniel explained, "that she could not preach openly now. So she took a job as a school teacher. But each day after classes, she would come home and weep before the Lord – telling Him she wanted to preach for Him again. The Lord always comforted her, telling her to wait on His timing.

"While she was praying one day in 1958, God told her to begin preaching anew. 'I want you to stand up and preach the Gospel. You are to be a boat of refuge in the turbulent sea of China. And I will stand beside you.'"

The same morning, a number of her former co-workers began to arrive at her home. Each one gave the same reason for coming. "The Lord has spoken to me. He has told me to stand up and preach the Gospel. Now is the time."

For two more days, they continued to arrive; some on foot others by boat. Each one had been prompted and led by the Lord Himself.

How could they start preaching again? Almost every suggestion seemed impossible, just too dangerous. So they threw themselves on the Lord's wisdom and asked Him to lead them. And that was the way it happened. God proceeded to lead each one of them to individuals or families ready to hear the Gospel.

"One time when my mother was in prayer," Daniel told us, "the Lord told her to go to a particular street, to visit an old lady who was on the point of death. 'Preach the Gospel to her and pray for her,' the Lord said.

"My mother did as the Lord had said. She went to that street, and to that house. When she arrived she could see through the window an old lady lying on a bed. Her face was pale, her stomach swollen, and she was groaning in pain.

"After praying on the door step for a moment, my mother went in and began to talk to this woman. She was very touched as she listened to the Gospel, and weeping, she accepted the Lord. Then as my mother began to pray for her, she was immediately healed.

"Her family could hardly believe it. They were amazed to see their desperately ill grandmother well again. My mother then began to explain the way of the Lord to the rest of the household – and each one accepted Jesus Christ that same day."

The Old Man – the old Christian whom God had fed with the food that a rat had brought – was led just as clearly in his ministry. As he asked the Lord to show him where he should preach, he was told to visit a nearby town and witness to a certain man there. The Old Man protested. "Lord, I have never been to this place. I don't know the man, and I don't know where to find him. How can I possibly do what you're asking?" But the Lord was not going to take "No" for an answer. "You go, and I will lead you."

So the Old Man went. He found the town, and once there, the Lord took him to the street and the home. As he stood outside the house, he protested a second time, "Lord, I don't know this man. I don't even know what he is called!" Through prayer, God gave him the name which

280

the Old Man promptly began to shout for the person inside
to hear.

The door opened, and his surprised host invited him in.
The believer entered with the words: "Today, the Salvation of the Lord is come to your home!" Once inside
the Old Man explained the way he had been led to the
house and the reason. He began to preach the Gospel to
the entire family and again, every one of them accepted
Jesus Christ and became believers.

Daniel's parents had been with us on the evening he recounted this story and had followed the conversation with
frequent translation from their son. Now Mrs Kwang interrupted him with a flow of enthusiastic words in their
dialect. He turned to me with a gentle smile. "My mother
wants you to understand," he explained, "that there were
many, many more examples like these. There was nothing
unusual in the leading she and the Old Man received – all
the co-workers were led this way. It was just the work
of the Lord Himself as He began to build His church
through the conversion of families or individual people."

His mother smiled with the assurance that her message
had been relayed, and Daniel continued his extraordinary
account.

In time his mother and the rest of the team came together for another meeting – this time to review where
the Lord had led them and what their future was to be.
For ten days they studied the Bible together and prayed,
asking God to show them not only His plan, but how they
were to carry it out. At the end of that life-changing period,
they knew they had their answer.

They were to set out two by two, to the surrounding
villages and towns and even further afield to preach the
Gospel. God confirmed their ministry with many signs of
His power and love. As the Chinese watched these miracles
being performed, their response was one of conviction.
Many were won to Christ. "Your God is both true and
living," they would declare. Each miracle was an occasion

to tell people about the greatness of the Lord. The believers increased in number and many new fellowship groups were set up.

Throughout this period, Mr Kwang had been teaching in order to support the family. "When my wife was also teaching," he explained, again through Daniel, "she had earned a lot of money. But of course once the Lord called her to preaching again, the authorities did not like it. Not only did we lose her income, but mine was also cut back because they knew I too was a practising believer."

There was no bitterness or self-pity in his face as he mentioned that point, but Daniel went on to add his commentary. "By this time my father's fame as a teacher had spread throughout the whole town, yet still they gave him the lowest salary possible."

He was earning less than £12.00 per month, and caring for six people on that wage. They were very, very poor. Yet this did not daunt his parents.

Whenever a co-worker was in need of rice, vegetables or even a ticket to travel for the Lord, they would give out of whatever they had. A few days after Mr Kwang's pay had arrived, they were often out of money again.

"We didn't have enough food to eat. One bowl of rice would be divided between the six of us twice a day. Frequently it was cooked in a great deal of water so our bowls could be filled to the brim – mostly with the water and just a little rice. This went on too long, and my brother and I often found our hands, feet, and bodies became swollen with the lack of food.

"Many times he and I would go out looking for vegetables. We would go to the markets, and bring home any old ones which the sellers had thrown away. One time we must have eaten something that was very bad. We got a very serious case of food poisoning – and both of us came close to death.

"Our life was very hard and yet," he looked across at his parents with a smile, "somehow it did not seem hard to us, because at that time our mother and father were not in prison. She could preach the Gospel. He could teach at the school. And we were very happy just because we had parents."

Even after the start of the Cultural Revolution, his mother's preaching forays continued from city to city. Because all church buildings in China were now closed, services would be held in private homes.

It was not unusual for a group of preachers to pray all night, waiting on the Lord for His message to the people for the following day. When their sermons were preached, it was common for hundreds to be won to the Lord.

"Every morning my mother would pray from three a.m. until six-thirty a.m. unburdening her heart to the Lord and praising Him for all that He was doing," Daniel told us. "We could see the Lord's power very clearly." The church was growing by leaps and bounds.

As the church grew, however, so did the attention of the authorities. Daniel chose a separate occasion when he was alone with Julie and myself to describe his parents' times of suffering and persecution.

The authorities had one particularly powerful weapon in seeking to control the local people. If persecution of parents did not succeed in persuading them to the Communist line of thought, they turned to the children.

"One afternoon," Danield told us, "my older brother Peter was walking through a park on his way to our home. Suddenly a group of people confronted him and beat him up. When he got home he was very sick; he had many wounds and he had been hurt very badly." Daniel was shaking his head at the recollection.

A few days later, when the boy had recovered only a little, the authorities struck again.

"One evening the Red Guards came to our home and took away everything we had. They did not leave any of our furniture, clothes, or anything else. The house was empty when they finished.

"The guards made us all stand up on a bench, and told us to deny Jesus Christ. When we would not, they became very angry and beat us with clubs: even my three-year-old sister. After that they took us to a public square and made a big crowd gather around us.

"The men took my father and mother and whipped them. They tied them at a forty-five degree angle with a heavy rope and beat their backs with shoes that had sharp spikes in them."

Daniel paused for a moment before continuing. "The worst moment came when one of the officials took some scissors and lunged towards my parents. My older brother was very frightened at that. He thought they were going to poke out one of my mother's eyes. He was badly shocked. He began weeping but then stopped when he saw what the Guards were planning to do.

"They just wanted to cut off my mother's and father's hair to make them look like fools in front of the rest of the town."

Still Mr and Mrs Kwang would not utter the words demanded by the Red Guards: "We deny Jesus Christ." They preferred to die than to do that.

"Right, Kwang, you are going to a labour camp, and let's see how long you hold out there," the father was told by a senior official.

"Even if I die, I will not deny Jesus Christ," he said. He was hauled off to a notorious camp, where people were dying daily from ill treatment.

Peter Kwang watched the sorrow in his mother's face to see her husband taken away. At the same time, however, he was aware that something strange was happening within his own body. When they returned home he knew it was serious. A number of veins had ruptured and he had begun to haemorrhage. The toll taken by the boy's earlier assault, on top of the beating and shock he had received that day, had proved too much for his body to bear.

We knew already that Peter's body had been frail to begin with. Daniel had told us of the long childhood years when the government had stopped their food rations. "Often we would be on the point of starving," he had said "and we could only eat scraps of food that other people discarded."

"But you see," he had added, "the people of China are so poor that they do not throw away food very often. We just ate the peelings from vegetables, or the bark of trees. And sometimes nuts and berries if we could find them. One time my brother was so sick, and he had nothing to eat, that I saw him –" he broke off, obviously finding it difficult to talk, "I saw my brother pick up chicken dung and eat it because he was so hungry."

With that background of suffering, and appalling treatment dealt out to him during that week of violence, it was no wonder Peter's body had given way.

Nevertheless the twelve-year-old boy "soldiered on" to support his mother in her own struggle. Not wanting to worry her further he retreated to a dark corner of the house. A few soiled rags had been left nearby, not taken by the soldiers. He reached out for them and unobtrusively began to mop up the blood seeping from his body.

After several hours he knew it was too serious to hide from his mother any longer. He called her to him and as she took in the situation she was close to despair.

Bending over the boy she prayed for the Lord to staunch the bleeding and immediately it came to a stop.

Lovingly she washed him and laid him out on the floor for the night, since their beds had been taken by the Communists. Aware that his condition was critical, she took herself into a separate room and fell to her knees before the Lord.

"Father, you know I can't stand any more. I've already had my husband taken from me. Please don't allow my son to die. It would break me."

And yet with a struggle she added, "If it is your will Lord, I'll be obedient."

As she sobbed in prayer she felt the certain presence of the Lord beside her, comforting her. His voice came in reply. "Your son has undergone too much persecution already. Now it is time to take him home. He has suffered enough. He is pure."

Within a few weeks Peter Kwang was dead.

Many years later, just before Mrs Kwang was to leave China, she received a message from a pastor who had been working in the Three-Self church movement. The man explained that he had been the one behind the attack on young Peter in the park. He wanted to ask her forgiveness.

* * *

The Lord did not allow Mrs Kwang to be crushed by the death of her son. As she reached out to Him, He comforted and reassured her in her grief. In time she was on her feet again and once more faithfully testifying of her God. She and her dedicated team would travel days at a time, proclaiming the Gospel from town to town.

On the final day of one of these trips, a desperately ill woman was brought to Mrs Kwang. She had not much longer to live. After the meeting, her friends asked the evangelist to pray for her, which she did. Instantly, the sick woman was healed. The news spread quickly throughout the village and everyone came out to see Mrs Kwang and her associates and listen to the Word of God. The Lord moved among them and many accepted Him as their Saviour.

She began to give further teaching, telling them more of the Scriptures and instructing them on how to pray. She also taught the newly-converted believers Christian songs for worship. The next day, Daniel's mother returned home.

But the children of these people had learned the Gospel songs well and, after the meetings, a large group of them took to the streets, singing their new songs with gusto. It was only a matter of time before the local cadres became aware of the music.

They were outraged, and began an intensive search for

Christians in the town. Those caught were thrown into prison and beaten until finally one of them cracked and began to inform on the others.

As the interrogators began to extract information, they learned of the evangelist's preaching and the healing of the sick woman.

The order was given: "Find that woman and arrest her." It didn't take much detective work to unearth Mrs Kwang – she was now well known in the district. One day, as she was at home with her children, the soldiers struck and made the arrest.

Mrs Kwang was taken for trial before a tribunal of Communist officials. Her wrists were tightly bound and she was forced to bend down from the waist at a ninety degree angle as they questioned her. If she gave an answer that they didn't like, a guard would be instructed to kick her or hit her viciously on the back.

Every six hours the officials would change shift and a fresh group would come in to question and torture her. During the three day period, she was not given any water, food or sleep.

Yet even as she was bent double in agony, all Mrs Kwang could speak of was the love of Jesus.

"I have seen God with my own eyes," she told her persecutors. She then proceeded to tell them of a period, some years earlier, when she had contracted five very serious illnesses together. Her weight had halved, and she had become desperately sick, with no hope of recovery.

"Finally I knew I was on the point of death itself. My family knew it too, and gathered round me to pray. I could breathe only with little short gasps, and I felt certain I would be dead within a few minutes.

"But just then, the Lord came to me and comforted me. He showed me a vision of the Second Coming when He will return to this earth to take home His children. And, at the same time, He healed me completely.

287

"So you see," she concluded smilingly, "now I must preach the Gospel. I must tell people of the greatness of our God. And let them know that He loves them – and wants them to live forever with Him.

"He loves you too," she added. "You can find new life in Him. Are you willing to believe?"

As Mrs Kwang finished her story, the officials at first were furious. But they could not deny that, in her attitude, they were seeing the forgiveness and love of the One of whom she had been speaking. Slowly a few responded. Some began to weep, and soon one said that he too wanted a faith like hers. Then others followed until many in that room accepted Christ.

*　　*　　*

"After the three days," Daniel continued, "my mother was thrown into a cell. It was terrible there. The room was tiny and it was underground – so my mother was in darkness. The floor was damp and the toilet had not been cleaned in a long time. There was no bed for her to sleep on, only the floor. When they threw her in there, she finally lost consciousness ..."

A little smile lit up his face. "But the Lord is faithful. He came to her in a dream and comforted her. Then He told her to go on preaching for Him, even in that shocking place.

"My mother drew on His strength alone. She told Him she would obey. But she could not see how she could witness – it seemed impossible. Then the Lord told her a way. She went to the prison authorities with a suggestion. 'I can see that this prison is very dirty,' she said. 'Would you like me to do some hard labour for you – and clean it?'"

The authorities were very responsive to the idea. Soon every part of the prison was open to her. She could preach to all the prisoners and they welcomed her enthusiastically. They were touched by her love for them, and recognised this as a reflection of the love of God Himself. As she preached of Him and the way of salvation, hundreds gave their lives to Jesus Christ.

And it was not only the prisoners. The guards too were touched by my mother's attitude to them and to the authorities. Instead of hatred and bitterness, they were meeting one whose Lord said "Love your enemies. Do good to them that hate you." As she taught them about the Lord, many guards became Christians as well.

"But," Daniel continued, with a shake of his head, "when the Communist authorities heard about it, they were furious.

"They beat her all over again. It was bad, very bad. Then a high officer sent my mother some blank paper and told her to write out her confession. She prayed to the Lord for guiding and began to write her statement. It was the biblical plan of salvation. She sent it to the official. He was furious with her for doing such a thing, but he had to read it before a large group of officers who were to pass sentence to her. When they heard what my mother had written, many of them too became Christians!"

Nevertheless when sentence was pronounced, Mrs Kwang, "dissident", was ordered to twenty years' imprisonment.

Her interrogation began anew after the judgement as officials tried unsuccessfully to extract names of other Christians and their meeting places. She was tied with a method known in China as "Super-binding", one of their most effective ways to get information from prisoners. Their system is to tie a rope from the base of the neck down to the hands which are bound behind the back. It is designed to make it impossible to get one's hands comfortable without giving the neck a rope-burn. And vice-versa - to make the neck comfortable means breaking the wrists.

This excruciating torture lasted for several days until unexpectedly, during one morning prayer time, Mrs Kwang was told by the Lord that she would be released that same day. Despite her twenty year sentence, she believed what He had said and waited expectantly for the promise to be fulfilled. By evening, she had heard nothing and she knew the prison rule that no inmates could be released after nightfall. But her confidence in the Lord remained unshaken, and sure enough at nine o'clock an official came to her cell.

"Okay, you! You can leave the prison now."

Daniel was not able to explain why they had broken the rule on that occasion. "We were never told," he said. Then, with a bright smile, he added the phrase which we were to hear so often: "It was the Lord ..."

Their final words to his mother were another warning. "Don't you tell anybody what has happened in here. Don't mention the torturing and beating – don't mention any of these things. If you do, it will mean trouble for you. Now – get out of here! Get home!"

The next day Mrs Kwang began preaching again.

Throughout the months that followed, hundreds of new believers joined the fellowship groups and Mrs Kwang trained more and more co-workers to pastor them. Among them were former Red Guards and prison officers who now addressed the woman they had once persecuted as "Mama Kwang".

*   *   *

Meetings were usually held every night at two or three a.m., when, Daniel explained with a cheeky smile, "the secret police would all be sleeping."

Often their meetings happened without prior notice – being called when Mrs Kwang or one of her co-workers was led during prayer to hold one. On arrival at the meeting place she or the other preachers would be met by a crowd of believers waiting expectantly for their time of worship.

Whenever the preachers would ask how the group had been brought together their reply was always the same: "The Lord Himself told us to come here for fellowship." No human method of communication had been used to gather them.

Signs and miracles often accompanied the preaching and worship at those meetings. Dumb would be brought, and leave the place speaking. Blind would leave seeing, lame walking. And all the time the numbers of believers continued to grow.

"How many believers are there now?" I asked Daniel.

"We have about three hundred fellowship groups," he replied.

"How many attend?"

"The small ones have just a few hundred. The big ones several thousand." He spoke quietly, unaware of the response his reply would bring.

"You mean altogether, surely?"

"No. In each group there is that number," he repeated patiently. Then, as he read the surprise on our faces, he added, with a cheerful smile: "It is the Lord's doing! He is very wonderful to us."

* * *

Finally however, the secret police caught up with Mrs Kwang again. She was imprisoned twice more. On her third time inside the evangelist was sentenced for life and, because of the seriousness of her "crime", her husband was brought out from labour camp to be informed.

"Your wife has committed many crimes against the State," the prison guard told him. "We consider her a maximum security prisoner. It would be too great a risk to let her loose in the community ever again."

He looked hard at Mr Kwang, hatred blazing in the official's eyes: "We regard your wife as China's number one enemy."

Mr Kwang tried to visit her inside the gaol, but was not

allowed. Yet he badly wanted to comfort his wife – somehow.

Slowly he began to walk around the outside of the prison singing well-known hymns, in the hope that, wherever she was, she would hear them and be strengthened.

Before his return to the labour camp, the father went to say good-bye to his children.

Daniel clearly remembered his father's parting words. "If you can get to see your mother, tell her that I am of the same heart as she is. Tell her I love her.

"Explain that because I was not permitted to see her in prison, I walked around it singing songs of the Lord. I wanted to comfort her, to turn her eyes to Him.

"Tell your mother these things."

* * *

After telling of his mother's imprisonment, Daniel requested politely that we break that day so he could rest. The very recounting of the suffering seemed to have drained his fragile body of all its strength.

The next time we met with him his parents were present, Mrs Kwang was beaming with obvious eagerness to share something with us.

"My mother is saying," Daniel explained as she spoke to him, "that there is a special prison experience she believes you ought to hear, as it concerns you."

By now I had come to know the evangelist well enough to realise that when she had something on her heart, it was worth listening to carefully. I sat down beside Daniel as she began her tale.

"While I was in prison the final time," she said, Daniel translating more rapidly now, "the Lord gave me a vision."

"I saw many thousands of co-workers in both the East and the West working side by side and digging a trench. That trench became bigger and longer, and then water started to flow into it.

292

"This water was the River of Life.

"I saw it flow first through China into all parts of the country, and after that into the whole of the world."

Daniel's father inserted his own word of explanation.

"The Lord gave her this vision in 1974, in a dreadful prison when it was hardest for her to believe. She had been sentenced to life imprisonment in an underground cell with no toilet facilities except a bucket in the corner which was never emptied. The cell was damp and crawling with lice and mosquitoes. The only food she was offered was rice cooked with sand. She had already been beaten and tortured terribly and was still being interrogated by the authorities.

"It seemed she could not even survive very long in such a place. Yet when the Lord gave her that vision she believed Him. And after He miraculously released her from prison she told us all what He had shown her."

Mrs Kwang herself finished the story. "It was the time, Brother David, when you were just beginning your ministry in the free world for those under persecution for their faith." She was smiling warmly as she continued. "It was as the Lord told me. I did not know it then, but East and West were already working together to dig the channel for the River of Life to flow."

If ever I had received confirmation of the Lord's authorisation in this work, it was at that moment. This time it was I who requested a break, to bow silently before the One who had brought it all together.

When we resumed, Daniel was himself keen to share one of his personal experiences in China.

"I would very much like to tell you a special story, Brother David. It happened during the time after my mother was released from her third imprisonment, when she had to hide away in Canton."

I nodded. That was the time that Joseph had first met her, in the university grounds.

If Mrs Kwang had returned to her home town, she would

immediately have been thrown back into prison. Thus it was most important for Daniel to conceal knowledge of her whereabouts.

Night after night, however, his house would be raided by the local authorities and he would be interrogated to obtain her address.

While she was away, his mother had sent him a series of letters expounding the symbolism of the book of Revelation. He valued these very highly and could not bring himself to destroy them even for security's sake. One night, at eleven p.m., a large group of secret police arrived to make a thorough search of the house. For Daniel, it was obviously very serious. If they found the letters he had left under his pillow, they would know where his mother was staying.

With typical simplicity Daniel explained: "I had to pray to the Lord to help me. At first I was shaking, but then I prayed all the more for God to protect the letters."

The police stayed several hours, searching every part of the house and reading every piece of paper they discovered. As they hunted, they positioned two guards to stand with Daniel. One was in front, the other behind. Both were watching to see if he reacted when the police searched in any particular spot. If his eyes so much as flickered, they would know to look in that place very carefully.

When they came to pick up the pillow that was hiding the letters, he cried out silently, "Lord, in Jesus' name, please blind their eyes so they will not see them."

At that precise moment, confusion broke out. Another official nearby tripped with an armful of pillows and they fell all over the bed. By the time the first man had helped his comrade gather them up, the original pillow had been forgotten. The letters remained in their place, undetected.

Finally, the secret police gave up and left the house empty-handed.

"You see," Daniel said to me, "I have witnessed the

goodness of the Lord with my own eyes."

"You must have given thanks when you went back to sleep that night, Daniel," Julie said quietly.

His face clouded. "Well actually, a few minutes after they left, another more senior official came to the house to begin the interrogation all over again. I suppose he thought I would be more willing to talk after what had happened earlier."

Daniel bowed his head. "Their ways of questioning are so hard," he murmured.

A few minutes later, however, he looked up again – his face shining once more. "But I have one last story I want to tell you.

"It happened a long time ago when my mother was first imprisoned and my father was in labour camp. She was taken away shortly after my brother died, just a little while after our house had been ransacked of all its furniture, money and food. We had to sleep on the floor.

"When the guards took my mother, they instructed our neighbours to torture and beat us children so that we would deny our faith in the Lord. But we didn't. After they had finished beating us we just went back home to sleep on the floor and cried in prayer before the Lord. My heart was very heavy. I was ten years old and I had to look after my younger brother and sister.

"At that time we had nothing at all in our house except a little bit of rice in a rice-jar. With no money we could not buy any more. And nobody could come to help us because the secret police were standing guard outside to prevent them.

"We realised that if we cooked the rice that day, there would be none left for the next. Then we would just have to wait for death to come. The three of us threw ourselves down upon the floor and asked the Lord to perform a powerful miracle. Then in faith we began to cook the rice.

"Next day when we woke up for our breakfast, we went to the rice jar and the Lord had answered our prayer.

There was just as much rice as there had been the day before.

"And every day it was the same. The Lord did not allow the level of rice to go down. We had enough until the day my mother was released from prison and then it ran dry."

He gave us one of his infectious laughs. "The Lord is very wonderful in my life."

I looked at him and the family with tears in my eyes. I could find nothing to say, but inside my heart felt ready to burst. They and their brethren inside China were a living testimony to the greatness of God.

In that moment I learned a lesson that I have never forgotten. I had come to this work thinking of the ministry we would be able to give the Suffering Church. Now the truth of the situation hit me. How much greater was *their* ministry *to us* – the free Western church with every opportunity to learn of God, yet needing to discover how He really works.

We were the ones who had Bibles galore and freedom to meet as often as we liked. We were also the ones who dragged ourselves out reluctantly to a Bible study or prayer meeting when a night at home would have been so much easier. We were the ones who claimed to be walking in the Lord's will, but found prayer times too difficult to wake up for, and stopped only occasionally to listen for the Lord's voice in our overcrowded daily schedules.

"Daniel," I said at last. "How is it that your brethren walk so closely with the Lord? In the West we cannot hear the Lord's voice in the way you do."

Daniel passed the question onto his parents and waited for their answer. At last he spoke. "One has to make the sacrifice, Brother David, to follow the Lord this way."

"You mean that one has to be persecuted before having this kind of faith?"

"No, Brother David, that is not the sacrifice. The sacrifice they are talking about is *prayer*."

I looked at them, blinking for a moment, trying to take

in their meaning. These believers, and the thousands in China, did not just give the Lord a few minutes of their day in prayer. The whole of their day was like one extended prayer, so great was their hunger for the Lord. At any given opportunity, they would seek His presence, His company, His fellowship – often praying for hours at a time as they poured out their hearts to Him, and offering themselves for His service.

"Daniel?" A last question. "Could you ask them how long it takes to reach that kind of commitment – to be so given over to Jesus? How many hours of prayer each day? How many weeks, months, years?"

In time the gentle answer came back. It was beautifully simple yet it spoke volumes.

"The Lord knows your heart, David."

There it was. If the heart was "sacrificed" to Him, if the believer so abandoned to the Lord that nothing else mattered ... then the rest would follow.

CHAPTER TWENTY

Let Us Run Together

"What's next, Daddy?" Dawn asked amid the clatter and chatter of our favourite Chinese restaurant in Manila. "Where will you go from here?"

I knew the answer. We had already heard reports of Christians travelling two or three days to get one of the thirty thousand Project Rainbow Bibles. The next step could only be the million which the Kwangs had requested the day they arrived from China.

"Can we trust the Lord for a million?" I grinned, watching their surprised reaction. Then the other three nodded with understanding.

"I guess it fits the vision the Lord gave you, doesn't it?" Julie said.

"You bet. After all, He said at the start it should be ten million. This is only one-tenth of that amount. Not so much after all, is it?" I chuckled.

"Good grief, Dad!" said David. "That's sure going to be one huge step! Just think of the people, Bibles, money and prayer support you'll need."

"I know," I replied. "Yet the other deliveries needed just as much. Do you remember how we started with small consignments – just forties and fifties – and then up to nine hundred and from there to thirty thousand? Each seemed enormous after the one before."

"Yet the Lord was bigger still," murmured Julie.

"And He can do it again this time," I smiled. "After all, He's the same Lord!"

* * *

On my next trip to Hong Kong, the Kwangs and I discussed this gigantic task. "You remember Joshua called on the Lord to stop the sun and the moon, so they could win the battle?" Mrs Kwang asked. "It will take a mighty work of God for us to be victorious in this battle too. And the hunger of the believers is so great, Brother David. Even with Project Rainbow, your Bibles are not enough."

Together we read some of the overjoyed letters which had begun pouring into our offices from the heart of China.

> *Dear Cousin,*
> *Just as we were filled with yearning for even the trickle of a brook, we were satisfied. Our thirst was not because we lacked water. Rather it was because we did not have the Precious Word which God has given us ...*
> *Our hearts are filled with inexpressible happiness. May the flow be unceasing and reach to the farthest places!*

Another read:

> *Beloved Cousin,*
> *What we had lost earlier, you have replaced: the Bread of Life.*
> *Cousin, after receiving it, we brothers and sisters here have been offering up praise and thanksgiving. At the same time, we have been devouring the Bread of Life. When we have eaten it, the Word becomes strength, enabling us to walk the path laid down ahead of us and to fight the good fight. We will not disappoint your concern for us.*
> *May God's grace to you be deep and wide, without measure and without limits.*

As I looked over the many letters, I wondered how many other thousands and millions of believers in the People's Republic needed that same hunger satisfied.

"I have a name for this project," I told the Kwangs. "I think we should call it 'Project Pearl'."

Their faces lit up. "The 'Pearl of Great Price'?" they asked.

"That's right. The one precious pearl for which the merchant gave all that he had."

"Just like the believers in China," mused Mrs Kwang. "They too have given all they have to belong to the Kingdom of God."

"Well, Brother David," said Mr Kwang with a beam. "Why don't we begin it right away – on our knees?"

*　　*　　*

A few weeks later Shan and I, together with Roger Winthrop, one of his colleagues, visited another believer who had sacrificed his all for the Kingdom of God.

Wang Ming-dao, along with Watchman Nee, had been a major leader of the Chinese church until his imprisonment in 1955.

After fourteen months of the rigours of prison life, the preacher finally signed a confession admitting his opposition to the Three-Self Movement had been "counter-revolutionary". He was released but became severely disturbed emotionally. He rejected his confession and returned to prison, where, this time, he stayed for twenty-one years and eight months. In January 1980, he was released to join his wife who had been freed two years earlier.

We expected to see a quiet, aged man, perhaps broken in body and in spirit. Instead, as with Mrs Kwang, we found a believer having the same fire for his Lord that we had heard about in his younger days.

"I remember the words of Jesus to His church in Revelation 2:10," he told us.

"Fear none of those things which thou shalt suffer: behold, the devil shall cast some of you into prison, that ye may be tried; and ye shall have tribulation ten days. Be thou faithful unto death, and I will give thee a crown of life." (Authorised Version.)

These verses had sustained him while in prison.

"I have been through twenty-three years of refining and the Lord has not allowed me to suffer loss through it all, but rather to receive an even greater blessing.

'Twenty-five years ago, I'd forgotten that Satan was waiting to use my weakest point to attack me. 'Aren't you afraid?' he said. And he brought me face to face with a terror that I had never conceived of before. Never in my life had I confronted anything so fearsome, and I, like Peter, was weak.

"Well, what happened in the end? After the Lord Jesus rose from the dead, He appeared first of all to this fallen Peter. Now my Lord has done the same with me. He has not remonstrated against me, but instead He has comforted me. The Bible says, 'A bruised reed he shall not break, a smoking flax he shall not quench.'"

The old teacher continued. "Now there is only one thing I fear. I fear God. So long as I do not sin against God, so long as I remain faithful to Him, then I fear nothing. Each day we spend on earth, we must be careful, be on our guard.

"There is an ancient Chinese saying: 'There are many beginnings but few endings.' The Bible records many stories of people who began and never finished. And I must warn myself: never be one who begins and cannot finish."

*   *   *

"His message couldn't have been more appropriate, could it?" said an exuberant Brother Andrew as I recounted my unforgettable meeting with Wang Ming-dao. Accompanied by James Wee, I was again in Holland for our yearly international meeting. The three of us were walking through the cobbled streets of Brother Andrew's picturesque home town.

James spoke up. "And we have no time to lose. The door of China has never been so open." With Zhao Ziyang in power, the country would be more open than ever in the immediate future. "Do you know," he continued, "one group in China has sent us an urgent message to get Bibles inside as quickly as possible? They are convinced God has been warning them that China will not remain so open for long. I have heard the same thing said by many believers throughout the country."

"And the Kwang family too, when they came out of China," I added.

The "smuggler" agreed. "That's what makes Project Pearl so important. I believe you have to make it priority number one. And be assured that the rest of us will be standing behind you."

By this time we had come to the market place in the heart of the little village. Brother Andrew steered us towards a little stall in its centre.

"Wonderful," he said, "I'm dying for one of these."

As we drew closer, I saw what he was referring to. The stall sold those wretched raw herrings I had been required to consume on my first visit to Holland. Our Dutch companion made it sound so easy.

"Just grab the fish by its tail and top it up with raw onion."

I winced as I remembered the earlier occasion. James' face paled as he also politely but firmly declined.

"Shame on you," Andrew chided, eyes twinkling, as his voice assumed mock gravity. "How can you two be effective missionaries if you are not prepared to identify with those around you? How can you be one with the Dutch if you don't act like Dutchmen when you're with us?"

James spoke first. "You are right, Brother Andrew. We should eat it. And knowing that, when you next visit the Philippines, you too will want to identify with the people there, we'll be only too pleased to buy you some 'balut'."

Balut is the Philippines' national delicacy – duck embryo

302

boiled in its own shell and sold warm by street vendors.

Now it was Brother Andrew who turned pale.

"You'll love it, brother," I reassured him, following James' lead. "The trick is to bite into it without looking. Once you get used to the initial feel of the feathers, the bill and the rest of it, you'll be asking for seconds!"

Andrew choked on the last of his herring as he burst into laughter. "Okay, you two win. I don't want to be morally obliged to eat that dreadful duckling next time I come to Manila.

"Why don't you give the herrings a miss?" he said graciously. Then, breaking into his infectious grin, he added, "This time, anyway."

* * *

We followed the road that led us to the nearby harbour. As we sat down on a wooden bench near the water's edge, I pulled my Bible from my briefcase. In it was a letter from China.

"I'd like you to hear this, Andrew. I've heard the translation before and it's really something."

The letter had been written by the Old Man who had been such a support to the Kwang family's ministry. James Wee translated it:

> *Beloved Cousin David, safety and peace!*
> *We thank God for his great mercy in loaning you to us to care for us. The precious books you mailed were received today ... Thank you for your love and concern for us. If you have opportunity, we are honouring and inviting you to visit our town. Then we can have fellowship together, share the grace of the Lord, and encourage each other to run for the Lord until He returns ...*

"Encourage each other to run for the Lord," Brother Andrew repeated. "Not just the two of you, David, but the body of believers inside China and the church in the free world. East and West encouraging each other to run for the Lord.

"Why not?" he continued. "If one million, or ultimately ten million, Bibles are to go into the People's Republic, they could do with at least that number of Christians behind them. That would mean one person praying for each Bible and for the believer who receives it."

I watched a pair of fishermen in a small boat approaching the shore. As they reached the shallow waters, one leaped out of the front holding a thick rope. The two men worked as one; the first carefully guiding the tiller while the other waded through the flotsam to guide the boat to the bank.

"Amen," I said. "We need to run together."

EPILOGUE
A Night To Be Remembered
A Look at Project Pearl

"Hey, men, there's a boat headed right at us!"

The captain of our tug squinted anxiously into the distance, tension gripping his body. Until that moment, we had been cruising quietly along the southern coast of China, our course outlined in silver by the bright moon above. The night was crystal clear and had been heralded by a breathtakingly beautiful sunset. Time seemed suspended in the serenity of that evening. The stillness was so great we could almost reach out and touch it.

Our sense of calm, however, was shattered by the captain's cry. Joseph Lee was at the helm and he peered through the bridge window to see the vessel for himself.

"It's getting closer, Captain. And what's that on the stern?"

Captain Karl's expression froze as he focused his binoculars. "It's a machine gun." He looked a moment longer, "And a manned one at that! Our 'visitor' is a Chinese patrol boat!"

All of us on the bridge strained forward, the colour draining from our cheeks. Loaded on the barge behind us were one million Chinese Bibles, and we were minutes away from delivery to the believers who had requested them.

"Are you sure that's a patrol boat?" I asked the captain.

"No question about it."

We watched the craft come ever closer, the machine gun and its operator now clearly lit by the moon.

I took a deep breath. "Lord, there's nothing we can do. Only You can take control of the situation. We know how greatly You love the believers waiting on that beach and how much You want Your Word in their hands."

Even as I prayed, I was comforted by the knowledge that, on our departure, Brother Andrew had alerted our prayer chains worldwide to intercede for three days. At this very moment, there were hundreds, even thousands, of people praying for our team.

"We rest in Your hands, Lord," I finished quietly. "We will just stand back and watch You at work."

After the prayer, I opened my eyes to see that the patrol boat was now right beside us, a mere seventy-five feet away.

Captain Karl fixed his eyes directly ahead and mumbled quietly, as if addressing the passing vessel, "If you don't look at me, I won't look at you."

The rest of us did our best to pass him a wintry smile, but we all knew that if we were discovered Project Pearl could come to a complete halt and the lives of the believers and our crew put in immediate danger.

Yet this was not the first time we had seen Project Pearl placed in jeopardy. There had been major battles from the very beginning.

*   *   *

On that moonlit night, as in every other battle, we had needed to stand on the authorisation given by God at Project Pearl's inception. It had seemed right to us, after Project Rainbow, that our next task would be the fulfilment of the believers' request for one million Bibles. We'd needed to be sure, however, that this was indeed what God wanted, and was not just man's idea.

He had left us in no doubt. His first encouragement had come for me early in the year when flat on my back with an illness. Visitors had left a leaflet, which gave scientific evidence that the sun and the moon had stood still at Gibeon as a result of Joshua's prayers.

The following days I studied the relevant section in Joshua 10, and a firm conviction grew in my mind. As surely as Joshua had prayed and seen God's power that day, so we could pray and see His same power for the million Bibles – even if their delivery required a miracle of the same scale.

Shortly afterwards, Sven, our executive vice president, and I met with the Kwang family in Hong Kong.

"We have a passage we would like to share with you," they said. "Joshua, Chapter 10. You remember when Joshua called on the Lord to stop the sun and the moon so they could win the battle?" Sven and I beamed from ear to ear as the Kwangs went on to say how it would take such an act of God for Project Pearl as well.

We rejoiced together. God had given the same message to us both – the one representing the believers inside China, the other representing those on the outside who longed to serve them.

There were many more such confirmations and during the weeks of research that followed, a plan of delivery was established. Long hours of meetings were held inside China, in Hong Kong, in the Philippines and in the States, all concurring that the Bibles should be delivered by boat at night. Subsequent research into China's shipping patterns, coastal conditions and beaches had followed until, at last, our team walked with local believers on the South China beach we codenamed "Mike", after the Archangel Michael. We all agreed this should be the site of the delivery.

It was while travelling to Holland to lay these plans before Brother Andrew and the international directors that I once more received encouragement from the Lord. On the plane, my Bible reading brought me to Exodus 14:19, 20, where the Israelites were seeking the Lord's covering from the sight of the Egyptians. The verses concluded, ". . . neither side went near the other the whole night long."

Like the Israelites, we would be seeking caves and I

smiled inwardly that God had allowed me to stumble upon the passage at that time. I felt an assurance that the coming days would permit us to see His same mighty protection on the night we would need it.

Later, in Hong Kong, Pastor Ward and I met with the Kwangs at our hotel. Mama and Papa Kwang had just returned from several weeks' prayer and fasting with the believers inside China.

"Our brethren are praising God for the wonderful news of Project Pearl," Papa Kwang reported. "They send you their love and are praying daily for you and for the delivery."

Mama, too, gave her confirmation. "They know it will take a mighty act of God to see one million Bibles in their land. And brothers," she added, "the miracle will not end with the delivery itself. After that there will be many lives touched by the Bibles."

There was a pause as each of us dwelt on the magnitude of the events in store. Pastor Ward leaned forward, his brow puckered in concentration. "You know, I don't think the results of Project Pearl will even be contained within China itself. At least I hope not," he said, breaking into a grin, then went on to lay before the Kwangs some of the other objectives we believed God had given our team for the outcome of the assignment.

First and foremost, of course, was the fulfilment of the delivery itself.

Second was our longing that when news of this enormous need reached the West, thousands of people worldwide would also respond and set about deliveries of their own to China.

Third, we hoped that public knowledge of such a request would provide opportunity for the voice of the house churches to be heard in the outside world. At present the dominant voice to reach the West is that of the official Church, usually through the Three-Self Movement's leader, Bishop K. H. Ting. Much publicity has been given to his statements that China is meeting the need for Bibles among its people. House church members, however, say that the need is far in excess of the supply. Only 135,000 Bibles have been published, while a conservative estimate places the Christians in China at twenty million. And not only were these Bibles miniscule in number, they were given only to those who complied with set government conditions. A double message therefore is currently coming from China: that of Bishop Ting who is able to travel abroad freely, and that of the house church members who are so restricted in communication with the West. How we longed that through Project Pearl their cries would reach the world.

Finally, our fourth goal concerned the government itself. We had often prayed that when news of this delivery reached Deng Xiaoping and the Communist Party, they would realise the people's desperate shortage of Bibles and begin publishing Scriptures in suitable quantities, making them available without strings attached.

As Pastor Ward finished his outline, I picked up his final point. "That would be the best solution of all, don't you think?" I asked the Kwangs.

"The greatest miracle we could hope for," Papa concurred.

Mama Kwang also smiled her agreement, then reached across for her Bible. "Meanwhile, Brother David, we believe the Lord has given us a verse regarding the fulfilment of the first miracle, the night of the delivery of Project Pearl. We received this verse while in prayer with our brethren inside China."

As they read, we were to witness again the leading of our consistent Lord. For the Kwangs proceeded to quote the very passage that had touched me so profoundly on the plane to Holland, Exodus 14:19, 20, culminating in the same phrase: ". . . neither side went near the other the whole night long."

I shook my head in gratitude, finding it hard to remain

309

dry-eyed as the godly pair read to me. Nothing more needed to be said. Together our little group gave jubilant thanks that God was so firmly authorising both East and West to trust Him in meeting the needs of His Church in China . . . with one million Bibles.

*   *   *

The following weeks brought constant activity on both sides of the Pacific.

In Singapore, Pablo, our research man, signed with me for a 128-ton, ocean-going tug. At US $480,000 we were getting it at the best price available. All the same, we knew we were signing up in faith alone for we had not even one cent to put towards the payment. Moreover, the owner wanted the full amount in just ten days.

Much prayer followed. Our bases in Australia, New Zealand and Japan were able to send, in total, US $100,000 in down payment. Then, to our joyful amazement, the remaining US $380,000 came through the prayerful giving of just one church, Calvary Chapel in Costa Mesa, California. On the day final payment was due, its pastor, Chuck Smith, made a telegraphic transfer of the enormous sum direct to the shipowners in Singapore.

In the meantime, after assessing quotations from publishers around the world, we ordered one million Bibles from the American firm, Thomas Nelson Publishers, in Nashville, Tennessee. The Bibles were to be printed as the believers had requested – in the new simplified script of China, Union Version.

Simultaneously, in the Philippines, a barge was being built to our specifications. It would need to accommodate 232 tons of Bibles, with provision for internal flooding so that, on the delivery night, the vessel could ride lower in the water for the Bibles to be offloaded and towed to shore. Further north in Manila, arrangements were being made for the importation of small craft that would be used to tow the boxes of Bibles to the beach.

310

It was time to recruit the crew. Men were invited from Open Doors' offices around the world to ask the Lord whether He would have them join up.

"Before they do so, we will ask them to share specifically how the Lord has led them to this task," I'd told Brother Andrew when we'd discussed the plans.

"Amen!" he'd responded. "And, David. I also ask that you interview all the men about their wives' feelings toward the assignment." It was crucial that each one be one hundred per cent behind her husband. This could be a life or death mission.

One further requirement we made was that each person be sworn to total secrecy. Not a word could be breathed to anyone, other than the explanation necessary for the man's wife.

That secrecy remained of paramount importance during the remainder of Project Pearl. We believe that in the spiritual battle, just as in general military strategy, the element of surprise is eighty per cent of the victory. In fact it was not until well after the delivery that we were able to share its completion with most of our office staff around the world.

We on the crew were a motley bunch, landlubbers for the most part whose only knowledge of the ocean was its colour. Just two of the twenty men had any previous experience at sea. This was never more evident than when, having collected our barge in the Philippines, we set out for Hong Kong.

During one training session, just after Joseph Lee had joined the crew, Captain Karl barked out the order: "All hands on deck!"

Men came running from every direction, but Joseph could not determine where they were running to. It was quite clear, however, that he was supposed to be running somewhere so he took off at great speed until he came across the captain.

"Captain?" he puffed. "Where's the deck?"

Our disbelieving captain stared at him, needing a moment to take in the question. Then, realising Joseph was serious, he said in astonishment, "You're standing on it, Joseph!"

The incident brought hoots of raucous laughter from the rest of the crew. But even as the guffaws died away, the truth was underlined for us one more time. If this mission was to be a success, it would not be through the cleverness of men, nor the training of our crew. It could only come about through God Himself at work.

*　　*　　*

The need for God's total control was all the more evident in the subsequent weeks. Our trip to Hong Kong brought us face to face with ten-foot waves which threatened to overwhelm our relatively small craft. And, after we had limped safely into Hong Kong, we were to be met with yet more problems. In a way, we were not surprised. We knew we were engaged in spiritual warfare, and had seen 2 Corinthians 10:3,4 come alive in a special way: "Although we lead normal, human lives, the battle we are fighting is on the spiritual level. The very weapons we use are not human but powerful in God's warfare for the destruction of the enemy's strongholds" (J. B. Phillips). Without doubt, the last thing Satan wanted in China was the delivery of one million copies of God's Word, the Sword of the Spirit. No wonder he wanted to make it hard for us. But the victory was not for his taking.

That fact became all the more apparent the day following our arrival in Hong Kong. Shirtless under the hot sun, the men began loading the barge, with its much anticipated cargo: 232 packages of Bibles newly shipped from the United States. After several hours' work, however, we were shocked to discover that the one-ton packages were simply not going to fit. The men had checked and double-checked the measurements. But all concluded the same;

somehow there had been a miscalculation. Perhaps the problem was the bulky waterproof wrapping. Perhaps the thickness of the ropes had not been allowed for. Nobody was sure what had gone wrong. We only knew that we now faced the prospect of putting twenty huge packages into storage, and thus leaving 86,400 Bibles behind.

"Surely no, Lord!" I cried. "You gave such clear authorisation for a million."

Daniel Kwang visited us that evening, and we invited him to pray over our dilemma.

With a gentle confidence in his voice, he called upon Jesus: "Lord, You are able to make the Bibles fit. And I am certain You mean all one million to go to my people."

To this day we cannot explain what happened. We don't know whether the Bibles shrank, or the barge increased in size. All we know is that when loading was completed at last, those packages which had not fitted before, now did so! Once more we rejoiced in Him who was so assuredly Master of every part of this project.

Several weeks later, immediately prior to our planned departure for China, we were to see His control with equal clarity. Just as our preparations were being finalised, we discovered a major typhoon was on its way.

If we waited for it to pass, we knew another could just as easily follow. We were now into June, the month when such weather patterns begin to cause constant havoc in Asian waters.

"David, how can I risk the lives of all these men by heading out into that storm!" a concerned Captain Karl protested. Our boats were certainly not big enough to survive the furious seas such weather would bring.

"I know it doesn't seem practical, Captain. I know it!" I replied, heavily burdened. Yet still I believed, as I prayed, that that still small voice was saying, "Have faith." And sometimes, I recognised, God did not ask His children to be practical, but rather to be obedient. It surely wasn't practical for Joshua to have requested that God stop the sun and the moon for one day. But Joshua was a man who walked by faith and not by sight, and that was what we needed to do. Practicality, I'd concluded, was the enemy of faith.

Two New Zealand crew members, Rod Bowen and Dennis Thompson, were listening as we agonised over our predicament. "Well, guys," they responded, "if the typhoon is the only problem, we'll pray it away! The Lord can deal with that!"

They meant business. The two retired for prayer until, several hours later, they reappeared to report happily: "It's gone. We're sure of it."

Later weather reports confirmed their conviction. The typhoon had indeed gone. Perfect conditions were forecast for our trip.

That night Pastor Ward, Joseph and I met with the Kwang family. During our weeks in Hong Kong we had spent hours with them in our hotel each day, planning in minute detail every aspect of the delivery. Together we would pore over maps of the harbour and surrounding districts. We also discussed at length the strength and movements of the authorities in that area. At the same time, seven Chinese "runners" had been going in and out of the country updating us all the time on the believers' preparation for the Pearl, and any changes which would require contingency arrangements on our part. To us it was an incalculable privilege to be working with these courageous organisers on the inside, all of whom had, at some time, been imprisoned for their faith.

During this final visit from the family, Mama Kwang put through several phone calls to the believers to confirm that they would be all set for our arrival.

"By faith we are ready to move the patient if the hospital is ready to receive," Mama told them in Chinese.

"We are ready to receive," they told Mama excitedly. "Just one thing we would ask of our friends. If the patient dies after the injection, neither of us is to blame the other."

Joseph translated, and we interpreted their message in

terms of our prearranged code. The believers and our crew constituted the "patient", the delivery, the "injection". If anything went wrong, they were asking, none should hold anything against the other. "They are saying we must all be prepared for any suffering that might take place, for Jesus' sake," Brother Joseph said gently. "Both sides now lay down their lives before Him."

"Tell them we agree," I told Mama Kwang. "We are with them one thousand per cent!"

She did so and then, to my delight, she handed me the phone. Neither I nor my Chinese brother could understand much of each other's language, but the joy and trust he communicated at the prospect of the delivery made words of secondary importance. Most moving of all for me was the love in his voice, assuring me I was being addressed as a member of the family.

I returned to our hotel and phoned Julie to tell her we were on our way. She then notified Brother Andrew who, in turn, sent out a message alerting our prayer groups around the world.

"*Chinese courier team in danger. Please pray for seventy-two hours.*" The call went to our bases in Africa, Europe, the Middle East, North America, Latin America and, of course, Asia. Immediately telephone lines all over the world ran hot while the request was relayed into thousands of homes. Their phones, in turn, buzzed as members of our prayer chains alerted others in their local areas.

We couldn't know for certain the total number of people interceding, but as we hauled in the tug's anchor that sun-drenched afternoon, every one of us knew we were covered by prayer.

The next day, with our boats making good progress, we sent a message of confirmation to the believers. We had a radio on board with a link-up to Martin Lord, our shore-based radio operator.

"*We're going to have a party. We will have eighteen bowls of rice and twenty-one cups of tea,*" we said. To the believers this meant that we were coming on June 18 at 2100 hours. Martin phoned this through to the Kwang family who, in turn, rang the believers inside.

Had anything gone wrong for them, the Chinese Christians could have halted the delivery even at this point. Indeed, right to the end they could have told us to turn around and go back if they had felt the Lord stopping the project for some reason.

The message they sent back next day, however, was a joyful, *"Welcome to the party!"* And what a "party" it would be! With every nautical mile, our spirits rose in anticipation.

Prayer dominated our days at sea. The crow's nest, high above the bridge, came to be dubbed "Ward's Prayer Tower", since Pastor Ward often prayed there for hours at a time, or even the whole night through. As a crew, we met daily in the mess hall for morning worship, and began each new watch with prayer before going about our duties. Spontaneously, too, small groups would often gather for intercession on deck or in our sleeping quarters.

In addition to that prayer, however, was individual preparation as the men examined their own lives before God. Rod Bowen spoke of a conviction from the Lord that, "Although He has a special work in store for us, *our hands must be clean to do it.*" If sin of any kind lay between us and God, we needed to have Him deal with it then and there so that no obstacle should impede His Spirit's working in us.

The morning of June 18 dawned bright and clear. I went on early watch, revelling in the sunshine and, best of all, the beautifully calm conditions, ideal for the later floating of the Scriptures. As the day progressed, the seas became even flatter until, at dusk, they were almost unnaturally still.

The ocean was a glowing mirror of light as we approached the appointed harbour. In front of us, the huge red sun hung low in the sky, bringing a rosy translucence to the glasslike sea. Behind the boat, the equally large moon was in ascendance, its orange rays diffused on the surface with those of the sun in a glorious blend of colour. Reflection of the water's hue lit each watching face, rather like the refraction of crystal when held to the light.

The beauty of the silent scene overwhelmed us. It was as though we had left one world behind and entered another. Previously we had witnessed many memorable sunsets at sea, but never anything approaching this night. All who saw it later shared a common conviction that it was the nearest we had ever come to a taste of heaven. Not just in a fanciful way, but in the comforting assurance that on this night of all nights the Creator Himself stood with us, using the unforgettable moment to display His absolute power over His world and the events that were shortly to take place within it.

Moreover, as we gazed on those two brilliant orbs seemingly stationary in the sky, our thoughts could not help but return to the very first confirmation God had given for the task before us: Joshua 10. The day that a servant of God called upon Him to stop the sun and the moon for twenty-four hours.

God had acted. And, in the midst of that splendour, there was no doubt He was telling every one of us that we were about to see Him act again, in His same mighty power.

In the following hours we were to draw upon that power as we observed, to our dismay, patrolling gunboats and an enormous troopship we estimated at 500 feet. Every man on board went immediately to prayer and subsequently rejoiced as no action at all was taken against us.

The scene had then seemed quiet until we noticed that one boat. It had left the regular harbour traffic and was heading straight toward us.

"Oh, Lord . . ., Oh, Lord," Brother Joseph called quietly as he gripped the helm and kept our tug doggedly on course.

The word spread rapid-fire among the crew, and one could almost hear each man holding his breath with the tension of the moment. Never had Exodus 14 seemed more real, nor more needed. I lay those verses before the Lord once more, and their account of God keeping His children hidden so that, "Neither side went near the other the whole night long."

The patrol boat came alongside at steady speed. Distance is deceptive on the sea, however, and to us it felt even closer as our lights illuminated the twenty-five-foot craft and its manned machine gun.

Then, without faltering, it was gone. Its captain had not glanced in our direction nor tried to raise us on the ship's radio. The patrol had behaved as though we simply were not there at all. Joyful alleluias were offered to the Lord from all points – from the men already aboard our barge, those in the crew's quarters and the few of us still on the bridge. It seemed that Jesus was standing between our boats and all passing vessels that night.

The reality of His presence continued to flood the whole crew during all that followed. With Mike Beach at last before us, we lowered anchor and cut the engine.

Joseph Lee, Pastor Ward and I climbed over the side of the tug. Pablo was in the rubber "Z" boat below, along with Michael Bruce, one of our Australian co-workers. The men had been trained to have all three inflatable boats lowered and operational in darkness in just four minutes. As our little boat surged toward the shore, I recalled that Grandmother Kwang had prayed on that beach every night for two months for this very moment.

The "Z" boat reached the shallows, and we jumped into the water. Wading toward us with arms outstretched were the leaders of the believers. As on so many previous occasions, traditional Chinese reserve was put to one side as they leaped into our arms, hugging each of us in turn.

Although none of them spoke much English, several delivered a well-rehearsed English greeting, one after the other in careful succession.

"Welcome to China, Uncles! Praise the Lord!" each

318

exclaimed, with glowing eyes bright in the moonlight. Our own were moist at the beauty of this simple gesture. Even in the midst of our joy, however, all of us were conscious of the urgency of the situation. We gathered on the beach to pray, as Michael and Pablo returned to the tug. Just a few minutes later, my walkie-talkie radio crackled into life. We were under way.

After that, everything seemed to happen at once. Our barge had been partially flooded during the preceding hour to lower it according to the plan. Now additional water was pumped into one half to tilt it down to water level. The side of the barge was lowered and the huge blocks of Bibles were manhandled into the water.

The "Z" boats then sprang to life. From the shore, Pastor Ward and I watched the three of them outlined against the moon. Michael and Pablo manned one; my son David and another American, Edward Dean, drove another; Amando Reyes, our Filipino team member was at the helm of the third, along with Todd Martin, our communications man. Behind the towing "Z"s, the blocks of Bibles spread out like dominoes, linked by rope into groups of four, five, six or even a dozen.

"Over here, Brother David. More to the right!" Joseph Lee translated the believers' directions for me to pass on to the captain and crew via our radios. The three-way communication would continue throughout the delivery.

I'll never forget the moment the first packages came to shore. Although of course our brethren knew what to expect, there was still a sense of disbelief as they cut them open and held the Bibles close.

Sheer joy rendered them speechless as "Oooohs" and "Aaaahs" echoed across the beach until at last they found their tongues and offered jubilant praises to God.

They fingered the books over and over, with faces alight. Well before the delivery these people had told us they would willingly die to see the Word of God come to their country. Now they held it in their hands.

319

Mindful, however, of the ever-present risk of discovery, they soon called upon their friends waiting among the nearby trees to carry off the Bibles. Inside each one-ton block were forty-eight boxes containing ninety Bibles apiece. We had deliberately planned this size of box so that the local Christians would be able to carry them, two at a time, suspended from a traditional over-the-shoulder bamboo rod.

Trucks were also on hand to whisk them away as quickly and as far as possible. We had already passed on US $75,000 of supporters' donations for the distribution of the Bibles within China.

The delivery took two hours in all. While there were twenty crew men in total, all worked as one – the captain and his assistants on the tug, the heavy-duty team pulling packages from the barge, and the men piloting the "Z" boats back and forth.

At last the unloading came to an end. "Brother David, they say we must leave now," Joseph Lee whispered urgently. Earlier that day the believers had seen soldiers combing the beach on the lookout after a robbery in the local area. They wanted to get us away as fast as possible in case a second patrol was planned for the night.

The tug's engine sprang into life as we said good-bye to our Chinese family, after two hours in which we had sensed God's presence more greatly than ever before. Every man among us was irrepressible when the crew later broke into joyful praise. We knew we had been with Jesus. And we had seen Him at work in such a way that there was a sense in which we felt we had been spectators as much as participants.

The believers felt exactly the same. One of the leaders was later to write, "*Ink and pen are unable to express my feelings . . . That night Jehovah appeared to us by the beach and reigned as King.*"

* * *

Satan, however, was still not ready to concede defeat. Indeed his anger was, as we'd anticipated, greater than ever. Past experience had taught us that intrusion into his territory always brought an attempted counter-attack from the forces of darkness, but precisely what form it would take on this occasion, we could not predict. Now we know.

Just four hours after the delivery, local authorities arrived on the scene after a tip-off from non-Christian fishermen. By this time, the believers had managed to remove most of the Bibles, but the soldiers surrounded what remained believing, so the Christians later informed us, that they had discovered the whole of the delivery. They then attempted to destroy the Scriptures both by fire and by water. Neither method was very successful, however, since the books were very difficult to burn, and those thrown into the sea floated and were later brought ashore by fishermen.

One of the organisers was later to write that this confiscation had actually been of help, since, while the soldiers were distracted trying to destroy the Scriptures, they unwittingly freed the way for the major proportion to be transported unnoticed. *"Even the plot of Satan accomplished the will of God . . . Satan thought he was destroying all of our apples, while we were delivering the bulk. God used this to keep us safe in the process of delivery."*

Satan continued to strike out, nonetheless, and a trusted Christian betrayed the organisers of the project to the Three-Self. Most of these leaders were then beaten, interrogated and placed in prison. We ached as we heard the news and called for worldwide prayer concerning their safety. (All have subsequently been released.)

The believers themselves remained undeterred by these tragic events, however. Indeed, they even began requesting further Scripture deliveries.

"In order to continue the work, please prepare two million pieces for us and send them in. Every group is waiting for the goods," wrote one key Christian who had managed to evade the authorities' search groups.

That request was soon to be followed by another asking for a third million.

In the meantime, the believers' network traced the distribution of the Pearl Bibles throughout the country, and fed their data to us. At first we had not know what proportion had been discovered on the beach, but we now know that no more than 10,000 were destroyed then, or in the following days. Within a few weeks we learned that sixty per cent were already delivered. Two months later that figure rose to eighty-five per cent as the Bibles penetrated further, north, south and west. At that point, the Christians sent us a list of the places of distribution.

"We have already sent the apples to the cities and villages of Hunan, Shensei, Anhwei, Chinkiang (of Kwangtung), Fukien, Shantung, Sinkiang, Hailungkiang, Henan, Hopei, etc. How grateful they were when they received the apples!"

It was to be nine months to the day, however, before we would receive the full picture. Such was the length of time needed for the distribution plan to be executed in full. That was not unexpected. In any delivery, even a load taken across the border by suitcase, time and careful attention must be allowed for well-planned distribution strategy. How much more so, then, in a task of this size.

At last, however, came the day in March, 1982 when Joseph Lee could phone me in the United States. He had been inside China and upon his return was able to put all pieces of the very complex research follow-up together. Counting deliveries both by sea and by land, the goal of Project Pearl was achieved. A million Bibles were now safely in the hands of believers, house church members in the main, as well as some committed Three-Self Christians. His report was confirmed by others who had separately researched the situation so that we could be sure.

"In China, hundreds of thousands of faithful Christians gave thanks to our God after they heard the news," wrote Brother Lo, a Beijing contact who, in years gone by, has suffered for the purity of his walk with Jesus. *"Hallelujah!*

Praise the Lord! Glory be to God! One million Bibles – this is what the Chinese Christians needed badly. In fact, we would greatly welcome another million Bibles!"

He went on to express the believers' feelings for Brother Andrew, the one whose original vision for the Suffering Church had been an integral part of our work in Asia from the very beginning.

"Brother Andrew must be a Christian wholly given over to God, one in whom Jesus Christ reigns supreme. He must also be very submissive to God . . . Thus one million Bibles have been smuggled into China.

"Hallelujah! Praise the Lord! We know that there's no one-man show in God's family. Nobody can take up all the burdens. There must be many, many Andrews – big ones, small ones – that will take up the burden unitedly. The great task can't be accomplished by Brother Andrew alone."

Finally, Brother Lo expressed his thanks to all those involved in Project Pearl, not only those on board the boats or who carried in parallel loads, but the people around the world who had prayed or supported the task as well. *"Thank you so much for your concern for the Chinese Christian brothers and sisters. Your act has really encouraged us. You love the Chinese souls so much that we feel we should love our own countrymen more. We will always remember you in our prayers. But you have already received the reward – the smiling faces and thankful tears from hundreds of thousands of Christians in China."*

Such warm gratitude encouraged us all enormously, but it did something more. It underlined afresh the believers' continuing need for the Word of God.

Project Pearl had reached its conclusion. But our work in China was only just beginning.

The largest Christian revival of this century is under way in China. Reports from many China experts estimate that there could now be 50- to 100-million believers, of whom at least 95 per cent are in the house churches. No man or organisation can claim responsibility for this. We are witnessing the outpouring of the Holy Spirit. There are many countries worldwide that have fallen to today's atheistic revolution. China, however, could be the very first among them where God Himself is turning the course of history in a new direction. Your involvement is requested by the house church movement. Open Doors with Brother Andrew is only one among many China ministries through which you respond to their call.

More information concerning Brother David's ministry and that of Open Doors with Brother Andrew, can be obtained from the following addresses:

P.O. Box 47,
3850AA Ermelo,
HOLLAND

P.O. Box 4282,
Manila,
PHILIPPINES

P.O. Box 6,
Standlake,
Witney,
Oxon,
OX8 7SP,
ENGLAND

P.O. Box 53,
Seaforth,
N.S.W.
AUSTRALIA

P.O. Box 6123,
Auckland 1,
NEW ZEALAND

P.O. Box 990099,
2053 Kibler Park,
Johannesburg,
SOUTH AFRICA

1 Sophia Road
#03-28, Peace Centre,
SINGAPORE 0922